NAZMY - LOVE IS MY RELIGION

EGYPT, TRAVEL, AND A QUEST FOR PEACE

SHARLYN HIDALGO

Phoenix Rising Publishing
New York, NY

NAZMY - LOVE IS MY RELIGION © 2014 Sharlyn Hidalgo

Published by Phoenix Rising Publishing
New York, NY 10280
Phoenix Rising Publishing is a division of Transformational Enterprises,
Inc.
Website: www.MaureenStGermain.com

Editors: Kelly Malone, Bèv Hays, Rianna Hidalgo, and Kim Baron
Cover and Back Cover Designer: Rob Allen
Back Cover Photo: Tarek Lotfy
Chapter Art: Ashley Werner

Library of Congress Control Number: 2014958431

ISBN 978-0-9911898-0-9

10 9 8 7 6 5 4 3 2 1

Printed in the United States of America

Dedication

With deepest gratitude, I dedicate this book to the freedom, democracy, and prosperity of the Egyptian people and to world peace.

To Carol,
Looking forward
to getting to know
you.
With love,
Sharlyn

Photograph by Giacomo Tosti.

About the Author

Sharlyn Hidalgo, traveled to Egypt with Quest Travel in 2007 where she first met Mohamed Nazmy. On this, her very first trip, she fell in love with Egypt. In 2010 she returned to Egypt twice, once on another pilgrimage and the second time to begin interviewing Mohamed for this book. Sharlyn became enthralled with the work Mohamed was doing in Egypt to promote peace through travel and especially through spiritual pilgrimage. In 2012 she led her first tour and has just completed her second one as of September 2014.

Sharlyn has an MA in Psychology and is a practicing astrologer, tarot reader, therapist, teacher, healer, artist, and writer. She teaches classes on the Celtic Tree Calendar as well as the Egyptian Mysteries and is author of the book *The Healing Power of Trees: Spiritual Journeys through the Celtic Tree Calendar* published by Llewellyn Publications. She is also certified, through Nicki Scully, as a practitioner and teacher of Alchemical Healing, an energetic healing form sourced in Egypt. Sharlyn currently teaches a yearly Druid Apprenticeship and holds ceremonies that celebrate the Turning of the Wheel in the Celtic tradition. She is dedicated to promoting peace and healing on our planet.

Website: www.alchemicalhealingarts.com

Table of Contents

Acknowledgments

Thank you Mohamed Nazmy for sharing your love of Egypt and vision for peace. You continue to build a network of love and light that is affecting the world in an immensely powerful way. You have changed my life. Thank you for allowing me to tell your story. Thank you Emil Shaker for your joy and laughter, your insight and wisdom, and your love of Egypt. My heart is open because of you.

Thank you to all the friends and tour guides, authors and contributors who gave time and heartfelt expressions of joy as you shared your stories about Mohamed and Emil and Quest Travel. Thank you for creating ideas and acting on insights that are shaping the new paradigm of unity and cooperation—a new vision that brings forward the spiritual teachings and mysteries of ancient Egypt. You show us how this wisdom can affect us today. Thank you for sharing this information with people all over the world to increase consciousness on the planet and create the understanding that we are one with our source and co-creators of our lives.

Thank you to Mohamed's family and the staff at Quest Travel who are all so warm and welcoming. Thank you to my husband Ricardo Hidalgo for your constant encouragement and for sharing the tour with me in 2012 where you too fell in love with Egypt and became friends with Mohamed. I want to thank all of those who chose to travel with me and who made my tours so fabulous.

I thank Spirit for prompting me into these unknown waters and consistently supplying me with the necessary courage and inspiration to stay the course. I am grateful to Egypt, both past and present, for its treasures and mysteries. I am also grateful to the kind and generous people of Egypt, who welcomed me with their warm smiles and infectious humor. I honor them for their courage as they face the challenges of carving out their own style of democracy. They have filled me with hope.

I am also grateful to my skilled and encouraging initial editor Kelly Malone. I couldn't have created this book without you. I also want to thank Jonny Hahn, Irene Iris Ingalls, Laura Bailey, and Susan Webster for your friendship and contributions. Thank you to Nicki Scully and Jean Houston for all of your teachings and for giving me your helpful suggestions and feedback. Thank you Nancy Nazmy for all your input when I first began the project. Thank you Danielle Rama Hoffman for your friendship and teaching, and thank you Friedemann Schaub *and* Danielle for taking me on my first trips to Egypt, when I first met Mohamed and Emil. Thank you Normandi Ellis for your encouragement and for your contributions on the magic and power of Egypt—you have a profound and beautiful way with words. Thank you to those who so generously shared their photographs with me, and thank you to Richard Fero for helping me prepare them for printing.

Finally, I want to thank the gracious Bev Hays for her mid-level editing and I am grateful for my publisher Maureen St. Germain of Phoenix Rising Publishing. Thank you to my daughter Rianna Hidalgo who worked on the final edits with me. You are one of the best writers I know and you made all the difference in the world. Thank you to Kim Baron for the final proofing/editing and over all midwifing of this book. Thank you to Ashley Werner, my niece, who is an amazing artist and who created the Eye of Horus to decorate the chapter headings.

And lastly thank you to the wide circle of Mohamed's friends all over the world as well as my own, who contributed to my Indiegogo Campaign so that I could make this dream come true. Without you I could not publish this book. And a special thank you to my friends and family who supported me throughout this project and are always there for me. This truly was a work of love supported by a global family of good will and generosity.

Foreword by Jean Houston

This is a book about a great and good man. With little of ego or arrogance, he brings the traveler to an essential experience of Egypt. A man of vast learning, culture and experience, a man of mythic kindness and generosity, Mohamed Nazmy is what this lovely portrait shows him to be—a universal human, a sainted scholar, and a unique and compassionate man of business, a dear and dedicated friend to all who come his way. He is one about whom it can be said that the human heart can go to the lengths of God.

I have brought my students to Egypt a number of times under his care and direction. Virtually all have been awakened to a remembrance of things past and future, while being deepened into a present of sacred knowledge and clarity as to one's purpose and destiny.

What then, is it like to travel with Mohamed? It is to lose the illusion of then and now, of ancient eras and modern times.

Under his guidance, in the pre-dawn call of the muezzin, in the late afternoon playing of a flute in the marketplace, I have heard the music that ripples across the friezes in the tombs of ancient musicians. On the curved lips of merchants in the night bazaar, I've noted the same beatific smiles as those that appear on the granite faces of the kings in Karnak.

The same dawn that bespoke the moment of creation to the ancient priestess washes across the faces of countless Egyptians—the light-skinned young businessmen in Cairo crossing the street, the dark Nubian children of Aswan weaving garlands, the sun-bronzed Bedouin camel drivers walking through the smoke of camp fires below the dusty yellow plateau of Giza, and the almond-eyed gatekeepers smoking cigarettes outside the temple of Edfu.

With Mohamed's help, in the dark heart of the Great Pyramid, I've spent the night staring into the dark, hearing the echo of ancient cantors, and feeling the timeless pulse of the universe. On the edges of the desert, at the foot of the pyramids, I have looked up and seen the vibrant stars that are the gods in hiding, the souls waiting to be born. As the wind blows across the desert sands, I can imagine the shushing sounds of the bare feet of dancing tribal women as they make supplications to their goddess.

Mohamed shows us that Egypt is not only a culture that existed in a certain time and place, with a certain history, geography, and economics, Egypt is also a state of being that exists eternally in archetypal realms. The historical Egypt was but a backdrop for the essential Egypt, the Egypt of the eternal return. In this view, Egypt did not have, but rather was a quality of intelligence.

In ancient Egypt, at least for a period of time, substance, and essence bloomed simultaneously. And the pattern of primary essence that resonates through archetypal Egypt—through the Egypt of our psyches—represents the creative potency of universal form and power. It is that which unfolded into what we know as the historical, exoteric Egypt. Mohamed retains this essence and creativity. Perhaps it is because he is a magus in modern dress. Yes, he laughs and jokes, and does business; he follows up on the countless rings of his mobile phone. But through it all, he remains a serene dweller in several worlds—spirit and nature, mind and soul, Egypt now and then and Ever Shall Be.

In our time of whole system transition we have extraordinary opportunities for both global and personal transformation. Mohamed tells us that if we look to ancient Egypt we may find the tools we need to recover and transform our world. These are tools of peacemaking and path finding that rely on spiritual and psychological growth.

Thus his tours are created to provide many shocks of recognition that cause us to remember who or how we are and what we yet may be. In this, he is a midwife of souls, a crafter of experiences that restore to us a Reality larger than our aspiration, more magical than all our dreams. With Mohamed we take steps to our own regenesis.

Sharlyn Hidalgo has written a true and potent story of Mohamed. And what you do not find on the page, you will discover in your own heart, a meeting with a remarkable and numinous human being who you will remember and draw inspiration from your entire life through.

—Jean Houston

The Introduction

I met Mohamed Nazmy, the president of Quest Travel, on my first trip to Egypt in October of 2007. Mohamed was the mastermind behind the amazing two-week metaphysical tour that I took, attending to every detail and ultimately providing me with some of the most heart-opening, enlightening, and fun-filled experiences of my life. Little did I know that I would take two more tours with Quest, and eventually lead my own tours *and* write a book about his work in Egypt. In the late summer of 2010 I went to Cairo to interview Mohamed and learned more about his life and work. In 2012, he helped me lead my first tour and my second in the fall of 2014.

Quest Travel is one of the top travel companies in Egypt today; arranging custom spiritual, archeological, and educational tours for a client list that includes important authors, scholars, and spiritual leaders. Quest also creates custom tours for celebrities and dignitaries. Some of the tour leaders and authors who have worked with Mohamed include Gregg Braden, Jean Houston, Lynn Andrews, Drunvalo Melchizedek, Carolyn Myss, Kevin Ryerson, Marianne Williamson, Jane Bell, Nicki Scully, Maureen St. Germain, Aluna Joy Yaxkin, Shelli Wright Johnson, Normandi Ellis, Graham Hancock, Robert and Olivia Temple, John Anthony West, and many others. This is quite an impressive list!

Mohamed has also arranged the archaeology trips for major universities and museums such as Harvard University, the Chicago Field Museum, and the Oriental Institute of the University of Chicago, and for established archeologists working in Egypt, including Mark Lehner and Kent Weeks. Quest has organized tours for many academic groups, including Christian Bernard and the Rosicrucian Order (AMORC), the Rosicrucian Egyptian Museum in California, and the American Research Center for Egypt. Harvard University has also worked through Quest to provide specialized trips for alumni and student groups. Some of the many travel companies Mohamed works with include Spirit Quest Tours and Greg Roach and Halle Eavelyn, Lumanati and Shelia Reed, Nicki Scully's Shamanic Journeys Ltd., George Faddoul's QC Travel, and Seven Wonders Travel with Janice Brannon. There are many impressive and wonderful people that lead tours through Mohamed and who are doing amazing things on the planet.

The Farewell Dinner in 2007

On the final evening of my first trip with Mohamed, he took our group—composed of thirty intrepid travelers—to a local restaurant for a dazzling farewell dinner. We had the whole place to ourselves. We sat at rows of tables in front of a raised stage that would later feature the evening's entertainment, complete with musicians and Sufi dancers. The restaurant staff brought courses of hummus and baba ghanoush with freshly-baked pita bread, fresh salads, falafel, and plates of fish and chicken, all topped off with a beautiful cake to celebrate my friend Joanie's birthday. As we feasted, local Middle Eastern music played and the room filled with the aroma of cumin and exotic spices.

After dinner, the performance began. A group of Sufi dancers, singers, and musicians, dressed in white turbans and long-sleeved caftans, drummed and sang while whirling dervishes enchanted us with their dance. The room was alive with their energy as they swirled faster and faster, their brightly colored skirts splaying out like spinning tops. As the musicians let loose with fast, furious drumming and the hypnotic spinning continued, I entered into an ecstatic union with Spirit. I wondered if I could hold any more ecstasy. It was the perfect ending to an amazing spiritual trip.

Afterward, as he always does at these farewell dinners, Mohamed stood in front of us. He spoke of his desire to create peace and understanding through his travel business. He explained how President

Anwar Sadat had been an inspiration to him and how, like Sadat, he too believed we all could make a difference. He told us we were now members of his family and that he loved us. Most importantly, he said he hoped we would become his *Ambassadors of Peace* by returning home and speaking well of Egypt and her people—that we could combat misconceptions about the Middle East by sharing the experiences of our trip.

Intrigued

As he spoke of his vision to create world peace one person at a time, it was clear his words were genuine and heartfelt. I was always intrigued by how highly my friends spoke of him, and now, listening to the kind timbre of his voice and the sincerity in his words, I found myself wanting to know more about this man. Danielle Hoffman, my friend, who leads tours to Egypt, had told me that Mohamed always sent a big bouquet of flowers to her hotel room whenever she arrived in Cairo to begin a new tour. I had been impressed by how kind that seemed, but now I saw for myself how Mohamed had a way of drawing people in.

Before this farewell dinner, I knew little about Mohamed and Quest Travel. I'd seen him at the Mena House, our hotel in Giza, for a brief moment at the beginning of the trip. He was friendly and "working the crowd," well-dressed in an expensive business suit and silk tie. I took it for granted that he was a typical businessman working on his public image.

After hearing this prominent and successful man talk about his vision for world peace, I was ready to drop my assumptions. Mohamed's speech struck a deep chord within me. The idea that running a successful business *and* fostering a vision of peace could co-exist opened my mind to new possibilities. It made me think of my heroes Martin Luther King Jr., Robert Kennedy, and Mahatma Ghandi. I thought of the Dalai Lama and Nelson Mandela. Amidst the flurry of packing up and heading back for the States in the morning, I tucked away this experience without an inkling of the adventure it would lead me to.

Returning to Egypt in 2010

I returned to Egypt three years later in 2010. On this tour, Mohamed traveled with us, and I had the opportunity to truly observe and interact with him. I soon discovered he is much more than a businessman—he is an unusual and amazing person with many layers. I was already impressed with his success, but as we traveled through Egypt I saw firsthand how people revered and respected him. I saw how he took the time to be with each of the participants on my tour, and how much he seemed to enjoy getting to know them. I watched as he established relationship after relationship. Everyone he spoke to seemed to brighten up and laugh, and he was just as kind to the people who worked for him.

I also met Emil Shaker, our guide and Egyptologist. I learned about Mohamed's friendship with Emil and realized how important their friendship was to the success of what they were both working so hard to do. They were a powerful team: brothers with a shared vision.

It was unusual for me to feel so comfortable so quickly. I felt like a kid again with my playmates and chums—free and fearless. I was deeply touched by Mohamed's warm personality, intelligence, and humor. Even more than that, I was affected by how he related to me. His authentic kindness and affection did something to me. My heart opened, and I felt more at home than I've ever felt before.

This was surprising. Although I had been to Egypt before, I still carried many fears and judgments based on my preconceived beliefs and misunderstandings about the Middle East, Islam, and terrorism. These misconceptions were based primarily on what I'd seen on the news and my country's response to the devastation of 9/11. The same may be true for many people of the United States. My trepidations about the Middle East melted away as I opened to the present and what was being offered to me. I received generosity, acceptance, and love.

Political Change in Egypt

Since that first trip to Egypt when the country was under Mubarak's rule, so much has happened. We have seen the country politically explode and reinvent itself over and over. The Arab Spring brought change on a global level. Given the Egyptian Revolution of 2011, the election of Morsi in June of 2012, the subsequent overthrow of his presidency, and the election of a new president in June 2014, many of us around the world are hoping this country can build a secular democracy.

It has been difficult for Mohamed and his business as the travel industry has been deeply affected because of the chaos and change. On the other hand Mohamed loves his country and is hopeful that prosperity will return. He is glad to have a new leader for his country and he hopes that travelers will return so that he can return to the business of creating peace.

As Egypt becomes more stable, it will become more important than ever that people travel to Egypt as a way of showing their solidarity with its people. Many believe that Egypt's struggle for democracy has reignited our own aspirations for freedom in the United States. We can't help but be reminded of the principles of a true democracy that the United States was built upon.

Mohamed's Words Ring True

What Mohamed has said is true. We *can* all come together and unite for peace and prosperity. This is not a time to be fearful, but a time to be courageous and stand up for what we believe. We are all one; we are all global citizens who have many more similarities than differences. This is what Mohamed believes and teaches. Given the dramatic changes and challenges that are occurring in the Middle East, Mohamed's story becomes even more relevant to each of us, no matter where we reside on the planet. We can all play a part in realizing this vision for peace, love, and understanding. Mohamed Nazmy shows us the way.

I'd like to share some of this magic with you as I share Mohamed's story and the many ways he manifests his vision for peace. It's true, he builds peace and acceptance one relationship at a time, but we can all follow his example. Mohamed's life shows us we can create peace at any moment no matter where we are or what we are doing. Who benefits the most from forgiveness, tolerance, faith, and helping others? We do. This is the biggest news.

Mohamed always encourages authentic spiritual teachers, whom he calls "Spiritual Alchemists," to bring groups to Egypt. Many of these people, from authors to tour guides to spiritual leaders, have contributed to this book. Nicki Scully, John Anthony West, Gregg Braden, and Jane

Bell were with Mohamed from the beginning of his work in Egypt. George Faddoul, Halle Eavelyn and Greg Roach found him through initial trips with the Rosicrucians, a world-wide organization that teaches spiritual principles, and then formed their own travel companies. Jean Houston, the world-renowned humanitarian, teacher and author, and Kathianne Lewis, minister of The Center for Spiritual Living in Seattle, bring large groups with them to Egypt. Daniele Rama Hoffman, Dr. Friedemann Schaub, Normandi Ellis, and Maureen St. Germain have led many tours. Authors such as Robert Temple and Olivia Temple have traveled with Mohamed for conferences. All of these people are very influential in their own right and were very kind to let me interview them for this book.

There are many spiritual truths in this book and it is my pleasure to share them with you through the lens of Egypt and Mohamed's life and vision. These truths have no dogma attached to them. They have nothing to do with religion, country, race, language, position in society, or culture. These powerful principles are ancient in origin and yet this knowledge applies to us today—even more so with so much at stake for so many. This wisdom can move you through fear and any need for judgment of yourself or others. So, sit down and relax and read this book at your leisure. It is my hope that you will find that the treasures found within its pages will enrich your life and help you to enrich the lives of those you touch.

Part One: How This Book Came About

Fig. Part One.1. Mohamed at the Sphinx.

Spirit Works with Us and Through Us

Chapter One: Traveling with Mr. Nazmy and Emil Shaker

As we sailed down the Nile during my second trip to Egypt in 2010, Mohammed showed two distinct sides of himself. One minute I saw the vacationer, taking time to enjoy himself by playing cards and backgammon with Emil or holding court with his fellow travelers. The next minute, I saw the owner of one of the most successful travel companies in Egypt, constantly answering his phone either in English or Arabic to resolve a myriad of work issues. He would speak in a low voice, even a whisper, save for those moments he raised it suddenly to press a point. He often mixed work and play, deftly handling both.

Before I ever had any personal interactions with Mohamed, I got to know him from afar by observing his relationship with Emil Shaker, one of Mohamed's Egyptologists and guides, and more importantly, a very close friend. After arriving on the boat, moving in and getting acclimated, I saw them sitting together on one of the couches in the living area. It was the first time I'd actually seen them together, side-by-side, as friends. They were laughing and teasing each other with great gusto. They seemed to be having a grand time while thoroughly entertaining some of the tour members.

I had heard many stories about Emil and Mohamed from Friedemann, Danielle, Nicki Scully, and my Seattle friends who had traveled to Egypt, so I was excited to get to know them and to observe their amazing friendship firsthand. It's hard to talk about one without talking about the other. Their friendship is marked by humor and practical jokes, or perhaps even constant competition as to who can tell the funniest story. Simply by being in their vicinity, you find yourself laughing until you're crying. They say laughing is the best medicine, and it worked for me.

Fig. 1.1. Mohamed and Emil at the Mena House, 2007. Photograph courtesy of Patricia Haynes.

There was more to their relationship, however. When Mohamed and Emil stood up, Mohamed walked slowly and Emil gave his arm to help support and balance him. It was then I remembered Mohamed had experienced a stroke in April of 2008, and I could see that his right arm, hand, and foot had been affected. This was the only real evidence that the stroke had any lasting effects. He didn't seem bothered in the least by this, and it certainly didn't impede his mental capacity, his humor, or his ability to socialize with and show deep interest in each and every one of us. In fact, what impressed me about Mohamed was how he interacted with those on the boat, from his clients to his crew. He seemed to enjoy building these relationships, asking people about themselves and sharing things about himself in return. People seemed to come alive in his presence.

It was a privilege to spend this time with Emil and Mohamed. In fact, I learned that it was very special to have Mohamed with us at all, because on most trips, he stays in Cairo to work in his office. However, it wasn't until the afternoon our group left the boat to tour the Philae Temple that I had the chance to speak with him one-on-one. It was synchronistic—I decided to stay behind since I had already seen the temple on my first trip and we were going again later that evening. When I went to sit on the deck, I discovered Mohamed lounging in a chair.

I was glad to have had this quiet time to make a personal connection with him. He was usually surrounded by others, and I didn't want to compete for his attention. As we began talking, I shared with him that my book, *The Healing Power of Trees*, was about to be published. This is strange in itself because I'm shy and normally wouldn't share my excitement so openly, especially since I barely knew him. He seemed interested, so I showed him a picture of the cover of my book that I'd received the day before I left the States. He was very sweet about it, saying he liked having authors on his trips. He told me that many of the leaders who book tours with him are authors, but he didn't name-drop or try to impress me. He was kind, humble, and easy to talk to.

The next time I had a chance to talk with Mohamed alone, the group had taken a short walk to a village along the bank of the Nile near Esna. I stayed behind to read, and Mohamed had decided to stay back too. I practice Alchemical Healing, which is a modality of energy work. I learned this healing form from Nicki Scully and have been certified to teach it for some time. Nicki is a long-time friend of Mohamed's, so he knew and was comfortable with her work. I offered to do a healing for Mohamed the first time we talked together, and he was now ready to trust me to begin the process.

Having this alone time was perfect for the healing. I mostly channeled loving, healing energy, envisioning his stroke-affected limbs returning to perfect health. Mohamed, whose eyes were closed, said he could feel touch even though my hands only hovered above him. He felt the life force energy for which I was merely a conduit. When I was finished, Mohamed looked me in the eyes and asked me if I thought he would get better. Without even thinking, I answered, "Does it matter to you?" He answered without missing a beat. "No, I am happy the way I am," he said. "Each day is a blessing." I understood him. We met in a moment of truth. He committed to continue physical therapy after I left, but that was it. I had no other opportunity to talk with him one-on-one for the rest of the trip. Nonetheless, we had created a bond.

Even after just a few encounters with Mohamed, I was impressed by the soul of this man. He emanated an aura of love and kindness. To me, he seemed like a modern day pharaoh, who exuded such love and warmth of spirit that I began to understand why people wanted to be around him. At the same time, I was intimidated by his worldly success and power, and chose to keep my distance much of the time.

I left Egypt with Mohamed's word ringing in my ears: "You're home!" He said this to me often, and I got this message again during the culmination of our tour's spiritual exploration. It happened on the last day at the Great Pyramid. When it was my turn to lie in the sarcophagus in the King's Chamber, I heard the words, "You will have many homes!" Now, I have come to feel that Egypt is my *heart* home. I didn't know at the time just how much more Mohamed's world and Egypt would open up to me, or that I would be returning in just a few months.

Chapter 2: Thoth Insists I Write a Book about Mohamed

When I returned to Seattle after this second fantastic tour to Egypt in 2010, I began "unpacking" my experiences. It wasn't long before I found myself missing Egypt fiercely. I felt an intense ache in my soul, and realized I had left my heart on the Nile. Egypt and my new friends there were all I could think about.

I awoke one night with the strange sense that Thoth, the ibis-headed Egyptian god of communication, science, language, and mystery, not to mention the master teacher of Alchemical Healing, was pecking at my head. For me, visits from Thoth are a regular occurrence. I am quite used to communicating with him in my mind's eye or in meditation, and I often rely on his guidance. To me, he represents divine wisdom.

This time, he was insistent. This was not our usual kind of communication, where I would meditate and he would talk to me. I hadn't experienced the power of his will when he has a specific job in mind. Night after night, his incessant pecking continued, until finally I recognized that it wasn't going to stop until I listened, and I certainly wasn't going to get a good night's sleep. He had a message for me—or perhaps more of an order—I don't think I had any choice in the matter.

That is how I found myself sitting on an Air France jet destined for Cairo. I was to write a book about Mohamed Nazmy and his work in Egypt. When Thoth insisted I write this book, I was baffled. I thought someone else should do it—someone who is an established author and who knows Mohamed better. The skeptical thoughts came in droves. 'He knows so many famous people,' I thought. 'I don't even have my first book out,' came another. I argued and insisted, but the pecking didn't stop.

It became such a nagging force that I agreed to act and asked Mohamed via email what he thought of the idea. I was sure he'd say no, and would have been relieved if he had. However, Mohamed replied with a casual "Yes, of course you can mention me and Emil in any book that you write." I wrote back and said, "No, you misunderstand me. I want to write a book *about you*!" He sent another email, without missing a beat: "Yes!"

As I read his response my stomach turned. I felt a sudden rush of nerves, I was scared *and* excited. Could I really do this? I felt a sense of doom *and* responsibility. What had Thoth gotten me into? I was also overjoyed at the opportunity to share Mohamed's story despite my reservations. What a wonderful project. And so the intention was set. I said yes, and I was embarking on the project of a lifetime.

I told Mohamed I would need to come to visit, and he offered me a ten-day stay in one of his beautiful apartments overlooking the pyramids of Giza. He owns an entire building with six large apartments, each taking up an entire floor. Although he rents these out, he reserves a few of them as living quarters for his tour leaders and friends who come a few days early to acclimate before their trips or stay a few days late to recuperate after a tour. People who travel with him on a regular basis advised me to go immediately, before the travel season started in September. Mohamed would be so busy, they said, it would be next to impossible to have much time with him. So I told him I would like to come right away and he said, "Yes, come now!" The project was a go. I had a place to stay. The timing was perfect. How could I say no?

Mohamed invited my husband to join me, but Ricardo couldn't take time off from work to go with me, so I asked Mohamed if Kelly, my roommate from our recent trip, could come along. Like me, she had left her heart in Egypt and was eager to return. Besides, Mohamed and Kelly had become good friends, and she wanted to help him improve his website. In his most generous fashion, he was happy to have her accompany me. After all, they were born on the same day of the same year!

Next came more doubt: I wondered how I was going to pay for all of this. I explained to Mohamed that I would need to know my expenses ahead of time because I was not a "rich American" but would, of course pay for my needs. When Mohamed offered to handle everything except the plane fare, I burst into tears of gratitude. I was overwhelmed with his kindness and generosity. With that taken care of, there were no more excuses. We bought our plane tickets, and a week later we were in Egypt.

I talk all the time about the "possibility of miracles" and "following your bliss" and "manifesting your desires," but when something like a trip to Egypt comes to fruition, or the publishing of a book happens, or a new wonderful project reveals itself, I'm in total shock. I was in a state of disbelief as I sat on the plane looking out of the window as the clouds rolled by and the cool air from the vent above me streamed down across my face. Kelly sat next to me and when we looked at each other we laughed and just kept shaking our heads back and forth in our shared wonderment. After all the rapid preparation, it was nice to be on the plane and just sit back and feel my excitement as the steady motion of the airplane vibrated gently under my feet and the hostess brought me a cup of coffee. It all seemed so unreal, and it had all happened so quickly. I just had to keep pinching myself. As I began to drift off to sleep, all I could do was count my blessings.

My Desire to Make a Difference

Mohamed's dream and vision for peace had stimulated a long-forgotten dream I'd had. I've always wanted to be part of the solution. I've wanted to be part of a larger effort to create unity and peace. All my life I've wondered how we can wed spirituality with actions in such a way that we create real change in our hearts and minds. Occasionally, visionaries come along who show us the way. They create a map. They're our "tour guides." By example, they show us how we can change our hearts and the hearts of our so-called enemies. They ask us to look at what brings us together, not what drives us apart. They encourage us to address the value in every individual despite our different beliefs. Mohamed is one of those amazing teachers and that is why I wanted to share his story, despite my fears and insecurities. When I got off the plane, I fell into the loving care and kindness of Mohamed, while simultaneously falling into Egypt and her cauldron of magic.

I'm so grateful for the experiences I've had on my journeys to Egypt, and for my time with Mohamed, Emil, and all the people at Quest Travel. Mohamed's larger-than-life love, humor, and vision to keep peace alive captured my attention from the start. He knows firsthand how minds and hearts are changed—through experiences at the temples, tombs, and sites of ancient Egypt; through the power of the Islamic, Christian, and Jewish holy places; through encounters with the kindness and charm of the Egyptian people, and through the care and love of his Quest family. My goal was to understand the puzzle Mohamed has pieced together so successfully in order to offer this gift to the world. Then, I wanted to share all of this—to offer up to you this banquet of magic, love, mystery, and humor. Enjoy! It is indeed a feast.

Part Two: Mohamed's Vision for Peace

Fig. Part Two.1. Mohamed loves his baseball caps. Photograph courtesy of Richard Fero.

We All Have a Special Purpose

Chapter 3: Mohamed's Special Purpose

In the book *Fate and Destiny: The Two Agreements of the Soul*, Michael Meade explains that fate has to do with the notion that the divine touches each human soul with special recognition and purpose. He writes, "Living out one's destiny reveals the divine word set within the soul and also causes others to recognize our true value and speak well of us" (3). Mohamed clearly has a special fate and destiny, and he has known this ever since he was a young child.

What is Mohamed's destiny? Mohamed would put it simply—"To be of service." In the early '80s, Mohamed and his friend Gregg Braden visited the Great Pyramid of Khufu at Giza. In the King's Chamber, Mohamed heard the words, "You are to be of service." From then on, he knew his purpose was to create peace and understanding wherever he went on this planet.

Mohamed's passion for peace is carried out every day in the way he treats others. He believes in unity, and he strives to create it through work, through business, and through the personal relationships he builds with those who are lucky enough to pass through his life. Whether it's someone on the street whom he stops to kiss and chat with, workers dressed in their galabeyas (the Egyptian common long robe-like dresses), farmers, service people, tourists, tour leaders, restaurant owners, salespeople, chefs, business associates, or friends and family members, he treats them all the same—with love and affection. He has a special way of connecting with each person he comes in contact with, and he is right at home in Egypt where people hug and kiss to show their appreciation for each other. There are large numbers of people who have been touched by his generosity, vision, and love. Whenever I spoke with someone who knew Mohamed, I left the conversation with their positive words echoing warmly in my ears.

Meade also says, "The greater life is found where destiny calls to each of us to become who we are in essence, to live far enough into life to reveal the inner story set within us" (3). Mohamed lives his essence, but he also blesses us all by doing so. All of us want to connect with our true life purpose. We all have a special "seed" that itches to grow, thrive, and bloom. This seed represents our genius, or life spirit, and has everything to do with our destiny. Mohamed is able to influence his guests in such a way that they, too, may choose to move toward their own special fate and destiny. Whoever is in his presence is affected. I've seen it, read about it, and heard about it; he has a special ability to activate this seed within each person so they can begin to answer the call and embrace their unique destiny and purpose. This is no small thing. Perhaps it is his utter acceptance of each person that makes them feel comfortable and assured enough to open up to their potential.

Mohamed credits both his father and Anwar Sadat for planting the seeds that inspired him to act upon his vision of world peace and unity—a vision the world sorely needs. Mohamed took these seeds and grew his business to the highly successful enterprise it is today. According to Mohamed, all of us need open hearts, faith and the guidance of divinity to help us grow. If we find the forgiveness and tolerance that already lives within us, we can appreciate the world's diversity. Egypt, he says, has a way of opening our hearts and helping us remember who we are and what is truly important. "I am able to create trips that ensure we have the interactions that will help us remember—we are more alike than different," he told me.

Chapter 4: The Influence of Mohamed's Father and Anwar Sadat

Mohamed's father deeply impacted Mohamed. You can see it in the way Mohamed's face lights up when he talks about him. He calls his father "the man." The love and reverence Mohamed expressed as I sat with him was palpable. His voice became more serious and he placed his left hand upon his heart as he talked about him. Mohamed described his father as a "very special" man who schooled him carefully and understood a father's responsibility as a guide, teacher, and guardian.

Mohamed's father was an Egyptian diplomat who was involved in many different organizations before and after the Egyptian Revolution of 1952, when the country abolished the constitutional monarchy, established a republic, and ended British occupation. Through his association with officers and others who had ties to the government, Mohamed's father was able to establish many important relationships. However, the relationship Mohamed's father held most dear was with Anwar Sadat, the man who made peace with Israel and was president of Egypt from 1970 until his assassination on October 6, 1981. Mohamed's father taught Mohamed to love and respect Sadat and his vision. "Anwar Sadat and my father are the two people who live in me," Mohamed said.

Teaching Tolerance

Mohamed's father also taught him about religious tolerance and how to find the good in people and circumstances. Even to this day, Mohamed says he chooses to take only the good and leave the rest.

When Mohamed was about six, he went to a co-ed Christian primary school called The Faith School. As a Muslim child, he was in the minority. In every class, students were paired up and they would sit together as a type of buddy system. Mohamed was paired with a Christian boy, so he asked his teacher to place him with a Muslim boy instead. She consented. Mohamed felt good about himself, thinking his family would be proud of him for being faithful to his religion. That night, he told his father, who showed neither approval nor reproach. Instead, the next day, he walked Mohamed to school and asked the teacher to place Mohamed back with the Christian boy. To this day, Mohamed and his former schoolmate are good friends.

Around the same time as this incident, Mohamed's father created a home office and library. Half the library held books about Islam, while the other half held books about Christianity. His dreams, however, went beyond the household. "All his life, he wanted to build a mosque to pray in," Mohamed told me. When Mohamed's father died at 63, it was up to Mohamed and his siblings to fulfill their father's wishes. They built the mosque, keeping Christianity and Islam together by incorporating the library. It still stands today. "Everyone goes into the mosque and asks, 'How come?'" Mohamed said. "We say, because it all belongs to God." According to Mohamed, just having these texts present in an Islamic religious center broadens the base for acceptance of both religions in the minds of those who visit, even if they don't read the scriptures.

Mohamed Follows his Father's Example

"If you are Muslim, you pray to God. If you are Christian, you pray to God. If you are Jewish, you pray to God," Mohamed told me, explaining the lessons he learned from his father. "He taught us how to love people and how to behave on a human level. He showed us how it is possible to ignore the nationality and religion of others, and just live together." Mohamed feels ever grateful to his father for instilling respect for religious and cultural differences, and has carried on his father's habit of seeking out the underlying shared qualities of all people. Ultimately, he said, he gained a sense of respect and love for the worship of God in "many forms and through many teachings."

Mohamed maintains this tolerance while being a man of strong Muslim faith who says he is not afraid of anything and believes everything in life is a gift from God. He makes friends with almost every new thought teacher, regardless of what country they come from, and he's drawn to people with open minds who teach compassion and unity. To this day, Mohamed enjoys his many friends and isn't concerned with their religion. He respects spiritual and humanitarian beliefs that encourage peace, and he accepts people as his brothers and sisters. He is apt to include you into his family if he likes you, and chances are, he will love you. I have seen those who come in contact with him feel his love and open their hearts. I have seen it over and over.

I asked Mohamed if he thought his father would be proud of him. Mohamed answered sincerely, "I wish he were alive. I really wish he were alive, because I would give him my success as a gift." Mohamed leaned forward in his chair and touched his hand again to his heart and his voice became very gentle and subdued. "I would say to him, 'Now, your boy will take care of everything.' I would give him everything he wants, no matter what. I would sell the shirt off of my back for him. It is really good to see that your kids have grown in the way you always wanted. I wish he could see this." That was the only time I ever saw tears in Mohamed's eyes.

Anwar Sadat

Anwar El Sadat was the third president of Egypt after it became a republic in the early 1950's. His peace treaty with Israel on March 26, 1979 earned him the Nobel Prize. Mohamed grew up with this man; their families were very close.

This association was instrumental in helping Mohamed believe in his vision of a peaceful world. When Mohamed's father passed, Anwar Sadat became a strong mentor and father-like figure to him. Mohamed wrote about Sadat in his book *The Modern Day Alchemist*, which he co-authored with his good friend George Faddoul:

From a peasant boy born on the banks of the Nile in 1918, in every respect, as if from Biblical times, Anwar El-Sadat's amazing journey was one of dedication to the welfare of his people. A true modern day alchemist, Sadat pursued the cause of right, the cause of liberty for his people and peace for the region.

Anwar El-Sadat turned despair into courage. Being the courageous man that he was, and as a true alchemist, Sadat in 1975 - just as I was coming out of my teens - reopened the Suez Canal once again to international trade. As a true alchemist and in a relatively short time, Sadat brought his country, my country Egypt the GIFT of the Nile, the land of the Pharaohs into the 20th century.

This is how my affinity with Sadat fueled my affinity with the search for the modern day alchemist [Mohamed's tour leaders], and how their lessons could inspire others, and how others could then continue the work of transmuting lead into gold, first the transformation of crude into gems in their own lives, leading into a personal peace which then opens the door for the possibility of having peace in the region, in fact the audacity of believing in a lasting world peace.

A true modern day alchemist, Anwar Sadat did more to bring peace to the Middle East and by implication to the whole world than anyone at the time [1970's] ever thought possible (11–12).

"What Sadat did with Israel," Mohamed said, "was the most absolutely unique and incredible act that we have up until now. Sadat was the first president in the history of the Arab world to do this. *He went to Israel to ask for peace.* He was not about war or killing, but he was looking out for the life of all of the people. He was looking out for their interests."

As he talked about Sadat, his facial expression grew somber. "When Sadat was assassinated, I felt that it was the assassination of a peacemaker." Mohamed stopped for a moment and took a breath. Then his eyes became sad, his voice softened, and he pushed his glasses to his nose with his left hand. "It is hard to find such men of vision. They are rare. So when we lose them, it is very hard." Mohamed keeps Sadat's book *Search for Myself* in his bedroom by his night-stand and confided that he has read it about 150 times. "Every time I read it," he said, leaning forward and looking intently over his glasses as if he were telling me a secret, "something new happens, and something new comes to me. Sadat is the person whose footsteps I wish to follow."

Mohamed's hand went to his heart as he stressed that his success in business came from following Sadat's example. "My vision is to bring people together, and I do not see Jewish or Muslim, Israeli or Arab. I only see human beings," he said. "I feel that regardless of color, race, religion, or nationality, we are all one family. What we all need is love, respect, and the acceptance of one another. Then we have no problem!" He leaned forward again and looked directly into my eyes. "If I love these people and they love me, then that means that everything people say about Muslims and Jews and Egyptians isn't true. Stereotypes mean nothing to me. I look to my relationships with people to tell me the truth." What he was sharing stirred up emotion in me, and reawakened my own dreams to live in a peaceful world where we are all accepted. I am so tired of living in a world at war. Mohamed's words uplifted my heart and made me feel hopeful again. Perhaps there was something I could do, something we all could do.

Mohamed told me he loves to visit Sadat's monument in Cairo. After Sadat was assassinated, the government chose this site for his tomb. Mohamed often takes his tours to see this memorial, and during these visits, Mohamed will often join to speak about Sadat and his influence. It is here that he also asks his groups if they will become his Ambassadors for Peace.

Learning about Tolerance through Relationships

Mohamed told a story about his good friend Nicki Scully, who has led tours to Egypt for years, and who happens to be Jewish. Whenever Mohamed travels to Oregon, she insists that he stay with her. One time in the '80s, he brought his daughter Nancy with him, who fell violently ill one early morning. Mohamed called upstairs to Nicki. Nicki ran downstairs, swept Nancy into her arms, jumped in her van, and rushed Nancy to the hospital. She didn't even stop to put on her shoes. After hours at the hospital, Nicki returned with Nancy, safe, sound and in recovery. "Those are the kinds of friends I have," he said. "Does the word Jewish mean anything to me? Yes, these are people I love. Does the word Egyptian mean anything? Yes, these too are people I love."

John Anthony West, the well-known author, is another close friend of Mohamed's. Mohamed told me that John never calls him by his name. Instead, he calls him "my brother." Mohamed asked me, "How can anyone turn that down?" His question was forceful—there was power and the full weight of true belief behind his words. When John comes to Egypt he stays with Mohamed; when Mohamed goes to New York he stays with John. John always invites people over in Mohamed's honor and cooks for them all.

The list goes on. Barbara Marciniak and Jane Bell have both traveled with Mohamed and become close friends with him. Barbara is a writer and shares teachings from a collective intelligence called the Pleidians, and Jane has been leading spiritual groups to Egypt for many years. "They stay with me here," Mohamed said. "And when I travel to the States, I stay with them. There is a lot of love between us. This love with my friends has made me question everything that we commonly hear about religion, race, and nationality. I do not believe in hatred or separation. There is no place for this in my heart. We worship in our own ways. It does not matter if we worship in a synagogue, a church, or a mosque." Mohamed believes it is our choice to live separately and to believe in separation, but that it is all fabricated. If the "people of the world would get to know each other," as he said, we would understand the kind of life that God wants us to live and the world would be completely different. "I encourage everyone I meet to care for each other from heart, not mind," he concluded. My heart melted once again as I heard these words. I was getting used to the feeling.

Mohamed shared some of his favorite videos with me as another way of explaining his vision. There was one about Gandhi and Martin Luther King Jr. There was another about a man who was born without legs who learned to run in races on his prosthetic legs. There was a theme. These videos were about how individual people had created personal, spiritual, cultural, and political change. As we watched together, he gestured to the screen when he wanted to emphasize a point, or quickly paused the action to explain something he didn't want me to miss. He repeated that one does not need to be a president or an ambassador or a rich man to do amazing things in the world: "Everyone can do something. Everyone can work for and encourage peace."

I realized that I too, can encourage peace in small ways. I can be kind to the clerk at the store, or to the person on the phone who's selling something or doing an obnoxious survey. Usually I hang up, or even worse, feel that I have the right to be rude because the call was unsolicited and they were bothering me. I hadn't thought about the fact that there is a person on the other end of the phone who needs a job and has the right to be treated with respect. His words have changed me. I can act with kindness in small ways in my relationships, and I can follow my own heart's desire by creating a book despite the challenges, obstacles, and fears that may threaten to stop me. I can be courageous and trust that Spirit will support me. Mohamed made me realize that every day, in almost every interaction I have, I can help foster peace.

Chapter 5: Religious Tolerance

In describing Islam, Mohamed once said, "It is really a beautiful religion. When you see a religion that respects everyone and every religion and every human being—that is beautiful." If Mohamed had said this to me years ago, I would have struggled to find the truth in it. Before I met Mohamed and had my experiences in Egypt, my thoughts, fears, and critiques of Islam were all based on what my own narrow Western world view claimed was true. I made judgments without really knowing much, considering I didn't know any Muslim people, and I feared travel for the perceived threat of violence. Perspective is everything.

Although Mohamed is Muslim, he separates himself from the term "religious," instead describing himself as spiritual and universal. "I do not want to put any separation between myself and others by saying I am this or I am that," he said. Yet he is faithful, and there is no doubt that being Muslim brings great comfort and stability to him. He even says that if he were reborn, he would want to come back as a Muslim because of the joy it has brought him.

However, he doesn't adhere to a set of rules. He may have built three mosques for his fellow Muslims to pray in, but he doesn't go very often himself. Mohamed believes people should be able to relate to God on their own, and develop this relationship within themselves. "I like to take religion into my heart," he said, placing his hand on his chest. "I feel very strongly that no one else can give me instruction on how to be spiritual."

Even after hearing him talk about his unique approach to being a Muslim, I was still surprised at what came next: "I myself am not religious," he said. "All these people who call themselves religious are causing a big problem in the world right now because they are trying to direct people to specific avenues of thinking and believing." There is great need, he added, for people to find a connection within themselves outside of religious dogma. I was so happy to hear him say this. I remember leaning forward in my chair in front of his desk at his office, full of anticipation. He leaned forward. "This is a better way."

Clearly, Mohamed is a proponent of finding personal paths to God within his own religion, and this tolerance extends to the many other religions of the world as well. "Let us agree on one fact," he said. "That we all aim to one God. He's everywhere regardless of the avenue we take, be it Islam or Judaism or Christianity." For Mohamed, being Muslim feeds him and provides spirituality, but Mohamed recognizes that there are many paths to the "source," whatever that may be. He insists, in fact, that we each find our own way to it. It doesn't matter whether the path stems from organized religion or a personal belief system. He is respectful of all, and he said this is one of the teachings of Islam.

Mohamed told me that when he reads the Koran, he finds in its pages a deep respect for Christianity and Judaism. "In the Koran it says you cannot become a Muslim unless you have faith in Christ and Judaism as these two religions come from the same place—the same God." This teaching, he said, brings unity.

In discussions, Mohamed focuses on the three major world religions. I assume it is because there is so much discord among these three religions in Egypt, the Middle East and the world at large. He doesn't mention Buddhism or Hinduism, nor the Celtic Native European spirituality that I follow. However, I can guess what he'd say if I asked. Likely, he'd tell me they are perfectly acceptable paths to the same God. "I believe that God is everywhere," he said once. "God is all around us, and below and above us, so why do we need anything in the middle?"

Through my conversations with Mohamed, I have become open to learning about Islam. There is an interesting dynamic at work in that Mohamed is Muslim, his best friend Emil is a Coptic Christian, and both have great respect for Judaism—a dynamic that made me want to understand all three religions better. Emil and Mohamed have such beautiful characters and such unbounded generosity, and I couldn't help but wonder if it was their faith that led them to be so kind. I began to see an entirely new portrait of what faith in Islam, or any mode of religion, can mean. I started to grasp how one could be "spiritual but not religious" (as I am too), while still loving one's faith. The teachings of respect for other religions and sharing what one has with others are not the Islamic teachings that usually reach our Western ears. We are conditioned in many ways to think of Islam and terrorism as one and the same, especially since 9/11. This belief is a flagrant distortion of the truth.

The result is fear. "Many Westerners believe it is a crazy idea to travel to Egypt," Mohamed acknowledged. He paused, shifted his weight, pushed up his glasses, and leaned forward in his chair. "But they do not really know the truth for themselves and they make their decisions based on programming and fear. What the media is feeding them is not truth. We know that the media is directed by people who believe in separation and it is to their benefit to keep this belief alive. American media is very invested in aggravating fear."

I was a prime example. Here I was, worried about traveling to a Muslim country because of the threat of violence. Judging by the daily news, there seems to be more daily violence right in my hometown of Seattle. The news is chock-full of muggings, break-ins, shootings, murders, and rape. Yet somehow, if I'm at home, I still feel relatively safe. I've speculated that if this were the only news about Seattle that reached the people of another country, they would be terrified to visit. Of course, I know to the contrary that Seattle is a beautiful city.

We can't know the truth without *real* information. Now, before I form an opinion about an incident taking place in the world, I also check news sources from other countries to gain multiple perspectives. After traveling to Egypt six times, meeting Mohamed and those around him, and interacting with Muslims and the people of Egypt, my attitude has changed. When I see a woman in my hometown wearing a hijab or a khimar, I like to say hello. I know not to judge, or worse, to be afraid. I never thought visiting Mohamed in Cairo would bring me around to a new respect for traditional religion. It's amazing how a personal relationship can change us and open our minds to new ways of thinking. This is something that Mohamed embodies—this is how he lives his life.

Chapter 6: The Spiritual Energies of Ancient Egypt

Creating Magic

Jean Houston calls Mohamed a "magus" in the foreword of this book for a reason. The more you get to know him, the more you realize that wherever he goes, magic happens. His clients have described him as "the mastermind" and "the magician." He has a way of breaking through barriers and making the impossible possible again. He has helped form the policies that allow groups to have private time at the sacred sites of Egypt, because he understands just how essential it is for travelers to have their own, unique experiences. He has arranged for groups to have the entire Cairo Museum to themselves after closing hours, attend magnificent feasts under the moonlight in front of Luxor temple, and slip up the Nile for late night visits to the temple of Philae.

Magic indeed. Mohamed made it possible for my travelling group to go into the Step Pyramid at Sakkara, Seti the First's Tomb, and the Tomb of Unas—all privately. These are visits that are allowed very rarely. I know every individual comes away from his tours with a unique story about the special experiences he provided for them. Some of these stories are in chapters to come. Mohamed loves to say, "If you can imagine it, you can achieve it. If you dream it, you can become it."

In the King's Chamber

There is a reason Mohamed works so hard to ensure his clients have the means of truly connecting to Egypt and its sites. Mohamed's own experiences with the sacred energies of Egypt helped shape his vision and purpose in life. In 1984, he visited the Great Pyramid with Gregg Braden's group. They went into the King's chamber in the evening for a private visit (Gregg's version of this story will be recounted in a later chapter). As they meditated in the chamber, Mohamed began to smell fragrant roses, a strange experience considering the amount of sweat produced by the participants in the enclosed, hot space. "I couldn't figure out where this scent was coming from," he said. Suddenly, he heard a voice repeating, "You are a server. You are a server." He didn't' know where the voice was coming from, but he began to have an inkling of what it meant. As he left the pyramid, he asked the inspector if he would smell him. The inspector replied, "You smell like a rose flower."

Gregg's group left the following morning to return to the States, but the words from the chamber echoed in Mohamed's mind and he felt a calling to go back. He asked Emil to stay in the pyramid with him from midnight until 6:00 A.M. In total darkness, without sound, they sat and meditated. Mohamed fell asleep. As he dreamt, he heard the words again: "You are a server. You are a server." When he awoke, he knew his role in life. There was no doubt. He was to serve others. Within the dream, he was shown that he was to use his business to help promote peace through travel. He was to be a bridge connecting people from other countries to the people of his own as a means of creating peace in the world and breaking down stereotypes.

From then on, Mohamed's life work has been to connect people through his travel business. He is dedicated to bringing people to Egypt and he is especially proud of creating spiritual tours. For Mohamed, this work has been the most wonderful thing to ever come into his life. "I started feeling that my life had meaning," he said. "I saw that meaning would come through serving other people and seeing joy come into their lives. Very simply, this is now my life story."

The puzzle pieces had come together: The influence of his father, his connection with Sadat, his growing vision of peace enhanced by his own religious and spiritual views, and his experience in the Great Pyramid. In tandem, these things had transformed why and how he does business. "Today when I travel, in my meetings, in my monthly program on TV, and even when I am eating, I am compelled to engage with people and bring peace to create harmonious relationships," he said. It is through this constant yearning to form bridges that those around Mohamed end up changing, and this is his true purpose.

God is There

"If God is there," Mohamed told me, "it has to be amazing." This is one of the reasons Mohamed loves going to the temples and tombs of Egypt. He said these places feel like cathedrals because God—whatever form of God—was worshipped within them.

Mohamed wasn't taught about the spiritual energies of the temples, tombs, and sites of Egypt. However, by going to these places by himself he was able to experience them, just like his revelation in the King's Chamber. He told me he doesn't need a guide or anyone else "to direct his eyes or his feelings or his thinking." He just sits and feels the energy of the place in his heart. He goes to the temples, gazes at the hieroglyphs, the sculptures, and the statues, and leaves with his own impressions. "The true guide of these places is Spirit," he said. "The spirit of the place connects you to the temple." Spirit is strong in these places, considering God was worshiped within them for thousands of years. These places are sacred ground, and the energy from ancient times can still be felt in their spaces. Mohamed said this is why he enjoys having spiritual groups come to Egypt: so they too can share the experience of being in the spiritual energy held by these sites.

Although we were sitting in Mohamed's office when we talked about ancient Egypt, it felt like we were at the sites themselves. I could see myself standing in the temple at Abydos, or visiting the holy of holies at Isis's temple at Philae. I could remember my own experiences with these spiritual energies as Mohamed continued talking. "Visiting these sites leaves you with great inspiration and connection, which is why people like to come here," he said. "These places bring us back life."

Our conversation was occasionally interrupted with little reminders that business continued as usual—a buzz at the door or a tour operator placing some papers to sign in front of him. He would soon turn back to me and pick up where he left off. He explained to me that when he first started doing spiritual tours, he would go to the places before he ever took a group. "I started to feel that I needed to know what was offered at these places," he said. "I went by myself."

Many of Mohamed's strongest spiritual experiences have continued to be in the sites of ancient Egypt. "When you have private time in the temples and just walk by yourself," he said, "the temples will give you all the explanations you need." Mohamed told me he talks to the sites and hears them talk back, but not without adding a defensive "I'm not lying—it's the truth!" I didn't need convincing.

Mohamed is adamant that nighttime is the best time to experience the energies of Egypt. During the day, he said, there are thousands of visitors and the energy is more closed off. "The sites come to life at night," he said. "Most Egyptians visit the sites at nighttime because night was the time for worship in these temples. You go in the evening and the temples are dancing with energy." He described the beauty and wonder of the temple of Isis on Philae at night, and suggests going to the Giza Plateau right at dawn. "You feel that each place is speaking," he said wistfully.

As he told me about the energy in these places, I was reminded of my last visit to the Temple of Philae in which I led a sunrise meditation in the sanctuary. We lit the altar with candles and my group entered the sacred space chanting, *Om Tara Tu Tare*, a Tibetan chant to the goddess Tara. As we sang, even the birds joined us with their songs, flying in and out of the small rectangular windows cut high into the walls just below the ceiling. We worked on forgiveness and self-love, and the presence of Isis was powerful. This is one of the precious moments in my life that I will never forget. I hardly remember what happened; it was as if I entered another dimension. I was filled with an overwhelming sense of love and peace. After the ceremony, my group left the temple and watched the sun rise above the Nile. It was a beautiful thing.

Chapter 7: Paying It Forward

On one of his visits to America, Mohamed watched the movie *Pay It Forward*. He liked the message, so he bought fifty copies and brought them back to Egypt. He gave them to his family, his colleagues, and the companies he does business with. He thought if they could really get the message of this movie it would change their lives—that if they followed the example set forth, they could become inspirations to others and help not only their societies, but humanity at large.

This encapsulates Mohamed's view that we are here to help one another. "This way of living," he said, "will end the word separation." If Mohamed could have his way, it would be deleted from the dictionary. He believes we can help each other regardless of nationality, religion, culture, or race. When we do, the seeds of good grow and we are changed. It's like a dose of vitamin juice or fertilizer for a plant. All of us on Earth have the good parts in our hearts, even the killer and the thief. The challenge, Mohamed says, is how to activate that seed of love. "If you neglect someone and say he is bad, he'll do worse. But if someone loves him and holds him with love and care, you will see that kindness come out of his heart."

Travel, it seems, is an effective way of helping people realize this and can be truly spiritual in nature. It brings people together; it connects us; it helps us release our judgments and find truth in the notion of equality. As Mohamed said, it doesn't matter if we are rich or poor, educated or not, or from Upper Egypt or Lower Egypt or the Lower West Side. "Here, we can deal with each other from the heart. Not from our bank accounts or our places of worship or the country we live in—but heart to heart."

I know firsthand that the trips Mohamed provides are transformative. When I was there, I found my heart again. Many who come to Egypt return over and over, and it thrills Mohamed to see this. He is especially happy when Jewish travelers return, considering all that is happening in the Middle East and Israel. He is happy that these people have trusted what they feel in their hearts: they know they are safe and loved in Egypt. He put it simply. "Nicki, Kelly, and Jane are Jewish, and I love them all dearly—by building these friendships, all of us can change the world."

Chapter 8: The Merchant Priests: Business and Spirituality

In *The Modern Day Alchemist*, merchant priests—specially trained priests of ancient Egypt—are described as follows:

> They imagined a global economy that empowered local economies around the world—from the largest to the smallest—to prosper and flourish with dignity and equality; a global market place where the spirit of partnership and responsibility transforms the emotions of anger, fear and jealousy into passion, compassion and empathy and where the natural flow of information, ideas, and resources between different segments of society and across cultures transcends the unconscious exchange of baseless commodities—uniting and exalting, rather than dividing people around the world. They dreamt of the rise of the global citizen movement to move the world closer to their ultimate dream of a global conscious evolution. They dreamt of global citizens all over the world participating through sacred commerce [business] and philanthropy, creating a new world rather than fixing or changing the old one (104–105).

In this sense, Mohamed is a merchant priest. He encourages us all to become global citizens. He promotes this vision through his business dealings, travels, friendships and relationships. He is also a powerful teacher, serving as a mentor and role model for many business owners.

Through my interviews with many of Mohamed's clients, it is clear that he has influenced each of them with his practices and values. Mohamed has done amazing things for the economy of his country. He has boosted tourism enormously through his business, providing a multitude of jobs and fueling the economy for people along the Nile. He has built mosques, assisted startup businesses, donated money to charity, and helped many individuals when they needed it most. He is generous while simultaneously teaching people how to become self-reliant and get the job done. He models efficiency.

Even more, Mohamed has taught them about kindness, generosity, how to spread prosperity, and above all, keeping their word. His bottom line is that he always keeps his promises. He has helped bring the heart back into business, teaching many how to create relationships that lead to positive success that isn't at the expense of others. I myself have benefited greatly from incorporating the values Mohamed exemplifies into my own business. I've watched Mohamed follow his generous impulses and witnessed the joy he gets from trusting his heart. Mohamed's life is a demonstration of how we can cultivate peace through business.

Alongside, and through, teaching good business practices, Mohamed has the ability to open hearts that are afraid and closed. It seems that his biggest joy is seeing others happy and he likes to do things for others for the mere pleasure of seeing them smile. It is his business that allows him to have these interactions on a daily basis.

It renews my faith to see that a business can prosper while helping others prosper: that exchange and commerce can be spiritual and improve lives. This seems revolutionary—just think of what we hear in the news about the greed of large corporations, banking, and Wall Street. Observing how Mohamed runs his business, and seeing how he uses his success to improve the lives of others, has impacted me greatly. I believe it is true that the more prosperity and opportunity we all share, the stronger our democracies can become. Thus, shared prosperity and freedom go hand in hand. This is the driving force behind the ongoing political chaos in Egypt. The people want opportunity and freedom, which cannot come from the dictates of oppression or power or religion—only from the heart.

Part Three: At the Office of Quest Travel

Fig. Part Three.1. Mohamed in the office at Quest Travel.

If You Can Imagine It, You Can Create It

Chapter 9: Meeting Mohamed: The Interview Begins

During the late summer, Cairo sizzles. A constant haze of pollution rests over the city, and after a few days, you can feel it penetrate your lungs and sinuses. It's super crowded with people and traffic. It's dirty. It's noisy. All day and night, you can hear traffic horns blare from the street. At daybreak, you can hear the calls to prayer broadcast over loudspeakers. It's all very exotic and a very fascinating place.

Fig. 9.1. View from the apartment.

Giza, where Mohamed lives and works, sits just across the river from Cairo. In 2010, during this stifling, bustling time of year, I flew into Cairo to spend ten days with Mohamed to interview him for this book. Mohamed provided me with a place to stay in his own apartment building. My gorgeous, three-bedroom apartment in his custom-made building overlooked the Great Pyramid and the two smaller pyramids that stand on the elevated plain of the Giza Plateau. In designing the building, Mohamed used every opportunity to capture this amazing view. In nearly every apartment, there is a bathroom with a wall of glass windows where you can sit on your "throne" and gaze at the pyramids. There is also a glass-enclosed elevator, from which you can enjoy the vista.

From my apartment, I could easily walk upstairs to the roof and enjoy a breathtaking panoramic view of the pyramids whenever I wanted. There, the three pyramids stood against a vast, turquoise sky. Resting on the horizon, these world famous pyramids of Khufu, Khafre, and Menkaure loomed like mountains. Every time I sat on the roof, I felt like I needed to pinch myself. They looked immense, as if I could reach out and touch them through the heat waves of the hot afternoon sun. Even when sweltering in the intense heat or enduring the cacophony of sound from the street below, I could look at these huge stone monuments and feel like I was melding with the ancient past.

So there I was, living under the influence and energy of the pyramids even in the apartment, seeing them every time I walked into the living room. Although the Sphinx wasn't in plain view, I knew it was just below the plateau to the east. A ten-day stint at the foot of these monuments proved to be incredibly energizing for me—not quite as harsh as sticking your finger is a socket, but still a jolt. Sometimes I couldn't sleep, and I often found it difficult to concentrate. I thought it would take me months to unwind from all that energy and process all the information I was absorbing.

Quest Travel, the apartment building, and Mohamed's own home are just a few blocks from one another. Each morning, Mohamed sits on his deck and drinks his coffee, staring out at the pyramids as he contemplates the mysteries of Egypt. Cleary, it's a more than suitable place to meditate on the meaning of life.

Having experienced the energetics of this special place where Mohamed lives and works, I now understand a bit more about his success, his creativity and vision, and his drive to share it with the world. There is something about Giza that enlarges and accentuates life. As I was looking at the pyramids from my window one day, my husband informed me via Skype that the Great Pyramids mark the exact gravitational center of the Earth. Perhaps we could consider this area to be the power chakra of the Earth, falling just below the bellybutton of the planet.

More About Mohamed

If I introduced you to Mohamed, you'd likely notice his vibrant smile first. He'd welcome you to your "new home and family" before asking you about yourself in a warm, heartfelt way. He would engage you. He would make you laugh. Soon, you'd feel safe and open-hearted. For some strange reason, you'd begin to see that all things are possible. You'd begin to think of your own aspirations and the possibility of manifesting them. He'd spark something within you, and your life would be richer for having met him. If I introduced you to Mohamed, you'd begin to feel that you'd known him your entire life. This is part of what I call the "Mohamed Phenomenon."

At fifty-nine years old (as of 2014), Mohamed is tall and impressive. With his smooth, swarthy complexion, he says (mostly out of humor) that in his younger days, he could be taken for Engelbert Humperdinck, a handsome pop singer of the '60s and '70s. A white streak stands out against his black hair—he has had this since his twenties, perhaps to mark him as the spiritual being that he is. He dresses the way he runs his business: impeccably. Sure, he wears his colorful Quest polo shirt and tan pants when he's in the office, but when he goes out, it's dark Armani suits and silk ties. During the daytime, he dons dark glasses that protect his eyes from the bright Egyptian sun. He looks like a movie star or the president of a thriving nation as he steps in and out of his chauffeured Mercedes.

One night, before leaving for an awards dinner, he joked about how smashing he'd look, teasing that he was pretending to be a "big man." When he left, he did indeed look smashing. Clearly, Mohamed enjoys the perks that come with his success, but he doesn't seem to take the glamour all that seriously. He's proud, but he's humble.

It is important to Mohamed that he stays humble. When he first became very successful he bought himself a brand new Mercedes. As he drove around in it he began to notice how his pride grew. He also noticed how this experience separated him from others. In that moment of recognition he made the decision to sell the new car and get a used Mercedes, which he has to this day.

Born and raised in Cairo, Mohamed is educated, cultivated, and articulate. He is guided by what he calls "the union of his heart and mind." Both generous and altruistic, he likes to share all he has, indulging those around him. He's active in charity work in Egypt and prominent in peace efforts. He regularly speaks on local radio and television programs, promoting his views.

As a businessman, Mohamed has studied the travel industry in England, where he lived for two years and the United States, where he lived for ten years in his twenties. "It is in America that I grew the vision of how I could bring efficiency and excellence to the travel business," he said, "and combine it with the love and the heart of Egypt." Mohammed is truly successful, but he certainly didn't start out that way. He is a self-made man, working hard to foster success with Quest Travel. His goal has always been to improve every aspect of his business, then improve upon that. He has, indeed, mastered excellence, winning many awards and acknowledgements for the quality of his service, and maintaining many famous clients who bring groups to Egypt. He has dedicated his life to providing the perfect experiences to his travelers, and in this sense, he has revolutionized the travel business in Egypt. Through the efforts of his company, he affirms, "One is cared for and has no worries." When I, for one, was travelling with his agency, they were always two steps ahead of our needs and wants.

As the land carrier for a variety of trips and tours, Mohamed personally customizes every excursion and sees to every detail from the moment his travelers land to the moment they board their plane for the journey home. If there is a hitch, he's on the phone in a flash to ensure it is taken care of. And believe me there are many hitches in Egypt. Although Mohamed manages educational tours for groups involved in archaeological and academic studies, he specializes in spiritual and metaphysical tours. These tours involve spiritual leaders who apply metaphysical principles and use their time in Egypt for teaching, holding meditations, ceremonies, and sacred rituals within the sites and monuments. Mohamed realizes the spiritual power these sites emanate. He knows they promote healing and heightened insight.

It's clear that much of Mohamed's success has to do with the relationships he cultivates—with employees, clients, other business people, officials at the top of Egyptian society, and everyday people on the street. Among his clients and friends, Mohamed counts popular new thought leaders from the States, Europe, Australia, and South Africa. He has close ties with authors and scholars who write about their studies and views of the Great Pyramids and the Sphinx of Giza. He also works with orthodox Egyptologists. His friend Zahi Hawass is an internationally acclaimed Egyptologist who has served as Director of the Giza Plateau, Secretary General of the Supreme Council of Antiquities, and Minister of State for Antiquities Affairs. This relationship has certainly helped Mohamed provide special experiences for his clients. Other friends, including Kent Weeks, lead important excavations and studies. Mark Lehner, a world-renowned Egyptologist who runs the international Giza Plateau Mapping Project, is also a close friend of Mohamed's. All these ties help him formulate incredible tours.

Mohamed's worldly success is impressive, but it's his warm, unassuming way that steals hearts. He emits an energy and warmth that is all his own, and he is more than willing to share this love and light. He has a twinkle in his eye and a charming, mischievous giggle. His sense of humor has everyone around him in stitches within seconds. He's full of laughter and joy, and when he shares his big, wide smile, he emanates charm. He has a way of breaking down defenses, making people feel totally safe, understood and acknowledged. There are no pretenses with Mohamed. Many friends, fellow travelers, and interviewees told me that within minutes of meeting Mohamed, they felt encouraged to be better people and make the world a better place. He is a master politician, but one who keeps his promises and dedicates himself to helping others. Mohamed truly cares about everyone he deals with.

Chapter 10: Notes from the Office

As I walked to Mohamed's office on my first day of interviews, I was terrified and full of doubt. Could I really do this? I tried to remind myself, however, that I was genuinely interested in Mohamed and his work. I tried to remind myself of my love for Egypt. So, I gathered my courage and put my trust in the process. I opened my heart and realized what a wonderful gift it was to have this special time with Mr. Nazmy.

Mohamed's office is an intimate space that feels like a cool oasis after coming in out of the bright, intensely hot Egyptian sun. The ample office is richly appointed with a beautiful Persian carpet and comfortable sofa and chairs. The heavy silk drapes are pulled to keep the room cool and dark, assisted by an air conditioner that emits a low, steady hum. The room is lit with a variety of wall sconces and lamps that have a soft, muted glow.

A usual day of work at the office will find Mohamed sitting behind a massive desk of polished, gleaming hardwood, with his landline phone placed directly in front of him. Stacks of pink folders, some a foot high, cover the right half of his desk. His computer stands to the left of his desk on a separate table. He moves his head back and forth so that he has a constant eye on the screen, now and then turning his chair to answer an email or edit an itinerary. He's surrounded by gifts and framed letters from friends and clients complimenting him on his service. Awards for Quest Travel, pictures of famous people, and photos of the famous sites of Egypt cover the walls.

Everyone at the office dresses as Mohamed does—in a colored polo shirt with the words "Quest Travel" stitched just above the left pocket, along with a pair of tan pants. This is the uniform for everyone but Emil, who seems to prefer wearing his own shirts. Emil's dress code is a constant source of light-hearted bickering between Mohamed and Emil. Mohamed complains that Emil has gone rogue. Emil usually retorts that Mohamed intentionally buys Emil's shirts a size too small so that he has nothing to wear.

All day, staff members ring the buzzer on the office door. Mohamed releases the lock by pushing a device at his desk, and they enter and stand by the door, waiting until he has a moment to acknowledge them. Mohamed eventually turns, addresses them, and then, as often as not, the phone interrupts. Mohamed holds up a finger, pushes his glasses up to his forehead, and leans down to the phone on his desk, placing his eye as close as he can to the phone to decipher the caller ID. From where I sit, it looks like he is placing his eyeball on the phone. Apparently, he is in need of bifocals. This will repeat throughout the day. It's a constant flow of answering the phone, reading and sending emails, answering questions, signing papers, and directing business as people come and go from the office. Sometimes there are lines of people seeking his attention. Once in a while, the rhythm is broken when Emil or other employees come in to laugh, tell stories, and joke around. This goes on all day long at a frenzied pitch.

The first thing Mohamed told me was, "Egypt belongs to the people of the world." He said the holy sites of Egypt contain mysteries that are part of our heritage as human beings, whether it's the three pyramids of Khufu, Khafre, and Menkaure or the Sphinx. I'd never thought of Egypt in that way before, and it was the beginning of an understanding that these places are part of my heritage as well as his. It was a good start. I began to settle down and feel more comfortable. He put me at ease, and I felt part of something bigger—something that united me with everyone on this planet.

Our First Interview

Before we started, Mohamed told me, "No phone calls." That seemed like a good omen until the phone rang. He began the process I grew so familiar with, holding up his finger, leaning forward, and checking the caller ID. Mohamed is very comfortable with multitasking. As we talked, his eyes would shift from my eyes to the computer screen, to the caller ID on the ringing phone, to my eyes, to the computer screen and back again. Occasionally he'd asked me to stop my recorder, saying he'd just be a minute while he took an important call. Sometimes, he'd recognize a client's number from Europe or the States, then break into a wide smile and pick up the phone. He'd greet them with a laugh and a larger-than-life hello before conducting business in English. Otherwise, he'd answer in Arabic. Sometimes the discussions were quiet and officious. Others were warm and friendly, and still others terse with rapid-fire orders.

It was not unusual for one of his many friends to drop by for a chat. When I was there, his friend George Faddoul from Australia was visiting, and often came to the office. Tour leaders and travel company representatives would show up to sit with Mohamed and hammer out plans. He often left the office for business matters.

At one point, I said, "You are in demand by everybody." With a twinkle in his eye, he nodded. "Does everything have to go through you?" I asked him. "Is there any way to change this?" Mohamed thought for a moment.

"If this changes, then it changes everything. I am here for people and when I am not here for them it doesn't work. It has to be like this." We were interrupted by another phone call. Mohamed answered, and I witnessed a lovely conversation in which he told the person on the other end, "I am missing you, and I want to thank you very much for what you did for my son on his birthday. I want you to know that I am a good friend of yours."

He hung up the phone and waved his hand to indicate that we could begin again. I got the feeling it's a good thing to be friends with Mohamed.

As I sat in his office, it was obvious that Mohamed is the captain of the ship. Everything must go through him, and he must make every single decision. Mohamed puts one hundred percent into his work, but it was those moments during the day when he would stop to listen to music that I saw he still takes time for himself. He likes anything romantic, classical, or meditative. He especially loves Andrea Bocelli and Engelbert Humperdinck. Sometimes Mohamed talks to friends via phone or Skype, or watches videos that inspire him.

It is quite evident that Mohamed's employees fear and respect him. Mohamed is a sort of benevolent dictator, and this works very well in his business. He only chooses dedicated helpers like Emil Shaker, his guide and Egyptologist extraordinaire, and Ihab Rashad, his vice president, who both admitted they have had to "marry" the business. Ihab is divorced, while Emil spends a great deal of time away from his wife and home in Luxor.

Regardless, there is a jovial atmosphere underlying the office chaos. The employees are like family to Mohamed (two of his employees actually *are* family—his daughter and his wife). Although his team work very hard, they also take time to talk and enjoy themselves. There's a sense of trust and companionship.

Mohamed and the men in his office joke all of the time, often at the expense of one another. They would say they tease "without mercy." They seem to relish gaining the upper hand, although Mohamed, who is top dog, is rarely the recipient of the teasing. I realized that this kind of joking is just part of life, a way to pass the time and amuse themselves, and they don't take it too seriously.

When I was sitting in the office one day, Mohamed introduced me to Farag el Sayed, a freelance guide who was hired to lead an upcoming British group. Farag is a highly educated man who had just written a book about Ramses the Second, who he believed was pharaoh at the time of Moses. As Farag discussed his book, his beliefs, and his various skills, Mohamed interjected.

"He's brilliant," Mohamed said and then he went on to joke, "Not like Emil." I'd seen Emil laugh when the joke was at his expense before, and I wasn't worried because I know that Emil gives as good as he gets. I had seen many instances of this kind of teasing with Emil, and I'd seen Emil tease others in a similar manner.

Mohamed joked again about Emil. He told me that Emil doesn't represent Egypt and we can tell this by the way he dresses. He said this with a twinkle in his eye and a mischievous smile. I'd seen Mohamed tease Emil before about not really being from Egypt because he is from the streets of Luxor. A man from Cairo in Mohamed's mind is cultivated and a man from Luxor is more like a country bumpkin. And I am sure Emil has his opinions about this as well. So this seems to be a common theme for joking between these two men.

In looking at Farag's dress, it was clear that he was extremely pulled together. I suddenly realized that indeed Emil isn't the best-dressed man on the planet. A few days earlier, when teased about a tear in his pants, Emil had complained that his wife couldn't repair it because she was in Luxor, so he had to wear them as they were. I hadn't really paid much attention to how Emil dresses, until I compared him with Farag. I had paid more attention to his humor, his knowledge of ancient Egypt, his zest for life, and his huge heart.

Don't worry. Emil got even in his own way. Being that it was Ramadan, and Mohamed was fasting, Emil pulled out his lunch and a soda and placed these on the table in front of Mohamed's desk. Then he sat down and ate and drank with relish. He turned to me and said that because he is a Coptic Christian he doesn't fast. He also said he enjoys eating in front of Mohamed in this way. Then they both started laughing!

Our Time Together

I especially liked my time alone with Mohamed. While interviewing him, I found myself wanting to be a better person. I wanted to participate in his vision for peace and understanding, and I felt totally loved and accepted. Isn't that what we all want? There was something contagious about his joy, his perspective, and his manner of being. Did I fall under his spell? Was he just the best salesman in the world? If so, isn't being a salesman for peace a good thing? It was all a bit confusing.

There was so much I wanted to discuss with Mohamed, but I knew I would only have a few hours a day with him. I took full advantage of our time. We talked about how to truly experience the spiritual energy of the ancient sites of Egypt. We talked about his affinity for the Egyptian deities. We talked about ancient culture as the beginning of culture for *all* people, not just Egyptians. We talked about spirituality. We talked about his father and how he had gone out of his way to teach his children respect and tolerance for other religions. We discussed the Afandina, the beautiful boat he had designed and had built. He shared with me what it means to him to be a Muslim. He explained how his marriage to his wife, Hanan, helps him keep his life smooth and balanced. He told me how happy he is with his children, his wife, and his life.

And yes, we discussed his notoriety and success. He told me that he believes the reason to have money is to help others, to give back, and to share the abundance one has been blessed with. Mohamed has wealth, but he is not overly impressed with it. He takes nothing for granted and attributes his success to the travelers who come to Egypt, and ultimately, to God. He enjoys simple pleasures. When Mohamed was visiting France, he was invited to a ritzy lunch at a luxury hotel with some very wealthy people. The next day, when he finally had a day to himself, he grabbed a sandwich, sat on a bench, and watched people on the street walk by. "This is who I am," he told me.

Part Four: Mohamed's Story

Fig. Part Four.1. Photograph courtesy of Richard Fero.

Follow Your Heart

Chapter 11: Growing up in Egypt

As I sat across from Mohamed in a comfortable chair, I imagined all of the other tour leaders and guides who had sat in the same place. I thought about all the lively conversations that had occurred, all the jokes that had been exchanged, and all the lives that had been touched. I felt eager to learn more about Mohamed, and began to ask him about his early life. What were his formative years like? With his approval, I turned on the tape recorder, pen poised, and Mohamed began to tell me about growing up in Cairo.

"I was born on April 1, 1955 at 10:00 P.M. in Cairo, Egypt," he said formally. That was plain enough, but what came next was a truly unexpected story. He suddenly grew shy and quiet. "I have a secret and I don't talk about this very much," he offered. I moved forward in my chair and nodded encouragingly. He went on to tell me what his parents once told him: After he was circumcised as a baby, he wouldn't stop crying, and soon his parents realized that he was bleeding relentlessly from the procedure. They rushed him to the doctor, who said that such bleeding was very rare. Though worrisome at the time, this bleeding is, in fact, the mark of a holy man in Islamic tradition. It is considered a blessing.

Mohamed said he remembers when he first asked his father about the story of his birth. He was about six. So, his father told him the story about the special blessing indicated by this bleeding, explaining to Mohamed that this marks a baby boy as a special person. Mohamed always felt he was different in some way from his playmates, and he wanted to understand more.

Years later, when Mohamed visited Saudi Arabia and Mecca, he met with an imam who told him more about the meaning of the bleeding. "The imam told me that this marked me," Mohamed said. "That it foretold something about me—something special, something elevated, something that carried meaning for my mission in life and my special purpose." The imam explained to Mohamed that such a person is holding, carrying, and acting from a higher consciousness. He is gifted with a special aura of love, if he so chooses to use it and this gift of the spiritual understanding of unity makes him different. Thus, he is not limited, but understands the realm of all possibility in his consciousness. Mohamed spoke of this as a gift from God and it was clear that he takes this as a serious responsibility. He said he has always felt he was destined to be of service and to bring people together.

Mohamed asked me if I would like something to drink and I nodded yes. He got on his phone, spoke in Arabic, and soon the door buzzed and a young man came in. Mohamed spoke to him in Arabic, and then asked me if there was anything that Kelly or I needed at the apartment. He suggested eggs, milk, butter, fruit juice, cola, water, or bread—the list went on. At first I said no, but Egyptians are generous people and Mohamed continued pressing, sure that we must need something. I wasn't sure as I was still so jet lagged, but realized that this could go on for a long time, I said yes to it all. Mohamed smiled, nodded, and gave instructions which prompted the young man to leave and close the door behind him. Finally we moved on with the interview and he shared with me more about his early life.

Mohamed grew up with privilege. He had a nice home with several staff members who attended to the family's needs, including the household chores. Because his father wanted him to focus on his studies, Mohamed didn't work until he went to the States when he was nineteen. His father's appreciation for education set Mohamed on a long path of higher learning. Mohamed attended the Faith School, the Shobra Secondary School, and the University Alsun, where he studied various languages. He also attended Nain Shams, which is known as Cairo University, where he specialized in language and hotel management, and received a degree in Business Administration from the American University of Cairo.

When Mohamed spoke about his parents, his eyes welled up with tears. He told me that he missed them immensely now that they had passed on. He seemed surprised by this emotion, uncomfortable even. He stopped talking, took a breath, and shook his head ever so slightly. I looked at the floor, just to give him a bit of privacy. He asked me to turn off the recorder—he needed a few moments to gather himself. I was taken with how much affection, respect and gratitude he had for his parents and what they taught him.

Mohamed's mother was a homemaker and great support to both her diplomat husband and children. She was the one Mohamed could easily talk to. It was his father, however, who guided him carefully alongside his nine siblings. From the eldest to the youngest they are Sohier, Ahmed, Amal, Amina, Abdallah, Mohamed, Omayma, Ashraf, and Somaya.

From an early age, Mohamed knew that he would either be involved in the travel industry or become a diplomat like his father. He told me that when he was five years old, he had a vision from God in which he saw what his life would be like. He looked at me softly and said, "I always felt different from others my age. I was old for my years in understanding things of the heart." He touched his chest with his hand as he spoke. "It has always been my ambition to bring different people together." It seems that ever since he was a young child, Mohamed has had a direct connection to God, and was always comfortable with this gift.

Chapter 12: Mohamed and the United States

Mohamed has had a love affair with the United States his entire life. Whenever he mentioned it, he would light up. He would grow animated, face beaming, and flash those vibrant smiles. He said he is fascinated with the United States in the same way so many from the States are fascinated with Egypt.

The Lunch Box Story

While I was on a Spirit Quest Tours trip in June of 2014, Mohamed traveled with us. While traveling down the Nile, a fellow traveler Jude Belanger, insisted that Mohamed retell what Jude calls the lunch box story. Jude had met Mohamed through friends when Mohamed had visited the States in 2011, and this was his very favorite story that Mohamed had shared with him. Mohamed smiled and was glad to recount the story.

Mohamed's affinity for the United States began when he was five or six years old. On Thursdays, the end of the week in Egypt, the children at his primary school would receive boxes of cheese, milk, and mixed sweets. There was writing on the boxes saying the snack was a gift from the American people to their Egyptian friends. Every Thursday, as Mohamed ate his snack, he'd think about the lovely gift that the people of the United States had sent him. He'd think, "What is this America? Who are these Americans and what do they look like? Why do they love us so much? Why do they give us this gift?" Gratitude and curiosity grew in the innocent heart of this young boy. He was so touched that from then on, he was determined to visit America to see who these people were who loved him so.

Thus, growing up, Mohamed loved all things American. He admired President John Kennedy. "It is no secret," he told me, "that this American president is loved by most of the people of the world." I had to agree with him that many Americans of my generation felt the same way. Even though I was in high school during Kennedy's presidency and knew nothing about politics, I found him engaging, interesting, and intelligent. He seemed so different from most politicians at that time.

Mohamed also reminisced about his favorite television show, *The Fugitive*, about Dr. Richard Kimble. In the series, Kimble is falsely convicted of killing his wife. He then escapes from the van that crashes in route to death row and spends the next four seasons traversing the nation to find the true killer. Mohamed said watching this '60s hit show made him feel more connected to the States. Suddenly, I realized that from 1963 to 1967, Mohamed and I were both watching the same TV show. I smiled.

Off to America

When Mohamed was young, he promised himself that if he had the opportunity to travel abroad, he would go to America. He even turned down a less-expensive trip to Europe in 1974, deciding that if he was going to travel, it was going to be to the United States. And so at the age of nineteen, he decided to fulfill his dream.

At that time, airfare from Egypt to the States was 50 dollars, a lot of money in Mohamed's world. Mohamed's father didn't approve of his desire to live in the States, hoping instead that he would continue his studies. Although he respected his father immensely, he knew he just had to go. So, instead, Mohamed turned to his older brother, who was working in Saudi Arabia at the time. His brother sent him 100 dollars—50 for the plane ticket and 50 for travel expenses. Even as he told me the story, Mohamed seemed to relive the excitement he felt when he finally had his ticket. "I was so happy!" he exclaimed.

When Mohamed makes up his mind to do something, he does it. Mohamed never spent time brooding over the notion that going to

America might not be an option. He didn't take no for an answer, and his goal manifested quite easily. This is a pattern in his life. It seems he has always been supported with what he needs as he moves towards his greater destiny. As he once said, when his heart and mind are joined, there is no stopping him.

On the way to America he had to stay the night in Copenhagen and his hotel room cost him ten dollars. That only left him forty dollars to his name and he was worried that immigration might not let him into the country with so little money. He remembered hearing that he would need fifty dollars to get in, and he stressed about this. It just so happened that the day Mohamed landed in the States, many of the people going through immigration spoke only Arabic. An officer asked if anyone in the group spoke English and could help with the processing of the papers and passports. Mohamed spoke up. "I knew I could do it," he told me. Once everyone was through, with Mohamed translating, the officer told him that he had worked very hard. "She stamped my visa without asking me anything further," he said.

Mohamed looked at me and threw his left hand up in the air, as if to say that life was out of his control and in the hands of God in those first confusing moments in this strange new place. When Mohamed got to New York, he was amazed by how different it was from Cairo—the air felt cold even though it was summer, the buildings were tall and looming, and pedestrians rushed by. "Everything was new and overwhelming," he said. "This was nothing like Egypt at all. Life here was very, very different."

As I sat with Mohamed, it was hard for me to imagine him as he had been then—a frightened and insecure young man in a foreign country. Given the cultural differences between America and Egypt, I'm even more astounded by his resolve and courage to travel to a country so different from his own, especially considering his age and lack of experience. Clearly, Mohamed had a need for independence and was fearless in pursuing his dreams.

Needless to say, luck was in Mohamed's favor. He found a cheap hotel, asked at the front desk how to find a job, and went from there. He was able to find work, a place to live, and people to help him with his new life. Mohamed doesn't spend a lot of energy worrying about "what ifs" and worst-case scenarios. This has always been true for him; if he needs to do something, he finds out what he needs to do, and then he does it. His optimism works in his favor. The universe was looking out for Mohamed, helping him have this experience in America that would play a vital role in the development of his business and in the fulfillment of his life's purpose.

Working in America

That doesn't mean the path was easy. As he talked about finding a job in America, Mohamed shook his head and smiled. He explained that he went to the employment agency on 14th Street, where a man asked him if he had ever worked before. "I answered yes," he said, "although I had never worked a day in my life before that point." Each time the man asked Mohamed if he had this skill or that skill, Mohamed said yes. Eventually, the man referred him to a place he could go in the morning to meet a "woman named Mary who would hire him."

By that time it was late afternoon. Mohamed returned to his hotel, planning to eat and get a good night's sleep. Mohamed didn't understand how hotels worked in the States, so he was shocked to find his luggage waiting for him in the lobby. He had only paid for one night, so after the 2:00 P.M. check-out time, they'd given his room to someone else. "Why is my luggage here?" he asked. "Where do I go now?" Hotel management sent him to the YMCA in Queens, and said they'd already made reservations for him.

"I did not know where this place they called Queens was," Mohamed said, shrugging his shoulders and looking to the side. "I had no idea how to get from Manhattan to Queens. So all I could do was try to ask somebody. I found out very quickly that life in New York is not at all like life in Egypt. In Egypt we help each other, so I was not used to people ignoring me or looking at me like I was from outer space. I was learning about the style of life in America!" I could only imagine how lonely and afraid I would have felt if I had been in the same position.

He took a moment to stretch, so I followed suit and took a sip of water. Mohamed was observing Ramadan and couldn't eat or drink, so each time I drank, I felt a pang of guilt. I was thirsty, but I'd gulp down as much water as I could in a single moment to get it over with. Mohamed cleared his throat and waved his hand to say he was ready to talk again.

"I finally talked to a woman who was about eighty," he said, "and she told me she would take me to Queens on the subway." He was grateful, but when he arrived at the YMCA, there was no reservation for him, and he couldn't help but take a moment of self-pity: "I thought to myself, 'Poor Mohamed!' I was alone, had no place to stay, and had to work in the morning. So what could I do?"

Before Mohamed left Egypt, a family friend had given him the phone number of someone in the States he could call if he got in trouble. "I thought this was the time I had to either make the call or go back to Egypt," he told me. "So I made the call." Luck was on his side, as usual. The man *lived* in Queens and offered to come pick Mohamed up. And so, George and his mother and sister welcomed Mohamed into their home, giving him a meal and a bed for the night. "I was overwhelmed to say the least," he said.

During the night, George's mother heard Mohamed snoring heavily. "She thought it must be because I was so worn out and exhausted," Mohamed said. In the morning, she announced that she wanted to invite Mohamed to stay with them until he was on his feet. He had a good night's rest, food to eat, and a place to stay with good people. He'd found a place of refuge and relief. Suddenly, my tape recorder stopped with a snap, interrupting our conversation. I flipped the tape over, turned on the recorder again, and nodded to him.

In the morning, George's sister, who worked in Manhattan, took Mohamed to the restaurant to meet "Mary" and apply for a position as a delivery boy. They wanted to hire him, but there was a problem. "She told me that since this was a Jewish restaurant, the name Mohamed just wouldn't work," he explained. "She told me from then on, I would be Joe." There he was, going by the name Joe in a Jewish restaurant with mostly Jewish customers, working as a delivery boy. Again, twists of fate fostered the growth of acceptance and tolerance in Mohamed. A young Arab man found his way to a job in a Jewish restaurant with Jewish customers, and he had experiences that he would never have found if he'd stayed in Cairo.

Mohamed beamed as he remembered this time in his life. Besides his obviously non-Jewish name, he wasn't well-equipped to be a delivery boy. "I had no clue where I was or where anything else was," he said. "I didn't even know what street the restaurant was on." Whenever Mary gave him an address to find, he would start asking anyone he ran into for directions, getting lost and re-lost along the way. "But I always took what Mary gave me and delivered it," he said. In his first week, Mohamed made 80 dollars, which he keeps in an album to this day. Soon, Mohamed was making about 120 dollars in tips per week and was able to save money. Meanwhile, he became good friends with George. They played soccer together and walked around the city. "George helped me feel less alone," he told me.

Eventually, Mohamed came to understand that he would make more money as a waiter. When he heard he could make 100 dollars during a single lunch service and even more during dinner, he thought 'I need to go and get this job.' He returned to the employment agency and told them confidently that he was well-qualified. He lowered his chin and peered at me over the edge of his glasses, raising his eyebrows. "Of course, the only job I'd ever had was as a delivery boy."

The agency sent him to the St. George Hotel, which had a French restaurant with a French menu. He didn't know the language. He didn't know what the food was, what people were ordering, or how to communicate with the chef. It didn't last long. After a five-hour shift, he was fired. "I couldn't argue," he said. "All I could do was say okay." Mohamed still wonders how he managed to make it through that many hours before they found him out. He must be an excellent actor and a suburb bluffer. He has a certain audacity, and thrives on pushing the envelope. His bravado has certainly served him well.

As usual, our conversation was interrupted when Mohamed's phone rang. He did the dance, eyeballing the caller ID, holding up a finger, and taking the call. He spoke rapid-fire Arabic and laughed deeply. As he spoke, he tapped his desk with his index finger for emphasis. After a few minutes, he said goodbye with a tone of loving endearment and turned back to me.

"What was I saying?" he asked me. Before I could answer, he launched back in. "The coffee shop," he said. "So that day I went for another job at a coffee shop." This job seemed more manageable: serving donuts, coffee, tea and sandwiches sounded straightforward after what he had just done.

Mohamed cherished the experience of working. "With every new day I learned something new," he said, "because there was so much I did not know. I loved the challenges. I learned things by making mistakes." Mohamed worked at the shop for a couple months, then left to try to find a job where he could earn more money. "I worked, got fired, worked, got fired," he said. "I made it through difficult lessons—everything was new—everything." For Mohamed, it was all an expected part of learning how to live life in America. There was no room for getting discouraged, only a chance to thrive on the challenge of new things. One job led to another, then another.

He had only planned to stay in the States for three months, but before he knew it, it had been a year. The longer he stayed, the more he liked it, and the more he trusted that his fighting spirit would get him through challenge after challenge. "I realized I didn't want to go back," he said. Mohamed brushed back the hair on top of his head with a sweep of his palm.

Eventually, he moved from Queens to an apartment in Brooklyn, where he got to know a Greek man called Joe from across the hall. "We understood each other well because we were both foreigners and from places on the Mediterranean," he told me. It wasn't long before Joe offered Mohamed a job. Joe owned a ship company, and asked Mohamed to be a supervisor right off the bat. Since Mohamed was eager to travel within the States and learn more about the country, this was a perfect job. "How could I say no to free travel, free food, and a higher salary?" he asked. So, visa well-expired, he continued his journey through the States.

His Education Continues

Mohamed worked for Joe for about six months, often traveling to Maryland. He said he liked Maryland because it felt more relaxed than New York. The lifestyle was slower and the dress was more casual. Next on his agenda was to pursue more education. "I heard the best thing to do in America was to study something," he said. "So I decided to go to school as a means of learning about the culture." A good friend helped him with the details and arrangements, and so he went to school in Maryland for the next three years, all the while growing more acclimated to life in America.

The Letter

In 1983, after ten years of living in America, Mohamed received a letter from home. As he sat as his desk, relaying the story, Mohamed tensed up for a moment. "I remember not wanting to open the letter," he said. The letter said his father had died. He was only 63. The news was a huge shock that sent Mohamed into a spiral of depression. "I kept to myself for months," he said. "I did not work or eat. I lost interest in everything." Mohamed's father was his true guide in life—a role model and mentor. "I am only ten percent of the person my father was," Mohamed told me. When Mohamed called his mother in Cairo, she told him she was afraid she would die before Mohamed came home and that she would never see her son again. It was time to go back to Egypt.

Mohamed's plan was to go to Egypt for a month or so, then bring his mother back to America with him. The States felt like home now, and he loved the lifestyle. "My mother is the one who birthed me, but my stepmother America is the one who raised me," he said. And so he made preparations to return to Egypt believing he would be returning very soon to the States and continue with the life he had created there.

Part Five: The Travel Business in Egypt

Fig. Part Five.1. Mohamed, Zahi Hawass, and Emil, 2008. Photograph courtesy of Richard Fero.

When We Embark Upon a Course That Involves the Good of the Many, Spirit Supports Us with Grace and Ease Along the Way

Chapter 13: Mohamed Returns to Egypt and the Travel Business

Mohamed was twenty-nine when he returned to Egypt for his father's funeral. He had spent ten years in the United States. In our interview, he kept his feelings hidden about this unexpected change in his life. As it turned out, his mother did not want to live in America and she needed Mohamed to stay in Egypt and help take care of the family. Duty to family simply won out over his desire to return to the States. He didn't mention having any regrets, but his love for America has never diminished.

Once he returned to Egypt, Mohamed set to finding work. In Egypt, the travel business is a major source of employment, and it is quite common for those who are young and well educated to take up tourism jobs. This is especially true if they are multi-lingual. Mohamed went to a big travel company and told them he spoke Spanish, French, and English. One can recall from his experience at the French restaurant that he certainly does not know how to speak French. One of the reasons Mohamed pursued the job was because it offered him an opportunity to be in contact with Americans. He had made many friends in the States and he missed them terribly.

As we spoke, Mohamed tapped his heart a few times with his palm. "Still today, something in my heart loves the American people and this has been true ever since I was five years old," he told me. "I can't really explain why this love and attention is focused all in one direction." To this day, Mohamed feels that he owes the American people. He explained that he wouldn't be the person he is today if he hadn't been given the chance to travel and have the experiences he had. When he gets an email or phone call from one of his American friends, he lights up. Mohamed has clients and friends all over the world, and loves them all equally, but America will always have a special place in his heart.

Working for Sphinx Travel

Mohamed worked for a travel business called Sphinx Travel for the next thirteen years. He started as a guide, eventually working his way all the way up to vice president. His experiences in the United States served him well; the company dealt primarily with groups from America. Mohamed was adept at quickly determining what they wanted from their travel experiences, and he would take the time to talk with them and explore their ideas. Mohamed worked hard to build this man's company, establish important contacts, improve service, and build a reputation that would later serve him well. More importantly, he worked hard because it is his nature to please others. He thought outside the box and had limitless expectations for what was possible.

At Sphinx Travel, Mohamed had to navigate a less-than-ideal situation. No one I spoke with had a single good thing to say about the owner of the company—a mild way of putting it. Mohamed, as is his nature, won't say an unkind word about this man, but he does say that the owner had trouble trusting others. Nearly every person I spoke with about Mohamed echoed that he was the only reason Sphinx Travel stayed in business. Those who witnessed Mohamed's skill had a hard time seeing him work for a man who was cheap, crafty, and unkind. Many encouraged him to start his own business.

While he was working for Sphinx Travel he was accruing important experience but also looking into the future and how he could best promote his own vision for creating peace in the world through travel. It would be a while before Mohamed was ready to go out on his own, especially given the climate of uncertainty in the travel business due to the negative impact of terrorism. In the meantime he made important contacts. For instance, while working with spiritual groups like the Rosicrucians, Mohamed began to understand that he could create a special niche for himself within the travel business that catered to spiritual pilgrimage. He was beginning to think about how he could make these trips better. The Rosicrucians brought large groups to Egypt which in turn brought prosperity but also brought a consciousness that Mohamed was drawn to. He continued to make new friends and provide better service to his employer's clients, while he was also expanding his own ideas about unity and what was possible to create through business.

Chapter 14: Meeting Emil

When Mohamed and Emil Shaker met in the early '90s as guides at Sphinx Travel, they didn't really like each other. Mohamed makes it clear that he and Emil are *very different*. Emil is a "country boy" from Upper Egypt, while Mohamed was born, raised, and educated in cosmopolitan Cairo. He calls the difference between them "day and night."

When Mohamed first met Emil, he wondered how they could possibly work together. Mohamed had prejudices about a "guy from upper Egypt," and made assumptions about what kind of person Emil would be. "I thought, 'could he be a good guy?'" Mohamed said, sweeping his hand upward as if to present the question to the air. Education in Upper Egypt was government run and had a reputation for being rudimentary in comparison to Lower Egypt. Mohamed thought Emil wouldn't be able to get things done or work well with people. "I did not believe that Emil and I were going to last very long," he told me.

On the other hand, Emil had his own prejudice against "city boys," from Lower Egypt, and thought he would never work with someone like Mohamed. Inevitably, they soon found themselves assigned to the same tour. The tour was led by Nicki Scully, the spiritual leader I discuss in Chapter 17. Jane Bell, who eventually began to lead her own groups to Egypt, was traveling with Nicki's group. As they cruised from Aswan to Luxor on a large boat, a "very arrogant" European man wanted to play poker. Emil and Mohamed quickly ganged up on him, outwitting him partly to win his money and mostly to bring his ego down a notch.

Through that noble joint venture, they became friends. "They discovered that they worked quite well together as a team," Jane said. Later that night, Mohamed and Emil formed a deep connection. "We shared the stories of our lives," Mohamed said. "We formed a strong relationship, which we have to this day."

Fig. 14.1. Mohamed and Emil in the old days from a photograph on Emil's desk.

When Mohamed formed his own company, he made Emil a promise: if he joined him, he would ensure Emil was a successful and prosperous man. He told Emil that his life would change. He would have more than enough to make sure that his family would be well taken care of, and he would have great things to do. Years later, all of this has proven true. Meanwhile, Emil has been instrumental in helping Mohamed become as successful as he is. Jean Houston, told me, "One is for the pure heart of Egypt and one is for the clinical details and the mind of what is there. These two have an amazing friendship."

Fig. 14.2. Mohamed, Nancy, Jane, and Emil in the early days. Photograph courtesy of Jane Bell.

They also have an entertaining dynamic, which Greg Roach, owner of Spirit Quest Tours and leads groups to Egypt yearly, described perfectly. He explained how Emil has to wait impatiently while Mohamed gives a good word to everyone on the street who comes up to him. While Mohamed gives a 'darshan' to everyone he connects with, Emil rolls his eyes and taps his watch, waiting for Mohamed to finish so they can get to their next destination. It happens every time they go out, but nothing ever changes. Mohamed is just being Mohamed and Emil is just being Emil.

Greg sees Mohamed and Emil as longstanding soul mates with a complex and fascinating relationship. He told me he thinks they must have a long history of incarnations together, considering how well they complement each other. "Mohamed is the opener of the way," he said. "He makes the precise arrangement and makes it as perfect as it can be. Then, Emil enters and works his magic. Emil is an artist of the highest order, in my opinion. Egypt is his canvas, and the people that visit are his paint." Both work and play off of each other to the benefit of their clients. Greg has seen them go from utter rage to hugging, kissing and joking five minutes later.

Maureen St. Germain, who is an author and a teacher of sacred geometry, the MerKaBa, and the Akashic Records, brings tours to Egypt frequently. She echoed that Emil and Mohamed are indeed so close that one might mistake them for a married couple. They seem to enjoy airing their differences in front of you, hoping you'll take sides. When Maureen first met Emil's wife, Faten asked her, "What do you think of these two men who are so close?" Maureen answered that they seemed like husband and wife. Faten thought that was hilarious.

One day, when I was in the office interviewing Mohamed, Emil came in and they began to argue quite vehemently about trust and betrayal. Sometimes they spoke in English, sometimes in Arabic. When they raised their voices, it was all in Arabic. As Mohamed argued that one should walk away from a person who breaks your trust, Emil paced back and forth. Mohamed leaned forward, pumping his left hand up in the air. "If they break your trust, that is the end of it! No argument," he said. He sat back in his chair, crossed his arms, and glared at Emil.

"This can never be true," Emil retorted adamantly as he stopped suddenly right in front of Mohamed's desk to make his point. "You cannot turn your back on someone you love." As they fought, they kept looking at me to see if I was going to side with one or the other. This seems to have been a longstanding disagreement and one of their favorite little spats—I doubt they have resolved it to this day.

When I asked Nicki Scully about the relationship between Emil and Mohamed, she described Mohamed as the alpha male, and Emil as the one with heart. When she and Jane Bell met the two men during the poker game, Nicki said it was clear they didn't like each other. Over time, Nicki and Jane watched these men, who both have huge capacity for love and giving, become the dearest friends. "Jane and I watched the two fuse until it was apparent that Mohamed wouldn't be able to be Mohamed and give the level of service that he does without Emil," Nicki told me.

The most tender and sweet sight for me was to see how Emil tends to Mohamed, who is still hampered by the results of the stroke he suffered in 2008. People have told me that following the stroke, Emil fed him, stayed by his side, and walked with him until he grew stronger. I have never seen such love and tender care. It is a good thing that Emil and Mohamed met and began to work together, as their relationship benefits everyone who comes in contact with them.

Chapter 15: The Effect of Terrorism on Tourism in Egypt

You can't talk about travel and tourism in Egypt without talking about the effect of terrorism on the industry. Long before 9/11 brought tourism in Egypt to a grinding halt, terrorism within the country wreaked havoc on the economy.

When I interviewed the author John Anthony West, who has taken groups to Egypt with Mohamed since the early days and is a good friend of Mohamed's, I wanted to know more about the effects of terrorism from his point of view. I realized it would be hard to truly understand Mohamed's story without a greater understanding of this. John told me about his first recollection of terrorism in Egypt. It was 1985, and a man named Leon Klinghoffer, who used a wheelchair, was pushed off a cruise ship in Alexandria. "This started a big uproar," West said. "It scared off Americans and brought a chill to the industry." The Egyptian economy relies heavily on tourism, as its ancient monuments draw people from all over the world. "Egypt is the only country in the world whose biggest industry is their past," West said. "Egypt *is* the attraction, except for the Red Sea and scuba diving." With a crippling lack of travelers from America and a dip in European tourists, Mohamed was concerned. "Tourism would get hit hard," West said. "Mohamed was scared...he had kids and a wife to support."

It was but a small group of militants who carried out occasional acts of violence who were responsible for deeply troubling effects on

Mohamed's work, livelihood, and the economy of his country. Although Mohamed eventually opened his own company, the terrorism in Egypt made it a bigger risk for him than usual.

Jane Bell is another tour leader who traveled with Mohamed when he worked with Sphinx Travel. She talked about how it used to be to travel in Egypt before Mohamed began his own company. She explained, "People shoved you out of the way and fights were going on and some people looked at you only for your money. Even though many didn't do this, to a foreigner it could be intimidating. There was no security and although you could go anywhere in the country, it was Mohamed who wanted to ensure the safety of his groups." Safety is what Mohamed worked so hard to ensure for his clients. And he has succeeded.

A Brief History of the Brotherhood and Terrorism

Although we often hear about the Muslim Brotherhood or the White Brotherhood, few truly know what it is. Founded in 1928, it was initially an organization that did educational and charitable work to fulfill Islamic values of altruism and civic duty. It later became involved in the nationalist movement, but it wasn't until 1936 that it grew militant in its opposition to British rule, turning to acts of violence and killings.

Over time, the Brotherhood began to embrace more hostile views about Jews and Western societies. The Egyptian government suppressed the Brotherhood many times after uncovering plots of assassination and overthrow. In 1948, the government ordered the dissolution of the Brotherhood, which had been involved in the assassination of government officials as well as arson attacks in Cairo. Although the Brotherhood supported the military coup of 1952, the military junta was unwilling to share power with the Brotherhood. In 1954, after the attempted assassination of Colonel Gamal Abdel Nasser, the leader of the 1952 Egyptian Revolution, the government again abolished the Brotherhood and imprisoned and punished thousands of its members.

Since that time, the Brotherhood has splintered into many sects. Some are Islamic extremists who have targeted terrorist attacks on government officials, police, tourists, and the Christian minority, increasing activity in the '90s. Splinter groups targeted high-level political leaders and killed hundreds of Egyptians with the goal of establishing traditional religious Sharia law. The leader of this extremist Egyptian Islamic Jihad is believed to be the mastermind behind the operations of al-Qaeda.

It's important to note that there are religious people who support Sharia law in Egypt but do not endorse or support violence. The Brotherhood's leadership actually distanced itself from violent measures and established a nonviolent, reformist strategy. The organization still remained technically illegal, but continued and was subject to periodic crackdowns. And splinter groups continued underground. Although Anwar Sadat released many political prisoners during his presidency, he himself was assassinated by a violent splinter group, after he signed a peace agreement with Israel.

After Hosni Mubarak took office in 1981 as the fourth President of Egypt, many educated students and professionals joined the Brotherhood and became involved in social service in neighborhoods and villages. To put a damper on the Brotherhood's renewed influence, Mubarak utilized repressive measures beginning in 1992. Despite government attempts to contain the Brotherhood, the organization continued to fight in what they called the war against the culture and identity of Islam, while the government in turn combated radical Islamic ideologies. Members of the Brotherhood who were never involved in violence or terrorism as well as those who had planned and participated in violence, suffered beatings and harassment, as well as arrests, torture, and imprisonment. This led to many random acts of violence against the government.

The Brotherhood has continued to be a strong political force in Egypt because of its grassroots support and strong organization. Given that people in Egypt were desperate for social services that the government failed to provide, and because the Brotherhood promotes Sharia law, which many conservative Muslims support, the Brotherhood continues. According to John R. Bradley in his book *Inside Egypt: The Land of the Pharaohs on the Brink of a Revolution*, it has been the largest and most organized political opposition force in Egypt and is still a major player in the country's unfolding political story (49).

It is important to remember, as in any country where a small number of people pursue violent tactics, the majority of people in Egypt do not support terrorism. Following Islam and being a Muslim is not a precursor for violence—that is a generalization that many Westerners make, ignorantly clumping "Islam," "Brotherhood," "Muslim," and "terrorist" into the same category.

The Deir-el-Bahari Massacre

In July of 1997, the Brotherhood employed a "nonviolence initiative." Four months later, terrorists from a militarist Islamic group killed tourists, police officers, and a tour guide on the West Bank of Luxor at the mortuary temple of Hatshepsut. This attack is thought to have been an attempt to undermine the initiative—purposefully carried out to wreak havoc on the economy and provoke the government into taking action against the Brotherhood, which they hoped would strengthen popular support for their anti-government movement. Although the attack *did* devastate the economy, it also led to internal divisions among the militants and actually resulted in a ceasefire that suspended hostilities against tourists.

Ironically, the massacre disrupted and curbed Islamic terrorist activity in Egypt. Egyptian public opinion was overwhelmingly against the violence. Within days of the massacre, spontaneous demonstrations against terrorism broke out in Luxor, with protestors demanding that the government take action. The militants quickly realized that violent tactics had been a huge miscalculation on their part and denied involvement. The majority of the Egyptian people abhor violence and are terribly sorry that any violence occurred in their country. This death-blow to their economy was extremely hurtful, so much so that the violence ended.

After the massacre, people stopped coming to Egypt, and the travel industry fell into a major slump. Checkpoints with armed guards were installed to protect tourists, and it took five long years to recover. Eventually, the government took strong action that, while curbing violence directed at tourist, also impinged on the rights of its people.

9/11

Just as tourism was increasing steadily again, 9/11 happened, and in an instant, all progress halted. Once again, Egyptian travel business was devastated. Kathy Ravenwood, a friend of mine who traveled to Egypt with Nicki Scully in October after the attacks, said that the sites were completely empty and there was barely a tourist in sight. She told me the Egyptian people kissed and hugged her group for returning to their country, imparting the message that these terrorists may have been Muslim, but the majority of Muslims are peace-minded people. Many Egyptians weren't even aware the attack had occurred. It was a very small group of Arab extremists who carried out the attack, and as the Egyptians became aware of the violence, they denounced it.

The Egyptian economy, which is largely dependent on tourism, took a nosedive. Although Mohamed's business with Americans dropped drastically, he fortunately had travelers from Europe, Australia, China, and other countries who continued touring. "The travel business in Egypt is always a big risk," said Jane Bell, "but after 2001, hardly *anyone* came to Egypt. Mohamed had a big overhead, and yet he still paid all his employees. Mohamed firmly believes that generosity pays off, and it is all in God's hands." In fact, Mohamed had prepared for an emergency, and even was able to give bonuses to three deserving employees at the end of the following season. As usual, the wellbeing of those around him came first, and the way he handled the situation impressed many. According to Jane, this is simply part of who he is. "Everything he does comes through his heart. He embodies the heart of Egypt. He is alchemy. He manifests his vision. His heart works it and his mind grounds it!" Nearly every person I interviewed for this book told me the same story of how he took care of his employees during a very difficult economic time.

Mohamed has an impeccable reputation for ensuring the safety of his travelers. However, during times when fear and prejudice were abundant in the United States, it was often his loyal friends and clients who helped him build business for Quest Travel—people like Gregg Braden, Jane Bell, John Anthony West, and Nicki Scully.

Chapter 16: An Important Relationship with Gregg Braden: Scientist, Visionary, and Scholar

Photo by Sean Kapera courtesy of Gregg Braden.

Gregg Braden is a writer, lecturer, workshop facilitator, and tour leader who believes the key to our future lies in the wisdom of our past. He has spent more than twenty years searching the remote monasteries of Egypt, Peru, and Tibet for secrets encoded in the languages of these ancient civilizations. Gregg's conscious-raising work, which has been published in 27 languages and 30 countries, continues to uplift and enlighten people around the globe. His past five books made the New York Times Bestseller List. He describes his goal as "to link the wisdom of the past that has been lost with the best science of today—to find solutions that are really concrete and applicable to what we are facing in our world."

I wasn't surprised to learn that his research began in Egypt, and that Mohamed was an instrumental part of Gregg's journey. Magic happened in their work together—magic that sparked insight, created opportunity, and deepened both men's resolve to follow their special purposes in life.

Gregg met Mohamed in the early '80s, when Gregg was just beginning his research and Mohamed was developing his skills as a travel guide. Their relationship was one of mutual benefit. Through Mohamed, Gregg was able to access the places he wanted to research and provide the experiences he wanted for his groups. Through Gregg, Mohamed was able to experience the spiritual revelation that set him on the path of realizing his vision of peace through travel. By working with Gregg, Mohammed learned what spiritual travelers wanted, and what metaphysical experiences were possible with the ancient, spiritual energy of the sites.

A New Style of Leading Tours

In 1984 Gregg took his first group to Egypt. After traveling many hours—New York to Paris and Paris to Cairo—Gregg met Mohamed who was working as a tour guide for Sphinx Travel. Gregg asked Mohamed to step into his "informal office" to talk. There was, in fact, no office, but the two spoke on the steps of the beautiful, historic Mena house that rests just at the foot of the Giza Plateau. Gregg had never worked with Mohamed, and he wanted the opportunity to connect with him heart-to-heart and brother-to-brother. He wanted Mohamed to know what he hoped to accomplish with his travel group. He told Mohamed: this was not to be just another tourist tour. This was to be a pilgrimage with the purpose of igniting creative and spiritual passions in each of his group members. Those in the group had been studying with Gregg for three years; before that, they'd never traveled beyond the borders of their own countries.

"All of them had agreed to leave friends, families, jobs, homes, commitments, and responsibilities behind," Gregg told Mohamed. "All had committed to a journey in which they would trust their own hearts to see where it would lead." Gregg wanted his clients to experience the beauty and history of Egypt, while "immersing themselves in the amazing culture and civilization that is the foundation of the world that we know today." Gregg was also adamant that he be a present and active part of the journey. At the time, the norm was for leaders to hold a conference at the

Mena House, then leave their groups with the guides. As Gregg explained his vision for the trip, Mohamed's eyes lit up.

Gregg told me Mohamed was the first tour guide who ever truly listened to him. Others would say yes to placate him, then do what they were used to doing. Mohamed, however, looked Gregg right in the eye and said he knew exactly what Gregg was looking for and that they were going to accomplish it together.

The end result was a fourteen-day trip from Cairo to Luxor and Aswan, then back to Cairo and east to the Sinai. On Gregg's trips in Peru and Tibet, he would always take his groups into the mountains, and it was important to him to do the same in Egypt. "A lot of tours didn't want to take the time," he told me. "But Mohamed really worked with me to get my group there." Today, it's fairly easy to get to the Sinai by plane, but at the time, it meant a long bus ride—across the desert, underneath the Suez Canal, and finally to Saint Catherine's Monastery at the base. Mohamed was able to arrange the ride, and Gregg's group had a beautiful sunrise meditation on the mountain.

For Mohamed, it was the first time he'd ever grown close to one of his tour groups. He felt like part of the family, and this set a pattern for Mohamed that would change the way he did business. "Relationships became as important as the tours," Gregg told me. That first trip established a strong professional relationship and friendship between Mohamed and Gregg that has lasted to this day.

In Gregg's book *The Isaiah Effect*, he talks about this tour with Mohamed, and describes a magical bending of time that they all participated in and could not explain. Normally, it took seven hours to reach Cairo by bus from the Sinai. On that first tour Mohamed led for Gregg, it took only four hours. The only explanation they could muster was that through the mutual excitement and anticipation of the group for their upcoming time in the Great Pyramid, they manifested a shorter travel time. Experiences like this challenge our beliefs about the nature of time and space. Indeed, it is much more fluid than we imagine.

Once they returned to Cairo, Gregg's group was to have the Great Pyramid to themselves from midnight to 4:00 A.M. Mohamed had never been in the chambers before, because normally he would leave travelers at the entrance and meet them outside when their time was up. This time,

Gregg invited him to come in with them. "You've been part of our family," Gregg told Mohamed.

"No one has ever invited me," he responded.

"Well, you're invited now," Gregg said.

The group filed through the steep and narrow passage that led to the lower chamber, often referred to as the pit. Although they all had flashlights, they struggled to maneuver through the small spaces. Gregg recalled being drenched in sweat in the intense, enclosed heat. As Mohamed made his way down, he dropped his glasses and stepped on them. I can imagine a great sense of claustrophobia overwhelming him as he moved down the corridor. Yet he continued to inch his way through the passage, somewhat blind even in the dim light of the flashlights.

Despite the discomfort, this was the place where Mohamed heard those guiding words: "You are to be of service."

"Mohamed had an emotional awakening and a huge catharsis by the time we reached the lower chamber," Gregg told me. Mohamed continued to experience revelations as they moved up to the King's Chamber and Mohamed heard again: "You are to be of service." Mohamed told Gregg that he had a clear vision of what he envisioned the travel business could be. "He saw that peace must come between people before it can ever happen between nations," Gregg said. "It was clear to him that in spite of their differences, people are able to recognize oneness when they experience each other and become members of each other's families." Suddenly, Mohamed knew that he had the ability to promote peace through the travel business in Egypt.

That trip into the Great Pyramid changed Mohamed's life, and he will tell you in a heartbeat that his association with Gregg Braden changed his life as well.

Emil and the Thanksgiving Feast

Gregg wanted his travelers to feel they knew the land, the people, and the culture—that they had a sense of family. To help manifest this vision, Mohamed arranged for the group to have Thanksgiving dinner with Emil Shaker and his wife. Thanksgiving may not have been a traditional Egyptian celebration, but the tour was in November, and many of the tour members were American. It was a chance for the group to build friendship with an Egyptian family and share a meal.

Mohamed and Emil worked together to make a plan—one that may have been slightly shocking for Emil's wife, Faten. Can you imagine your significant other telling you he's bringing home fifty people for dinner? Faten didn't have enough dishes, so she borrowed from neighbors. With these loaned dishes, Faten and Emil arranged a huge buffet on the kitchen table, complete with roast duck hand-raised by Emil (on their roof, no less). Thanksgiving in Egypt gave Gregg's guests a genuine taste of Egyptian hospitality.

At the house, Emil showed Gregg his personal library, which included copies of sacred manuscripts such as the *Nag Hammadi* texts. Coincidentally, Gregg told me, these texts were really the basis of his tour. If Gregg spent too long looking at a book, Emil would think he wanted it and offer it to Gregg. "Emil has the most generous heart," Gregg said. Gregg would always decline, not wanting to take a book from this man's treasured library. However, one seventeen-year-old tour member accepted Emil's gift of a three-foot-tall, black obsidian statue of Horus. The statue was part of a pair that stood on either side of the entrance to Emil's home, but when Emil saw the young man looking at it, he offered it without hesitation. "We had to be careful of admiring something too long," Gregg said. "Emil is very beautiful and amazing in his own right. He would give you the shirt off his back. The group was blown away by the generosity and hospitality offered to them."

Traveling Anyway

The travelers in Gregg's group became Mohamed's first Peace Ambassadors. In a fashion not so different from today, most people thought Egypt was a frightening place. If there were twenty people rioting in a village, Gregg told me, the news made it look like the whole country was in uproar. "It was really the combination of Mohamed and Emil, two beautiful men and powerful allies, who were responsible for showing the group what Egypt was all about," Gregg said. "These people then went home and shared their impressions and their experiences with friends, families, churches and organizations. They dispelled the fictions and they shared the fact that the images were not accurate. In this way the trip helped to correct those misconceptions."

After Gregg described his initial experiences with Mohamed and Emil, he talked about some of the more difficult times they shared together. "In that ten year period in which I worked with Mohamed, no one recognized terrorism the way that we do today."

As I spoke about earlier, on November 17, 1997, there was a massacre on the west bank of the Nile at Deir-el Bahri, and many tourists were killed. According to Gregg, a terrorist group had intended to wait for a bus of American students so they could capture them for ransom. When the bus came, the students were not American, and the group panicked and killed them. The headlines were filled with news that there had been a massacre at a tourist site in Egypt, and everyone fled. The tour companies pulled out, flights were cancelled, and countries refused to allow their citizens to go to Egypt. This put Egypt into a major economic slump for the next five years.

Gregg had a group of approximately forty-five people from the States who were scheduled to go to Egypt the week following the massacre. After the incident, he called each one of them personally and gave them the option to cancel, postpone, or go ahead with the trip. Only two canceled. And actually it was a good time to go because the Egyptian government stepped up security and made it very safe.

When they got to the Cairo airport, it was empty. No one greeted them. There were no personnel on the grounds and no other planes. As they walked through the terminal, they could hear their footsteps echoing in the marble floored hallways. "We walked in absolute silence," Gregg said. Eventually, a man came up and asked Gregg what they were doing there. When Gregg told him, "We came for a tour," the man looked utterly surprised.

When Mohamed picked them up, he had tears in his eyes. He told them, "It is such a difficult time for my country. The Egyptian people don't want the world to think that our Egyptians did this." When Gregg and his group arrived at the hotel, it was empty—completely devoid of tourists.

The next day, they visited the Giza Plateau. A reporter from a CNN news affiliate interviewed them. The reporter wanted to know why they were there, and why they weren't afraid. When President Mubarak saw this newscast, he wrote the group a letter and sent it to Mohamed, who knew Mubarak because his father worked alongside him in Sadat's cabinet. Mohamed brought the letter to the hotel and read it to Gregg's group. It said that the Egyptian people were grateful to them for coming to Egypt at such a difficult time, and that the Egyptian sites and temples, even those that hadn't been open to the public for over one-hundred years, would be available to them.

Everywhere they went, they had permission to enter. The guards would scramble for the keys, and both guards and guides would go in to see for themselves the places that had always been closed to them. The group's arrival was a signal to the rest of the world that it was safe to come back to Egypt; it was a catalyst that helped tourism start growing again. Once again, Mohamed and Gregg provided each other with sacred gifts. Gregg and his group helped bring health back to the industry that Mohamed relied upon for his vision, while Mohamed provided a remarkable, once-in-a-lifetime Egyptian experience.

The positive results of Gregg and Mohamed's relationship didn't end there. In the late '90s, an Egypt Air flight crashed off the coast of New York. When people heard about the accident, they were afraid to fly with Egypt Air and cancelled their flights. By chance, Gregg had a group scheduled to fly with Egypt Air the following week. Once again, his group decided to go through with their trip. Again, both Mohamed and Egypt were grateful to Gregg and his group.

The fact that a United States tour group used Egypt Air one week after this tragedy helped to bolster the travel business in Egypt. Gregg explained, "Americans have the reputation of being pretty discerning of where and how we go and historically, if it is not ok, we won't go." So during two very intense times, Gregg played a large part in fostering travel and tourism in Egypt. For Mohamed, it was a life and death matter for his business, his vision and for the economy and wellbeing of his country.

Making Things Happen

Over and over, Mohamed showed Gregg that when one has a heartfelt goal, nothing is impossible. At one point, Gregg wanted his group to visit the library at St. Catherine's at Mt. Sinai, something that had never been done before. To see the library, one has to go through the crypts, seeing the dead bodies along the way. For fifteen-hundred years, Gregg told me, the monks of the monastery have kept the bodies of their fellow monks there, believing their energy must be preserved. After a year, they disassemble the skeleton and separate the bones by body part into a room. If a family member wants to visit, they will re-assemble the skeleton, a practice that may seem bizarre to Westerners. "It was through these crypts that my group had to go in order to see the library," Gregg said. "Mohamed made it happen." As a result, Gregg was able to see and study manuscripts that were vital to his work.

On another trip in 1996, one of Gregg's tour members wanted to marry an Egyptian man she had met on an earlier trip. Mohamed surprised them by having a horse-drawn carriage delivered by ship for their ceremony at Philae. "It was all about creating an over-the-top experience for the couple," Gregg said. "It was beautiful…it brings Mohamed great pleasure to surprise people. He gets a real kick out of doing special things for his guests, and he is most generous in this way."

Gregg's next story was about a trip to Abydos where the government was so concerned about the safety of the group that they "made the journey a military operation." They secured each town and intersection for ninety miles so the group could visit the Osireion, an old and sacred place dedicated to Osiris. "You can find the symbols of *the Flower of Life* on the granite walls of a pillar there," Gregg explained. At the time, the site was being excavated by a German team, and no one was allowed in. Mohamed made some calls on his cell phone, and the group was given access. "Mohamed loathes saying no," Gregg told me. "He is always willing to provide his guests the opportunity to have a trip of a lifetime and receive much more than they could have imagined."

Mohamed also arranged for his groups to travel on a smaller boat that gave the group the flexibility of when to sail and where to stop. This allowed Gregg to see sites that were not on the itinerary and to stay at those sites as long as he wanted to stay. Gregg also appreciates the people that Mohamed hires. This is not the first time I have heard that Mohamed is skilled in his ability to hire good people and how the team he builds helps him provide the special service and feeling of family he's known for.

Gregg attributes his successful work in Egypt to Mohamed. It was Mohamed who gained him access to the sacred sites. It was Mohamed who helped foster a feeling of love and family. It was Mohamed who made these trips more than tours for "looking at stuff." They were heartfelt, emotional experiences. "I am honored to have Mohamed in my life," Gregg said. "We really did good work together. He has a brilliant mind and a really big heart.

Final Words about Mohamed and Egypt

Egypt was the first step of Gregg's long and beautiful journey. He describes the period from the late '80s through the '90s as a "window of opportunity." "There are windows in time," he said, "when the opportunities are ripe to explore and share human and cultural relationships." Egypt was the first country he had ever been to, and what he found in its temples and sites led him to the high Andes and Peru. Connections there led him from Tibet to India and Nepal. "There was a logic and a sequence to that journey," Gregg said.

After his visits to Egypt, Gregg often took his groups to Greece, Madrid, or Paris for a few days before returning to the States. However, there was a warmth in Egypt that he didn't find in other places. "Perhaps there was more efficiency," he said, "but not the hospitality and love. In Egypt, there is an outpouring of kindness that extends from the Bedouins in the Sinai to the people on cruise ships, the shop owners, and people on the streets." Gregg's description echoed my own experiences in Egypt. When I had a layover in Amsterdam, the airport was clean and controlled, but my heart ached for the smiles and eye contact of the loving people of Egypt.

After 9/11, Gregg couldn't find people to travel to Egypt. He takes his hat off to Nicki Scully, who was able to assemble a group and travel to Egypt right after 9/11. He knows this was immensely helpful to Mohamed. Since those days, he's spent immense amounts of time writing books, shifting focus to communist China and autonomous regions of Tibet. Gregg told me the principles within these books stem from the insight he found during his time with Mohamed in the beauty, mystique, and mystery of Egypt.

I asked Gregg what he has learned from Mohamed. "When we drop ideas about borders," he said, "and we drop ideas about religion and culture, and when we make the effort to travel to one another's country and look one another in the eyes and hold one another in our arms, we find we are a family. Although we may not like everything about each other's culture, we can learn to accept one another. The Egyptians have always, always been so warm and so loving. During the late '70s, Egypt was not popular in the Arab world because of their ideas of peace. They stepped forward with Jimmy Carter and signed the peace accords. The Egyptians maintain themselves as Egyptians first, not Arabs. They go out of their way to be open and welcoming. Mohamed allowed me to see this.

"Mohamed is a friend of peace in the world," Gregg said to me, "but he is also a true brother to me." Gregg is reminded of this bond whenever he receives a Christmas card from Mohamed, sometimes Santa on a camel. Although Christmas is not part of Mohamed's culture or religion, he sends the card just to acknowledge that it is part of Gregg's. "He is a beautiful man," Gregg said. "I am honored to have him in my life."

Chapter 17: Nicki Scully: Shamanism and Ancient Egypt

Photograph courtesty of Nicki Scully.

Nicki Scully is also important to Mohamed's story. In a way, Mohamed and Nicki Scully have "grown up" professionally together. She has known Mohamed since he first started in the travel business, working as a tour guide for Sphinx Travel. Once Mohamed opened Quest Travel, Nicki booked her tours exclusively with him. Since her first trip to Egypt in the late '70s, she has led more than sixty tours, and in doing so, has supported Mohamed's work of sharing Egypt with the world. They've encouraged each other, complementing each other's styles, interest in higher consciousness, and business acumen.

Every trip to Egypt has helped Nicki develop a better understanding of the Egyptian Mysteries and furthered her relationships with the ancient Egyptian gods and goddesses. Her travel company is called Shamanic Journeys, Ltd., and she has led up to four tours a year, and these often happen back to back. She developed *Alchemical Healing*, an energetic healing form that many of her students describe as "Reiki with power tools." This shamanic work incorporates imaginative and archetypal realms and the universal life force to promote physical healing, therapeutic counseling, and spiritual growth.

Nicki shares her understanding of ancient Egypt through her many enlightening books, classes, workshops, retreats, and conferences. She has written forewords for many authors, especially those who focus on the genius and knowledge of the Ancient Egyptians. She teaches about the Egyptian Mysteries, as well as other resonant spiritual and metaphysical subjects. Her books sing with personal stories and connection to the teachings, meditations, and mysteries of Egypt.

Jean Houston, a formidable expert on the development of human potential, sees Nicki as "the soul and substance of Mohamed's spiritual travel." She believes that "Nicki is a great esoteric scholar of Ancient Egypt and is the one truly responsible for the deeper aspects of Quest Travel." In this way, Nicki's work and Mohamed's work is fused.

It is truly as if fate drew Mohamed and Nicki together so they could spur each other on to progress toward their destinies. Those around them benefit greatly from their collaboration and the many ways they share the magic of Egypt with others. Like Mohamed, Nicki has an amazing story full of magic, synchronicity, spiritual experiences, and service.

Epiphany at Giza

On Nicki's first trip to Egypt in 1978, she was travelling with the iconic rock band the Grateful Dead. Her partner at the time was band manager Rock Scully, and the band was playing three concerts at the pyramids on the Giza Plateau. In her book *Alchemcial Healing: A Guide to Spiritual, Physical, and Transformational Medicine* she writes:

> At dawn each morning I would walk from the Mena House, our hotel, to the Sphinx, where the guards would let me stand between its

paws and spend sunrise offering cornmeal and making prayers. Later I would sit quietly in the "pit," a chamber deep beneath the pyramid that was neither lit nor open to the public at that time. A friend and I had convinced the guards to let us enter the narrow passageway, and with stubs of candles (flashlights felt out of place here) we could inch our way down the deep shaft on our butts. There in the darkness we entered the uniquely expansive energy of a great, unfahomable mystery (29).

… My first "ohming" [toning to the sound of ohm] was in the King's Chamber, with a number of our entourage. To this day I cannot be in the presence of ohming without remembering the peculiar resonance that so startled me the first time… Although most of us were ignorant of the Egyptian Mysteries at that point, we nevertheless sensed that we were responding to something big (29).

They certainly were. On that trip, at the top of the Great Pyramid, Nicki had an ephiphany. In the late '70s, before rules for preserving the monuments were enforced, one was able to climb the ediface. She climbed to the top of the Great Pyramid at dawn. This is no easy climb. The stones are huge and as you climb you have to hoist yourself up and onto each individual block. The air gets thinner and the heart pumps fast; one feels dizzy with the height and the exertion. You dare not look down for fear of falling. There, finally reaching the top she could see the huge globe of the Egyptian sun beginning to rise in the east. At that moment, she realized that her purpose in life was to bring forth the hidden alchemical and shamanic teachings of Egypt. She was one more teacher who'd fallen under the spell of the Great Pyramid and found her vision.

Nicki Meets Mohamed

In 1991, Nicki took thirty-two people to Egypt for a tour. She didn't know Mohamed at the time, and booked through another land carrier company. Her group stayed at the Mena House, along with another group that had traveled for a conference with Toby and Terry Weise of Power Place Tours. She couldn't help but notice that Toby and Terry seemed much less stressed than she was—they didn't seem burdened with the myriad of details and hassles that she found herself enduring. As it turns out, Mohamed, who was working for Sphinx Travel, was the one orchestrating the conference for Toby and Terry.

However, Nicki stayed away from Sphinx Travel because she disliked the owner of the company. She wanted to work with Mohamed and Emil, but their boss gave her the distinct impression of being a "shyster." She continued using other agencies while developing a friendship with Mohamed. When she had a question or concern, she would call him, and he would guide her through the situation. As she led groups through Egypt, Mohamed coached her about both her business and her work. Nicki was waiting for the day he left Sphinx Travel. "I kept encouraging him to move out on his own," she said. When he finally began his own business, she hired him as her land carrier.

Everything changed. Before working with Mohamed, Nicki had grown accustomed to paying bribes to the man who assigned rooms at the Mena House. This time, Mohamed walked up to the man and said, "I am working with Nicki now." Nicki never had to bribe him again. Over twenty years later, Nicki and Mohamed are still working together. "We became family really quick," she said.

Nicki found that Mohamed had an unexplainable "magical intuition" for getting her into special sites and offering rare opportunities. She remembered a day when they sat together in his office and he looked at her intensely, drumming his fingers on his desk. He said he had a special perk, and was wondering who to give it to. The "perk" happened to be a visit to a site that Nicki had been thinking about the night before—a place she felt was vital for her vision. It was all synchronictic and remarkably perfect. Although Mohamed did not know all the details of her work, Niki explained, he was always invested in the growth of consciousness that she works toward with her tour members.

Egypt and Nicki Today

Between Mohamed's investment in Nicki's work and her own determination to fulfill her purpose, Nicki has gone on to touch countless lives and be a witness for how Egypt affects and changes people. For years, she has brought well-known teachers and authors on her tours, enlarging the pool of luminaries that Egypt can influence in a positive way. During the last few years, Nicki has co-led Egyptian tours with Bruce Lipton, author of the *Biology of Belief,* and author Joan Borysenko, who brings spirit, science, medicine and psychology together for healing. Nicki has led groups with Gloria Taylor Brown, Normandi Ellis, Brooke Medicine Eagle, and artists Alex Grey and Allyson Grey. Danielle Rama Hoffman and Dr. Friedemann Schaub travel to Egypt through Shamanic Journeys with Nicki's endorsement. Nicki brings people to Egypt who have the power to spread the word to many. These already-respected leaders then return to their homes, expanded by their experiences in Egypt, and affect even more people through their subsequent teachings.

Like Mohamed, Nicki proves through every action that she is here to serve. With great compassion and generosity, Nicki offers a free Cancer Phone Bridge, a teleconference that provides a healing guided journey for those with cancer as well as their family members and supporters. Many lives have been changed through this offering. I've seen firsthand the positive influence that Nicki has had on so many people I know. Their lives bloom as they became teachers, business owners, healers, and authors in their own right, all sharing messages of love, light and healing that move us toward becoming what Jean Houston calls "the possible human, the finest possible achievement of the human being who understands its responsiblity in creating peace and harmony." Nicki is immersed in a dance with the mysteries of the universe, and it expands everyone who joins in.

When I asked Nicki what she'd like the world to know about Mohamed, her response came quickly. "That he really cares," she said. "He has a diplomatic mission as someone who brings worlds together, opens his country, and offers its riches and its magic to people who would otherwise have no way of experiencing it as regular tourists. No one is going to go the extra mile for them like Mohamed does, and he does this out of love."

As Nicki continues to take tours to Egypt, she helps support Mohamed's travel business in lean times. The fact that she keeps traveling to Egypt no matter what, demonstrates that bridging gaps between our countries is always worthwhile. Even after the revolution, Nicki took a group to Egypt, paving the way for other groups to follow. After the ouster of Morsi, she took a group in March of 2014 and traveled again in the fall. Meanwhile, Mohamed continues to provide the Egyptian experiences that Nicki's heart calls out for, acting as a true friend and mentor. Mohamed and Nicki are mutually and eternally grateful to each other. At one point in our conversation, Nicki described a memory that is very meaningful to her. She and her group gathered in a circle at Philae and sang John Lennon's *Imagine*. It is Mohamed's favorite song, and even the guards chimed in.

Part Six: The Story of Quest Travel

Fig. Part Six.1. Mohamed at the Mena House. Photograph courtesy of Tarek Lotfy, June 2014.

Trust the Universe

Chapter 18: The Beginning of Quest Travel

It's hard to fathom how risky opening one's own travel company truly was at the time Mohamed started Quest Travel in Egypt. As author and lecturer John Anthony West explained to me when we discussed Mohamed, business in Egypt was precarious. After the 1997 terrorist attack, tourism was in steep decline. "He was not prepared for the difficulty and risk that his own company would have to endure," John told me. "It really was a leap of faith."

Regardless, Mohamed knew he couldn't stay at Sphinx Travel. His usual routine involved heading to work around 8 A.M. and staying until almost 2 A.M.—somewhere between sixteen and eighteen hours in the office. He'd been there for thirteen years, and was familiar and comfortable with the work. However, one morning, everything felt different. "I went in at the usual time in the morning, and I felt very, very disconnected," he told me. "The next day, I just couldn't go to the office." The next day, Mohamed drove to the office, opened the door, and quit.

It was no simple process. The owner of Sphinx Travel refused to accept his resignation, and offered to raise Mohamed's salary six times. Besides the feeling that he had not been fully appreciated, considering how much his boss thought he was worth (but hadn't raised his salary before), Mohamed knew it wasn't about the money. "I had no alternative but to listen to the sound of truth in my heart," he said.

Mohamed was terrified of what would happen next. He had a daughter and a wife, and had no idea where he would find a well-paying job. "This was a very scary thing for me to do," he told me. "Egypt is not like America where you can just go and find another job." When Mohamed asked himself what he was going to do, the answer he kept hearing was to do nothing and trust the universe. He told me, "I kept asking myself, 'What is this trust the universe?'"

Despite his anxiety, he was inspired to follow his heart. I was struck by his courage, and was reminded of how he is guided by belief and faith in a greater power. "I had to just wait and live with the not knowing," he said. For the first time in longer than he could remember, he went home and spent time with his family. I know that this was a meaningful time in his life. In spite of his worries he had an opportunity to be with his wife and daughter and he enjoyed this.

One evening in August, Mohamed received a phone call from his friend Barbara in New York. She told him she wanted to come to Egypt and hoped he would organize a trip for twenty friends in October—a birthday gift from her mother. He agreed. With the skills he had refined at Sphinx Travel, he contacted hotel owners, cruise ship operators, and restaurant owners that he already knew. He had developed a rapport with them through Sphinx Travel, and they trusted him. More than that, they agreed to support him. Based on the excellent relationships he had established and developed while working for Sphinx, he was in business.

Barbara helped him launch his new life. From there, the requests came in. John Anthony West asked him to arrange a tour, and he was asked to make arrangements for a conference. Each request helped Mohamed understand what "trusting the universe," really meant. With these experiences under his belt, Mohamed decided to open his own company.

First, he opened a travel company called Right Direction in New Jersey, bringing large groups to Egypt. Those in Egypt who knew him when he worked with Sphinx Travel now recognized him as the owner of his own company, and many of them had been eager to see it happen. Around the same time, the minister of tourism of Egypt visited the Unites States, where he met with Mohamed and asked him why he hadn't opened his company in Egypt rather than America. Mohamed told him the

Egyptian government charged too much to open a company, and the minister promised that if he returned to Egypt, he would get the help he needed. Mohamed followed suit. In Egypt, another company in transportation already claimed the word Direction in its title. Out of the blue, the name "Quest Travel" came to Mohamed, and his now successful travel company sprang to life.

Mohamed began Quest Travel with four others. His wife, Hanan Abdallah, became the financial accountant. Mostafa Abd El Rahman became the HR manager. Emil Shaker became the Egyptologist and guide. Ahmed El Masry became the financial manager. These are the people who helped build his company into the thriving business it is today.

The Rosicrucians

Associations that Mohamed made while he worked at Sphinx would prove to serve him well in the future. His work with the Rosicrucians was important because it allowed Mohamed to focus on spiritual groups and see that he could provide a special niche of service within the travel industry in Egypt. This early association helped him evolve his business into what it is today. He was touched and expanded by his association with the Rosicrucians. He was able to realize that he was interested in promoting consciousness.

The Ancient Mystical Order Rosae Crucis, more commonly known as the Rosicrucian Order or the AMORC, is a non-sectarian group that studies the elusive mysteries of life and the universe. Since 1915, hundreds of thousands of students have used the Rosicrucian teachings, carefully preserved by mystery schools for centuries, to find their own inner light and wisdom. Delivered in a series of weekly lessons, the Rosicrucian home study course presents the collective wisdom of humanity on topics such as metaphysics, mysticism, and philosophy. Free from dogma, Rosicrucian students are encouraged to ask questions about the world around them and to use their insights to benefit not only themselves, but also humanity.

Although Mohamed began working with the Rosicrucians in 1990 while he worked for Sphinx Travel, they hired him when he began his own business because he had established such good relations with them.

"I found that I really had a deep understanding of them," he told me. "I saw that the Rosicrucians were calling for the unity of the whole world." He discovered that they didn't care what religion one was—they were for the promotion of unity and peace through deeper understanding. In preparing tours for them, Mohamed made sure he understood the tenants of this organization, reading books and researching. He did his homework to ensure he would provide the type of trips they would enjoy, a level of service that certainly isn't common in the travel business. Mohamed became their go-to travel planner, and dozens of other groups came to Mohamed on the recommendation of Christian Bernard, the Imperator of the AMORC— who he became good friends with. Big groups traveled with the Rosicrucians and so this connection proved to be a valuable resource.

This spiritual work of the Rosicrucians of course was right up Mohamed's alley, so it was a good fit for all concerned. In fact, many of the people Mohamed encouraged to come back to Egypt originally came on these earlier Rosicrucian tours including Greg Roach and Halle Eavelyn of Spirit Quest Tours and George Faddoul who owns Quantum Change Travel with his daughter Roberta. And so Mohamed had sown the seeds that would eventually feed his new business.

Success

When Mohamed received his initial license, he was given three years to increase his capital and earn 2 million dollars as a condition of retaining the license. In only eight months, he was at the ministry of tourism, asking for a reinstatement. In three years, he made 6 million. "Everything started going so well," Mohamed said. "Step by step, I improved my business. I made great friends and met new clients." I quickly understood, Mohamed's clients *are* his friends.

Mohamed's philosophy is to bring love, peace, light, and unity to the people who travel with him. He hopes that when they go home, they'll share the truth about Egypt as Ambassadors for Peace. As I witnessed, at the end of each tour he personally attends the goodbye dinner, asking his guests to return to their countries and speak well of his. Because he knows he has provided them with enriching experiences that connect them to the people of Egypt and open their hearts, he trusts it will be easy. By the end of a travel experience with Mohamed, I believe most people share the same sentiment: they are honored to become part of his agenda for peace, and they are happy Mohamed followed his intuition to leave Sphinx Travel and start his own company.

Chapter 19: The Quest for Excellence

Mohamed applied what he learned in the United States to his business in Egypt. He wanted to provide the best, most efficient service possible—even better than what he'd already seen in the States. Whether it was a tour for a college, museum, sponsor, archaeology group, celebrity, dignitary, or metaphysical group, he wanted to make it special.

Mohamed expects excellence, first from himself, then from his employees. When I interviewed Mohamed's friend John Anthony West, he touched on this. "He *does* expect perfection from those who work for him," he told me. I saw how his employees hold him in awe. They enter his office respectfully and try very hard to do well in his eyes. They fear him as well as admire him, and they avoid displeasing him or provoking his anger. He is kind and caring, but a hot temper is waiting to burst forth if something doesn't go the way he expected. "Mohamed is blessed with unfailing good humor," John said, "but when he loses his temper, he can rail." According to John, Mohamed is quite the "sight to see" when he is cross. He described Mohamed's temper as not so much mean-spirited as "a calculated response to a situation that demands that level of retaliation." In a sense, John said, it's under control and not counter-productive. When it's over, it's over.

One of Mohamed's first challenges was to ensure efficiency in the way his workers approached things. He still gets frustrated with the inefficiency he deals with in Egypt. For him, it is important to understand that when hiring an inexperienced workforce, setting standards and guidelines allows them to understand what they need to do to succeed. His methods may seem harsh or strict at times, but he is a benevolent boss. Those who are lucky enough to get a position with Mohamed know they are blessed *and* that they'll be challenged. Mohamed always takes care of his workers, as was reflected in how he maintained their pay-scales even after the drastic plunge in tourism after 9/11.

When he first began training his employees, he went as far as to test their loyalty and motivation. He sent one of his tour guides to the airport to wait for the incoming flight of his travelers. What the guide didn't know was that there were no tours coming in. He kept calling Mohamed, and Mohamed kept giving him excuses: the flight was delayed and it would be there soon and he was to wait. The guide waited 24 hours before leaving the airport and returning to the office. Mohamed's reasoning? From that point on, his guide would have boundless patience when waiting for a tour. Mohamed never wanted to have anyone in his care waiting or stranded at the airport. At that time, airport-stranded tour groups were a common occurrence, but Mohamed wouldn't accept it. He looked at me firmly and said, "This is the only way."

Another time, he dropped off his crew at the Giza Plateau during a sand storm and told them to wait for a bus of tourists. Of course, Mohamed had no intention of sending a tour group to the plateau. "No one goes to the pyramids in those conditions," Mohamed said, "No one." The staff waited for a long time before realizing they had to get back to the office on their own—at that time a much further trek than just across the street. Mohamed rationalized that those were the worst conditions the guides would have to endure. After that, they'd be ready for anything.

This approach may seem strange to us but Ihab, the vice president of Quest, helped me understand. "Egyptians are a little bit lazy," he said, "and they often have to be motivated by fear." George Faddoul, Mohamed's good friend from Australia helped me understand Mohamed's training tactics in the context of Egyptian culture. He said employees who are inexperienced may not always understand how to go about a task, but don't want to appear ignorant by asking questions. Mohamed was similar when he first arrived in the States, but took initiative regardless.

I saw firsthand how Mohamed works with his employees. During my trip to interview Mohamed, I underestimated how many tapes I would need for recording, and thought I would easily be able to pick up some more. When I ran out, Mohamed asked one of his workers to find some for me, showing him the tape and speaking in Arabic. The next day, there were no tapes. Mohamed called the young man to his office and reminded him. I didn't understand what they were saying, but I saw the man pick up the tape and turn it over in his hands before heading out on his mission. The next day, there were still no tapes. This time, when Mohamed called the man into his office, his voice was deeper, and it was clear he was tired of asking. The man's face flushed and he lowered his head. I am sure Mohamed said something along the lines of, "Get the tapes or don't come back to the office." The next day, the tapes were sitting on Mohamed's desk, covered in little hearts that indicated they had probably been made for a child's use.

George explained to me that Mohamed did not tell the young man how or where to find the tapes. The young man likely had no clue where to look or even what a tape was. Even if he had gone to Radio Shack, the employees might still not have known anything about this particular kind of tape. Or, the young man might not have had money to travel to a particular store on the other side of Cairo, a huge city that is difficult to navigate. The employee might not even have known where the store was. Regardless, Mohamed teaches and expects self-reliance, and the young man is faced with losing an incredible position if he fails his mission. To this day, I don't know how he found the tapes.

Because of Mohamed's reputation and generosity, no one wants to lose their job. On that last day, the man probably asked everyone he knew for help. If Mohamed had gone through the steps of educating the young man about how to accomplish the task, I would have had the tapes sooner, but that wasn't the point.

Danielle Rama Hoffman spoke to me about Mohamed's quest for excellence. "He knows what he wants," she said, "and he receives great respect from his employees." His employees are well aware that if they don't do what he needs, or if they cross a line, then the journey ends. For Mohamed, following his rules is a matter of honor. "This may be old cultural ways alive in the world of modern business, but it works for him,"

Danielle told me. "He brings the detail and the love together. He loves what he's doing, and he wants to give people the best, so he's not just a control freak."

Those who don't demonstrate the dedication or forbearance Mohamed is looking for don't stay in his employ. On the Afandina, Mohamed's special sailing boat, my friend Susan asked an employee if he would move some tables together on the deck so she could sit with a large group and chat. He failed to do this and so she told Mohamed who let him go on the spot. Susan felt terrible and asked Mohamed to rehire the employee, which he did. The next day, the same man dropped an immense stack of china plates. It was over. Susan said she then understood that while Mohamed was willing to give him a chance, he had quickly realized this man wouldn't be able to provide the level of service that he needed. Mohamed wants the best and he takes whatever steps necessary to create it. He is proud to say that every one of the tour leaders who worked for him at the beginning and stuck with him now have their own companies or are very successful in the travel industry.

Mohamed requires his employees to do what he tells them. One of Mohamed's rules is that his employees wear beige pants and Quest travel shirts when they are working. One day, one of the tour guides showed up at the site, ready for work, wearing jeans. Before promptly dismissing him for the day, Mohamed "really chewed this guide out." Mohamed's client asked Mohamed why he was so tough with the guide, and Mohamed responded that if he had let the incident go, it would set an example for others to ignore the dress code as well. The tour guide showed up the next day in his beige pants and that was that.

This very same employee told me that he looks up to Mohamed and considers him his spiritual teacher. He added that he is very grateful to work for Mohamed, and that Mohamed has taught him everything he knows. Mohamed, in turn, told me he had trouble teaching this employee in the beginning, but kept giving him opportunities because he saw potential and an ability to learn. Today, Mohamed is very proud of this member of his team. When Mohamed sees something in someone, he is willing to put in the time and be forgiving.

Mohamed also teaches his *clients* about business. Many of his current tour leaders started out as tourists on one of Mohamed's trips. George

Faddoul and Greg Roach now have their own travel companies. They originally met Mohamed as members of a Rosicrucian tour that had booked through Mohamed. When they returned to Egypt again and dropped in to visit, Mohamed suggested they gather a group of people and conduct their own tours. All the while, Mohamed teaches them about generosity and friendliness. Greg Roach, who owns Spirit Quest Tours, said he learned how to treat his clients as friends by watching Mohamed, and operating in this way has enriched Greg's life. Jane Bell and Nicki Scully echoed the same sentiment.

As a result of watching Mohamed, I personally also take more time to be friendly and caring in my own business. I've learned that the work is more about the good feelings created between people than anything else. Mohamed follows his heart, and the result is random, surprising, and extremely touching moments of generosity. Once, he offered to arrange a wedding honeymoon on his Afandina to an American woman on a tour, and even helped her find her wedding dress. Spontaneous giving brings great joy to him and the countless others who have benefited from his generosity.

Always, Mohamed leads by example. "He gives you the sense that he sees *you*, and not a lot of people can do that," Danielle told me. Greg Roach explained that when Mohamed is helping you, it feels like he understands you completely. "He has such a deep and profound understanding for his calling and the mission that we tour leaders have when we are in Egypt," he said. "He understands what we are trying to bring to our friends and clients. He has empathy for the spiritual work we do that perhaps the Egyptian society and the tourism infrastructure doesn't have and is not sympathetic to. He sustains the one with his right hand while doing what needs to be done with the other."

Mohamed's diplomacy and ability to form relationships has helped him provide both access to sacred sites and the privacy that spiritual group's desire. Maneuvering these relationships takes a certain skill. "There is a political side of Mohamed that I have a great deal of respect for," Greg told me. "In the developing world, it is all about who you know, and what they owe you, and what you bring to the table." Greg considers Mohamed a political genius. "He is a savant in this regard," he said, "and that is proven by what he has accomplished for the travel business in Egypt. In over twelve plus years, he has been responsible for the tremendous outreach and advancements in bringing groups to Egypt from all over the world. So where the rubber meets the road, and where money actually changes hands, he is a significant engine for economic growth in Egypt."

Jean Houston, has also traveled with Mohamed for years, and summed up what makes him so successful. "He has a huge heart," Jean told me, "a deep passion for what he does, and an ability to make things happen. Where others run into walls, he simply sees no walls. Egypt itself is in such deep communion with him that it opens itself up to him, and this makes it possible for ancient Egypt to open itself up to you." She went on to explain that Mohamed has a wealth of knowledge, not just about Egypt, but about world affairs and the nature of tourism. She called him a "genius" of tourism. "I have been all over the world, in 107 countries, especially developing countries, not as a tourist but working with the UN and other agencies," she said. "and I have never, ever seen anyone who can open up a country for you the way he can. He gets you a sense of its culture, its land, its history, its tradition, and its possibilities." John Anthony West had something similar to say. "He brings a level of attention and understanding no one else gives," he told me. "He provides something special." He emphasized that Mohamed is really the go-to person for esoteric and metaphysical trips in Egypt.

As these tour leaders have attested, Mohammed is efficient, devoted, and has built a business dedicated to excellence. He has held fast to his vision, prospered, and helped those around him prosper as well. He is a man of faith, courage, and passion. He has met and surpassed his quest for excellence. I can say that we are lucky to have him and Egypt is lucky to have him, but he will tell you that he feels just as lucky—for all those who have helped him down the path he has been destined to follow. When I asked John Anthony West what he would like people to know about Mohamed, his answer was simple: "That he is here!"

Chapter 20: Emil Shaker

Fig. 20.1. Mohamed and Emil. Photograph courtesy of Richard Fero.

Emil Shaker made a beeline for a crude little stall in the Cairo Khan El Khalili market, owned by a man in the dirtiest apron I have ever seen—he is known affectionately as "Mr. Bean." As Emil pulled my friend Kelly and me along, he explained, "These are the best beans in Cairo!" We sat down at wooden make-shift tables near a counter manned by several men, and a shelf with a large shallow pan full of ready-to-eat pocket bread. He ordered us each a bowl of his favorite Egyptian beans called "foul." Emil used a garden hose in the back to wash his hands, and we chose hand sanitizer. The freshly baked pita bread smelled wonderful but buzzed with flies. We figured we'd deal with the consequences of our eating adventure later. Kelly loves foul, and although I couldn't seem to work up her level of enthusiasm, I ate the whole bowl just to see the smile on Emil's face. It was also a joy to eat with the locals, or in this case, four young local policemen who stared at us as we ate. They gaped, mouths open; they seemed shocked to see two Western women take a meal with them at the stall. I noticed, with a chuckle, that their wide-open mouths were making it hard for them to eat.

Then we moved on to another stall and Emil bought his favorite applet candy rolled in powdered sugar. We stood against a tin wall in the hot sun, eating our treat, with our faces full of powdered sugar. I felt like we were three little kids trying our best not to get messy; but it was useless. By the end we had powdered sugar all over us. It is true that I had to take a course of Antinal, the local intestinal disturbance fix, but it was well worth it.

This is Emil: a man eager to share his joy, his humor, and his love of life. I first met him on my second trip to Egypt, when he acted as my group's guide, trouble-shooter, Egyptologist, navigator, entertainer, and shopper extraordinaire. As guide and Egyptologist, Emil works with many of Mohamed's spiritual groups. Mohamed's association with Emil (the only employee to get away with defying the dress code) is one of the keys to his success, but even more so is the deep relationship they share. They have known each other for more than twenty years, and together, they make a remarkable team. Guests and clients share as many stories about Emil as they do about Mohamed. If you email Mohamed, you ask about Emil's welfare. If you email Emil, you inquire about Mohamed, and that is just the way it is.

When Emil stands at the entrance to the temple of Luxor, he can point to his birthplace just behind the left colossus of Ramesses. Emil was born in 1953. He told me he was born on these grounds, which in those days were still full of three-sided mud structures attached to the temple wall. When he was a child, the authorities came in, kicked everyone out of the temple, and proceeded to destroy their homes in preparation for the growing tourism business.

Today, Emil is married and has three grown sons. Although his primary residence is in Luxor, he also has an apartment in Cairo because he spends so much time there for business. He has come a long way. He now owns his own apartment building in Luxor. The floors that he inhabits are quite beautiful and there are floors above him where his sons will live after they have married. One already has an apartment there with his wife. If you ask him, he will take you to his home in Luxor to meet his wife Faten and to see where he lives. In this way he is most generous.

Fig. 20.2. Emil and his wife Faten, 2012.

Since his graduation from the College of Antiquities at Cairo University, he has led hundreds of spiritual and metaphysical groups. At Mohamed's side, he has worked with authors and spiritual leaders such as Graham Hancock, John Anthony West, Marianne Williamson, Carolyn Myss, Gregg Braden, Kevin Ryerson, and Tom Kenyon, as well as Egyptologists, including Mark Lehner, Kent Weeks, and Zahi Hawass.

Feel the Energy

His success stems in part from his immense historical and spiritual knowledge. He knows what the sites mean and what they have to offer. He always asks visitors to "feel the energy," whether it's Luxor Temple, a tomb in the Valley of the Kings, the King's Chamber in the Great Pyramid, or even in old Cairo at the shrine of Jesus and Mary, or the synagogue where it is believed Moses was found in the bull rushes. It's the same in a mosque: he wants you to feel the energy and let it work on you.

Emil offers tourists a wealth of information about ancient times, discussing the hieroglyphs and the meaning of each individual site. His spiritual attunement to these places is such that one could imagine he has spent many past lives in Egypt. Emil seems to understand the extraordinary influence the energies of Egypt can have on people, perhaps from years of leading these tours, or because he was free to roam so many of the sites as a young boy. It was Emil who helped Greg Roach, who now owns Spirit Quest Tours and travels yearly to Egypt, integrate a powerful spiritual experience and awakening at Abydos. Emil's awareness of what is transpiring at many different levels allows him to help visitors interact with the energies of the sites in profound ways. I would describe him as a seer who can open veils at the optimal moment.

Maureen St. Germain, a spiritual teacher who has led many tours to Egypt, tells a story that demonstrates Emil's attunement to the sites. "Emil and I are one mind when we travel together," Maureen told me. "In all of the years that I have traveled with him I have only had one argument with him and the argument was at Aswan in the big temple of Abu Simbel. It is like a circus at this site as it is one of the most popular places to visit. You will see throngs of people of every nationality—it is like a carnival. I walked into the temple and I was blown away by the disrespectful tone...it offended my sensibilities. I didn't want to do a ceremony in there even though that is what I had planned with Emil. Emil said we are going to do this ceremony over in the corner, and I said, 'I don't think so.' He said, 'Yes we can do it over here and we will be fine.'" No matter what Maureen said, Emil would not take no for an answer.

"And so we did a beautiful chant where Emil indicated and the harmonies were beautiful and we sang in a very hushed way, very softly, and it transformed the temple and the people in the whole place stopped what they were doing and entered into a prayerful mode. Everyone stayed with that sweet tender respectful tone while we were there. I went back to see if they were still in this respectful mode after we left and they were. It would not have happened if Emil hadn't insisted. This was quite amazing!"

And so Emil is our trusted leader on many levels. When you travel with Emil, you're like his flock of sheep and you give him your trust. We follow him, hustle, and flock together when he barks, "As one!" He takes care of you, answers your questions, explains things to you, provides insights into the ancient spirituality, and makes sure you get from place to place and have meaningful experiences.

The Bad Boy

At sixty one, (as of September, 2014) Emil might not be the dashing figure that he once was, but it doesn't seem to matter. Flattering women brings him great joy, and he enjoys giving women his attention. He adores them and they just adore him. Emil's not partial to younger or prettier women. He likes women of all sizes and shapes and ages. He is a charmer, an outrageous flirt, full of sexual innuendos and yet I suspect that it's all a front because his heart belongs to his wife and he is dedicated to his boys and his family. But his flattery and attention, though harmless, work wonders.

Emil describes himself as a "bad boy,"—often inappropriate or even crass, but he incites fun and laughter whenever he gets going. Perhaps Emil, who is really incorrigible, gets away with what he does because of his friendship with Mohamed. But while Emil just won't stick to the straight and narrow, he does such an amazing job as an Egyptologist that Mohamed has just had to shrug his shoulders and love, accept and value Emil for who he is. It is not just what Emil knows, but his personality that has brought him such success. All of his quirks are in the name of fun and frivolity, for he is one of the kindest, most intuitive, and spiritual men I know.

Just like Mohamed, Emil gives of himself one hundred percent. Both Mohamed and Emil have had health issues over the years. They've paid a price for their intense dedication to their work life. Emil has had a couple of heart attacks and he has a stint in his heart that keeps a valve open. This doesn't seem to slow him down too much though.

His joy energizes the group, for Emil loves to laugh—at his own jokes the hardest of all. As Irene Iris Ingalls, who has travelled with Emil three times, said, "Emil is one of those people who laugh so hard that tears easily roll down his cheeks." He loves to play jokes on the guards at the temples and sites. You have to be careful when Emil asks you play along with one of his jokes. He says, "Let me tell this man that you are looking for an Egyptian husband." I always shake my head no. Some say yes, and play along, but consider yourself warned because this may cause some chaos for sure. He also gets a lot of joy out of teaching us to swear in Arabic and then getting us to swear at the guards. The guards look forward to seeing Emil bring his groups because they know they are in for more laughs. They think it is hilarious to have foreigners swear at them in Arabic!

I can think of a host of adjectives to describe Emil, and not all of them are congruent. He is very open and extroverted, and yet sometimes shy when it comes to taking a compliment. He can be described as naughty, bawdy, and lascivious. Such words as arrogant, masculine, audacious, and over the top come to mind. Sometimes he is so sweet and sometimes his is just so obnoxious. He is also the most generous man I know. He would do anything for you.

Emil's Point of View

On my second tour, we paid a nighttime visit to Philae Island to see the temple of Isis. As we approached in our little motorboat, the beautiful temple loomed above us. When we arrived, a sound and light show about the story of Isis and Osiris was in progress. Loud, dramatic music and multicolored lights accompanied a story of the two lovers, which boomed from the loudspeakers. Once the extravaganza ceased, we all breathed easier.

We waited quietly upon the calm waters of the Nile in our boat for the okay to disembark. Apart from the water lapping on the edges of the boat, it was silent as we all waited in eager anticipation under the full moon. We gazed in awe at the amazing temple above us, its huge edifices now lit solely by flood lights at its base. I felt as if we had entered ancient times and were a group of priests and priestess about to set out on our holy purpose.

Mohamed had arranged for us to have a special visit, and close to midnight we left our boat and made our way up the hill to the temple. We entered and proceeded toward the sanctuary, known as the "holy of holies." Single file, we walked through a long, dark hallway until we reached the small room that held the altar. In a beautiful moment of silence, we placed our candles upon the altar and stood in a reverent circle around it. After the guards turned off most of the lights, we began our meditation.

Unfortunately, we were interrupted when a single guard ran in with his gun and told us we must leave and were not to "do religion in here." The guard had not been told that we had special permission to visit the temple. It is unusual for visitors to come at night, and he persisted, so we had no choice but to file out and head back to the boat.

Angrily, I began walking back from the temple toward the docks down below. It was so dark that I was barely able to see, and I ran smack into a large temple stone and went flying, scraping and cutting my shin fairly severely. Emil came right up to me and said, casually, "Not to worry. This is a good thing. Isis has initiated you!" He said it as a matter of fact. Still seething that the guard had evicted us for "doing religion," I, for one, was not thinking of my bleeding shin as a blessing.

Sometimes, however, blessings come in surprising packages. Mohamed, disappointed that our night trip to Philae had been foiled, arranged for a private visit to the Pyramid of Unas upon our return to Cairo. Without the snafu at Philae, I wouldn't have realized my dream of visiting the Pyramid of Unas. In the end, Emil was right.

Adventures with Emil

Although he would never say it himself, it is Emil who transforms the experience of those he guides. Emil told me that he likes to ask people to go with him on adventures, but they're often afraid. Greg Roach regrets turning down one of these adventures: Emil wanted to take him to *The Field of 1000 Sekhmets* on his motorbike at midnight. Greg, however, was being a "chicken shit," as he would say, and declined. He described how excited Emil had been at the prospect of taking Greg along, and how crestfallen Emil looked when he said no. "I wish I had gone," Greg told me. Years later when Emil and Greg were visiting the Temple of Mut, Emil was finally able to show Greg *The Field of 1000 Sekhmets*. Unfortunately, the site had been excavated, and most of the 1000 statues are gone. "This is where I wanted to take you," Emil said to Greg. "Do you remember?"

Greg learned his lesson. "Always say yes to Emil," he told me. "I wonder what it would have been like to be unfettered, with no rules, riding on the back of Emil's cycle to this most amazing site at midnight." Today Greg is always up for Emil's adventures, even if it takes place at

4:00 A.M. "If Emil says, 'You will love it,' just answer yes. He never disappoints."

This applies to culinary adventures as well. Greg confided that he never refuses Emil, but he always pops an Antinal tablet before he visits another favorite eating place of Emil's.

Shopper Extraordinaire

Emil is always game for shopping and he continually takes his clients out to the markets in Cairo, Aswan, Esna, and Luxor. He takes his clients to various stores to help them purchase papyrus paintings, essential oils, carpets, statues, jewelry, shawls and scarves, and galabeyas. Emil loves to barter, and he's one of the best. When he was our guide, he would get us the best deals. He would warn us: if we went into a store or shop without him, we'd be on our own and he wouldn't be able to help us. I came to the conclusion that if Emil told me to buy something, I should buy it. As a result, I have lovely Egyptian mementos at bargain prices. More than souvenirs, anyone who travels with Emil brings home treasured memories of their time with him.

Emil loves to haggle and it gives him supreme joy to get the very best deal possible. He haunts second hand stores for bargains, travelling to find these treasures so that one day he can open his own shop. In the summer of 2010, he went to Bali and bought more than he could lug on the plane; he gave it away at the airport with great delight. He is a well-known shop-goer in Egypt and knows all the shopkeepers at the markets, often doing business with his friends. He is also aware of how hard business has been for the vendors since tourism has slowed, and he will ask us to mercy shop. He says, "Buy this for someone you don't like!" We all buy, knowing that we are helping out the families of the various vendors. If we are reluctant to buy, he will buy and eventually sell his stores or give then away. He always does this at the various sites and temples to help the people out.

When I was in the "Khan," the large bazaar in Cairo, Emil and I bartered with a man on the street for three small glass pyramids. After we agreed on a price, the vender changed his mind and added another fifty cents. I didn't think that was too much, but Emil walked away. According to Emil, once you agree on a price, upping that price is not acceptable.

Sometimes he intentionally visits the shops with the most notoriously greedy merchants, just to see if he can change their ways. That was true of the man selling the pyramids, and indeed he hadn't changed his way. It will be a long time until Emil revisits him and gives him another chance.

Descriptions of Emil

My friend Jonny Hahn has been on many tours to Egypt, all led by Emil. Jonny is a well-known street musician in Seattle, where he has been playing his piano at Pike Place Market for twenty-five years. He is a singer and songwriter who creates his own instrumental music, and also works as a healer with Matrix Energetics. Of Emil, Jonny says:

> I see Emil as personifying the energy of Zorba the Greek in the body of an Egyptian. He is bold, brash, bawdy, warm-hearted, irresistible, and eminently knowledgeable when it comes to Egyptology and leading groups visiting ancient sites.
>
> As a participant in three tours led by Emil, I felt like Karnak, Luxor, Edfu, Philae, and Abydos were all akin to Emil's "hood", his backyard, his stomping ground. He shared what felt like intimate insights at each locale with passion, intelligence, and vibrancy. The history that was already jumping out at one by the sheer physical spectacle of the temples was fleshed out and deepened by Emil's explanations of the hieroglyphics, archaeology, geology, and culture.
>
> Everywhere we went—be it markets, restaurants, museums, hotels, shops, the airports, or temple complexes—Emil was the savvy shepherd of a flock of bedazzled, dizzy, awe-struck, often sleep-deprived Western tourists.
>
> In his hometown of Luxor, he led a small group on a literally off-the-beaten-path stroll through his childhood neighborhood. He related not-for-primetime anecdotes about local characters and introduced us to the woman who was his nanny in an unannounced visit to her tiny apartment.
>
> Also in Luxor he rented two donkey pulled produce wagons that the group piled into for a rollicking, slide-splittingly hilarious ride through the local Luxor nightlife scene. The locals sitting at the sidewalk cafes or an apartment building terrace or out for a stroll,

broke out in ear-to-ear grins and spontaneous laughter as we, also laughing heartily, bounced on our rumps as our carts ambled through the narrow streets. It was Emil's gift to us, one not mentioned in any tourism brochure. It was his opportunity to show off his home, a slice of modern Egypt, to his guests from far way places in a most human and generous way.

Irene Iris Ingalls, an accomplished visual artist, Light Language scribe, and sound and energy healer in Seattle, has traveled with Emil many times. Like Jonny, Irene's experiences with Emil expand beyond those of a typical tourist in Egypt, largely thanks to Emil himself. Regarding one of her favorite memories, she says:

Emil's reverence for the temples we would visit always set the stage for our group to enter. Once things were going smoothly—after connecting with the guards and exchanging the monetary 'tips,' so the group could proceed uninterrupted—we would enter behind Emil, and when the inspiration struck him, he would start singing 'Om Namah Shivaye.' For me, singing a prayer such as that in such a sacred place and having it spring spontaneously from Emil, an Egyptian Christian man who holds all faiths in reverence, was such a delight! We would all sing in chorus 'Om Namah Shivaye' each day of that trip, several times, whenever the mood struck Emil. It was always so much fun and so purifying singing all together.

At the end of our trip, on the very last night, for our celebratory goodbye meal, some in our group had gifts they had brought for Emil. One woman in our group, Rose, who had been relatively quiet in our group, now handed her gift to Emil. When he opened it, he found a tape she had brought him from her own library at home. Rose had never met Emil before this trip and had been holding the tape in her suitcase for the two weeks. The tape she had brought for Emil was a 60-minute tape of the chant 'Om Namah Shivaye.'

Emil gasped when he opened it. He had lost his own tape a year ago and had been fervently wishing and wondering how he was going to be able to replace it. Rose who is very intuitive had picked this for him not knowing anything about Emil. She had not uttered a word for two weeks as we sang and sang that very chant everywhere we went. Now, whenever I find myself chanting that song, it always brings me right back to all those magical moments in the temples in Egypt and Emil leading us all in chorus.

Irene sent Emil a note for his birthday, and it was a message that reflects what many of us feel about Emil. In a bundle of birthday wishes I collected for him in October of 2012 from his Seattle friends, hers stood out as wonderfully expressive:

Dearest Emil!

This blessing is for your strong heart and love of life. I see and feel your laughter and joy, remember you singing blessings to the temples and forever doing so. The temples in Egypt will always have your beautiful vibrations resounding within, mixing with the thousands of other sacred songs sung there. Think of all the wonderful gateways you have opened for so many people from around the world and the hundreds of hearts you have opened and witnessed opening. This is a blessing for your heart. May it always be full of song and joy, strong in love and life. May your family be well and happy and may your life continue to be full of abundance and creativity! You are always in my heart when I think of Egypt. You are the heart of joy! So much love to you, and I cannot wait to see you and hear your laughter again one day soon. Happy Birthday Emil!
—*Much love, Irene Iris Ingalls, Seattle, WA, USA*

When I asked Danielle Rama Hoffman, who I first traveled to Egypt with, to describe Emil, she could only say, "Emil is Emil and there is no one like him." She and her husband Friedemann spoke of how Emil gives extra love and attention when he recognizes that someone needs it. When they lead Egyptian tours, they count on Emil to help their participants feel safe and included, weaving the group into a sort of unity.

"Regardless of the group's size," Friedemann told me, "Emil has an amazing sensitivity, and he feels who needs help, who is shy and insecure, and who is the underdog." Emil sees the person who may need a little extra support, or who is having a hard time. According to Friedemann, the person on the tour with the least confidence gets the most attention from Emil. "Both Mohamed and Emil use the energy of love to act as an elixir to integrate the group—Emil embraces the group. He doesn't play favorites. He pays attention to what they need."

I've seen firsthand how Emil seems to fall in love with everyone he meets. He has told me leading tours is hard for him, because he knows he will have to say goodbye and never see his new friends again. When people return to Egypt, he is overjoyed.

Emil is also invested in the spiritual work that takes place when people visit the sites of Egypt. Jean Houston explained, "Emil's incredible sense of the frequencies, the energetic systems of Egypt, is such that one rarely encounters; such that he has to stop at a place where he may have been a thousand times." Jean laughed as she described Emil standing in a temple, saying "Feel it. Feel it." She went on to say, "Emil is utterly lovely, a pure heart man. He is very youngish, robust man. I love Emil." I do too, along with countless others.

Fig. 20.3. Emil on the Afandina, 2012.

Breaking the Rules

Emil had told us that if you follow the rules in Egypt you will never get anything done. Danielle told me about a time that she and Friedemann were going to Hatshepsut's temple. It was before 5:30 A.M. and Americans weren't allowed to visit that early. So Emil told the guards that they were Russian and the Friedemann's name was Vladamir. Apparently

Russian groups can go right in. They got into the temple as Russians, and to Emil, Friedemann has been "Vladamir" ever since.

Emil is willing to do whatever it takes to provide his groups with the experiences that they want. In the Valley of the Kings, groups are usually not allowed to have private time. He tips the security guards, and when tourists approach the entrance to a tomb, Emil keeps them out by telling them the mummy they wish to see is across the way. He directs them to other tombs. All the older guards know him and let him get away with his diversion, but it is much harder for him when they change the guards around or if they are new. He has many tricks up his sleeve, but usually he can only use them once before the guards catch on to him, then he has to come up with a new plan. As he explained to me, this is the only way to get things done.

Hanging out with Emil

One morning, on my interview trip, I received a call from Emil asking me to come to the Quest Travel Office. I was dressed, and the office was only a block away, so I was there in minutes. When I arrived, I saw that he had made me tea. After a brief hello to Mohamed and George, who was still visiting from Australia, Emil said he had something special planned, so we picked up Kelly and headed to his Cairo apartment. While Emil's home in Luxor contains the beautiful things he has bought over the years, he keeps those items he truly treasures in Cairo. We marveled at his collection—some amazing, some dubious. Every cupboard was crammed with stuff—it was as if we had entered his second-hand shop, or a cross between a museum and a junk store. Upon entering the apartment our eyes were met with a stack of old shoes. There must have been about fifty pairs, all of which looked the same! After escorting us in, he asked us to sit down, and then started looking for something. Minutes ticked by as he pulled out drawers and opened cupboards and closets. Eventually, he found what he was looking for.

Smiling, he proudly presented us each with an amulet of The Eye of Horus which offers us good luck and protection. These fit right into the palms of our hands, and were made of clay. They were once painted but now were old and muted. Extremely happy with our gifts, we settled in to relax and be together as he showed us more of the interesting odds and ends that make up his collection. I felt honored to see where he lived, and I finally felt I saw a glimpse of the man behind the jokes and bravado. He talked about missing his wife in Luxor and his twin boys, who have now grown up and moved out. "They are good boys," he said. His first year experiencing life as an empty nester frequently left him sad. And then he said with all sincerity, "I am a good man." Yes, Emil is perhaps coarse, irreverent, and an ever-boasting peacock, but he has an immense heart. His joy is in his work, and his work is opening the hearts of those he meets. He is, indeed, a good man.

Chapter 21: Mohamed's Family

For Mohamed, family is everything, and Mohamed's family is extensive. It includes a wealth of siblings, aunts, uncles and cousins, not to mention the fact that Mohamed includes "friends" in his definition of family. Mohamed was close to his parents, and never hesitates to express his gratitude for the love and guidance he received growing up. Susan Webster, who has traveled to Egypt with Quest Travel and is a good friend of Mohamed's, explained that he was fond of his mother and looked up to his father. He also did everything he could to ensure a better future for his sisters. "He knew that in Egypt, it would be more difficult for them to create a financially sound footing for themselves," she said.

Today, Mohamed has a wife and children of his own. Susan told me it was actually Mohamed's mother who sparked the relationship between Mohamed and his wife, Hanan Abdallah; she introduced them at a party she threw for Mohamed's friends. Susan told me Mohamed had always wanted a family and children, but never thought it would happen for him. Luckily, he was wrong. "He is a loving father, and his children bring deep meaning to his life," Susan said. To this day, one of Mohamed's deepest regrets is the fact that his father died before he could ever meet his grandchildren.

Mohamed has a son named Marawan, but Mohamed often calls him "friend." I first met Marawan when he was sixteen. Today, he is twenty-one and studying business in the German University in Cairo. He has grown into a kind, capable, confident young man. He has set his sights on becoming a pilot post-graduation, and will likely train in Germany or South Africa.

Fig. 21.1. Marawan and his mother Hanan, August 2010.

Mohamed's daughter, Nancy, is the apple of his eye. Susan described how his face lights up when he speaks of her. She brought up another point: while Egypt embraces a culture of strong male dominance, Mohamed has raised his daughter to feel like the world is her oyster. "It shows his enlightened spirit," she said, "that his daughter has been shown love and encouragement to see that all possibilities are open to her."

I had the privilege of interviewing Mohamed's daughter in the summer of 2010, and it was clear she thinks highly of her father. We met in her office at Quest Travel where she had the title of Tour Director. She spoke of how grateful she is for all the lessons she has learned from him. First and foremost, strength and determination. Nancy was with Mohamed when he had his stroke in 2008, and went to the hospital with him after discovering he couldn't walk or talk. She has seen him undergo therapy and face the challenge of recovery head on. "He didn't let this stop him," she said. "He was happy before the stroke and happy after." He might move slower, she said, but he has all of his faculties and is at the helm of the business that he loves so much." His resiliency is an inspiration to her.

He also taught her independence. "I know what I want," she said, "and I can do it myself." When she was nine, Mohamed began to teach her about the business and asked her to help with things in the office. When she was older, she would go with Emil to the airport to pick up tours. Mohamed included her in all his travels, so she learned to be around strangers. Until she was sixteen, she traveled with him every year to the States. In retrospect, she thinks it was a lot of responsibility for a child, and speculated that perhaps she may have started "training" earlier than she should have. Yet, she knows she wouldn't be the person she is today without those early experiences; they gave her a sense of efficacy and awareness of what she was capable of. When Nancy attended the American University of Cairo, she worked in the travel business *and* did her studies—no small feat. She attributed her ability to accomplish so much at one time to her early life and the responsibilities that Mohamed entrusted her with. Nancy loves a good challenge, and I've heard Mohamed also express his love for a good challenge. "He has passed down the idea to me that it is a good thing not to be ordinary in any way!" she told me.

Fig. 21.2. Nancy at the Mena House, June 2014.

After completing a two-year post graduate study at the London School of Business and Finance, Nancy is now the HR Communications

Senior Specialist for a company called T Data. At the age of twenty-four, she has her own life, but she still helps Mohamed with tours when she can. Mohamed doesn't feel it is necessary for Nancy to take over Quest Travel, because he wants her to form her own path. Nancy is on this earth to do important work, and she makes her father proud.

Another lesson Nancy learned from Mohamed is that you must fulfill your promises. It isn't a standard everyone always meets; she admitted to growing frustrated with those who don't do what they say they are going to do. When she and Marawan were children, Mohamed would ask them if they were going to do something. When they responded yes, he would respond, "Say you promise." It was very important to Mohamed that they keep their word, and this virtue is deeply instilled in Nancy.

Most of all, Nancy takes pride in the work her father does. Mohamed does not act out of a sense of duty, but rather pure passion. "He loves his work," she said, "and he wants people to come to Egypt and be around him and see Egypt through his eyes. He wants to share himself, his country, and what he loves. He is one who enjoys leading and creating." Echoing what I experienced personally, she praised his intelligence in forming relationships. "He has an understanding about people and what they need," she said. "He always affects the people around him. This begins with the way he shakes their hands and the way he looks into their eyes. People begin to feel happy." I can personally vouch for this "Mohamed Experience."

Nancy broke into a grin when she told me how much people love her father. "People just love to have him come on their tours because he is so much fun," she said, beaming. On her first trip as a guide in 2006, she saw how much joy the tours brought to the participants. People truly considered it a blessing to be with Mohamed.

"Mohamed never worries about his own future," Nancy said. "Although he does worry about what his children will do in the future. He worries about others, and he worries that he may not be able to take care of them. He is overly responsible. However, he doesn't share his worries. He keeps his troubles to himself. He does not like to burden others. This is his nature."

Nancy also spoke about the unusual environment at the Quest Travel office. She explained that everyone who works at Quest Travel enjoys each other's company. "You can always hear the sound of laughter in the halls. I have worked at two other companies, and it was very different. Mohamed's coworkers, with whom he originated the business, grew up together, so they share lots of memories. This company feels like family." Nancy's Mom, Hanan, still works in the finance department.

I asked Nancy if fellow Egyptians are critical of Mohamed for being so open to people from other countries and cultures, especially the West. The answer, essentially, was no. Nancy explained that Egypt is a country used to foreigners. "People from all over the world come to study archaeology and Egyptology," she said. She described Cairo as a cosmopolitan city that attracts people from all over the world. In turn, those tourists support the economy of Egypt.

When I asked her what she would like the world to know about Mohamed, she said she would like others to know more about his personal life. "He is just as effective in this arena of his life as he is in his career life," she said. "He has wonderful relationships with his family and friends." When he was young, Mohamed promised his father that when he became successful, he would try to help his siblings and make life better for them. He fulfills this promise to this day. "Family is number one," Nancy said. "He will do anything for them." He visits his sisters, who are housewives, whenever he can. Mohamed has a rich and vast circle of friends, many of whom he's known since kindergarten and grown up with in Cairo. As a result, Nancy was raised in a strong community, and those people visit Mohamed at home or in the office to this day. Of course, Nancy couldn't talk about her father's rich friendships without mentioning Emil. "They always have to be together," she said. "They are a couple, really. They have a great marriage...better than with my mother." Nancy laughed at her own words. She has a light joyful giggle. Sitting there across from her at her desk in her office, I had to laugh too.

As our interview drew to a close, Nancy spoke about her father's good will and big heart. She feels that even with all his success, he has remained true to himself. "He still has the true Mohamed inside of him that really is young and alive." Despite the stress and negativity that can permeate daily business, she said, "He is just loaded with life."

Chapter 22: Mohamed's Staff and Business Associates

Quest Travel is what it is today not only because of Mohamed's dedication and leadership, but also because of the people who work for him. Mohamed attracts amazingly loyal and hard-working employees and then works with them to develop a high level of expertise and service. Although I was unable to interview all of his staff during my short time in Cairo, it was clear each and every person is skilled, devoted, and vital to Mohamed's mission.

Fig. 22.1. Mostafa, Administration, Taher, Chief of Accounting, and Mohamed, Accountant, 2014.

In the office he has finance officers and accountants, administrators, a transportation officer, office assistants, and receptionists. He also has security guards, bus drivers in Cairo, Luxor, and Aswan, and his boat crew and captain, and many others he depends upon to keep the business running smoothly. He also has others that he can count on when he offers side trips to the Red Sea, the Sinai desert, the Eastern desert, Alexandria, and Petra in Jordan.

Fig. 22.2. Enas, Transportation Manager, 2014.

I got to know his guides/Egyptologists and his escorts/tour operators the best because we spend the most time with them when we are on tours. Quest Travel is a true model for how business can fuel prosperity for the owner, the employees, the economy, and the people it serves, and Mohamed's employees are always up to the task. As Jean Houston, who has led large tour groups to Egypt with Mohamed for years said, "The people that Mohamed hires are just extraordinary."

The Vice President

The Vice President of Quest Travel is a delightful man full of rye humor and rapid observational quips. His name is Ihab Rashad, and he has been working in the travel industry ever since he received his degree in business administration from Cairo University in 1983. He was the general manager for a prominent travel agency in South Africa before accepting his position as Vice President of Quest Travel in 1997. I have been told that Ihab is one of the primary reasons Quest Travel fared so well during Mohamed's stroke in 2008 and through his recovery.

Ihab described Mohamed as "amazing, precise, clear, and honest." He explained that Mohamed summons "fear plus respect," and that this is how he manages to get the success that he does in Egypt. He also credits Mohamed for "helping everyone to keep the peace inside." Ihab is a sure pleasure to know and is a kind and endearing soul.

Fig. 22.3. Ihab Rashad, Vice President, 2001. Photograph courtesy of Richard Fero.

The Guides/Egyptologists

Emil, Sameh, and Doaa are Mohamed's main guides. Each travels with a tour group for the entire time of the tour, or they share a group. For instance Doaa may stay and work with the group in Cairo and Emil will work with the group when they arrive in Luxor or Aswan. They share their knowledge of the dynasties of Egypt and the ancient history. They also share their knowledge of what each temple represents. They are essential to each group as they are linking us to Egypt's past and to the spiritual teaching. Sometimes the guides also act as the escorts depending on the group and how many tours Mohamed is running at the same time. Mohamed also hires various freelance Egyptologists when needed. The guides also help us with the shopping and do the bartering for us if we so desire. I am always amazed by the total devotion that I have seen in Emil, Sameh, and Doaa. They work really hard to impart to us what they know about ancient Egypt.

Fig. 22.4. Nancy, Emil, Sameh, and Mohamed, 2008. Photograph courtesy of Richard Fero.

Besides Emil, Sameh Taha is one of Mohamed's guides and Egyptologists. According to Jean Houston, when Sameh teaches about Egypt, "He gives you the information in a way that becomes part of your nerves and sinews." I was able to travel with Sameh on my first trip to Egypt, and I saw how much he enjoyed sharing his knowledge of ancient Egypt with us. He was always dramatic and full of enthusiasm, gesturing and explaining while imparting the heart of the ancient history of his country and the meaning behind the hieroglyphs carved into the walls. He was always joyful and full of life. I was astounded at his skill and stamina. He was with us all day, without eating or drinking (it was Ramadan), and attended to both his job as an Egyptologist and a tourist attendant. It is hard to imagine fasting at that time, given the heat and his workload. This speaks to his faith. At sundown every day, Sameh wolfed down his meal. I didn't blame him. Beyond his dedication, he is a kind and entertaining man who made us feel like part of his family. His wife and children came to our farewell dinner, and he was eager to have us meet them and have his family meet his new friends.

Fig. 22.5. Sameh Taha, Egyptologist and Guide for Quest Travel, 2007.

I also worked with Doaa Badawi on the first leg of my trip in 2014 while we were in Cairo. She is a dedicated guide who took wonderful care of us and supported our work at the temples. She was a tireless in her efforts to share her knowledge with us as well as her humor and high spirits. I really commend her for going out of her way to spend time with the folks on the tour, and for being present during our meditations. She was most respectful of the spiritual work that we were doing.

Fig. 22.6. Doaa Badawi, Guide/Tour Operator for Quest Travel. Photograph courtesy of Doaa Badawi.

The Escorts/Tour Operators

An escort or tour operator also travels with each tour group and handles all the logistics along the way. They answer a lot of questions and help people on the tour with their various needs. They get us from point A to B on time, and manage all of the details from baggage pick-up and delivery, to hotel and cabin room assignments on the boat, and to making sure that we get our meals on time,. Basically they trouble shoot on our behalf making it seem as if everything is seamless. Mohamed's daughter Nancy used to serve as a tour operator and sometimes she steps in to help with a group. An escort may also work with individual clients and take them on side trips, for instance to Saint Catherine's Monastery or to Jordon to see Petra.

Hatem Ali, a tour operator for Quest travel, is another loyal employee of Mohamed's. After a long plane ride to Cairo from the States, there is no face I would rather see beaming up at me as I ride the escalator down to baggage claim. I can always count on him being there, ready to attend to me and my group with a big, kind smile. He has been working with Mohamed for almost twenty years, and sees Mohamed as his spiritual teacher. Hatem is a conscientious worker and a very kind man who will tend to every detail for his clients, taking time to communicate with and help each individual. Hatem attributes his skill in the travel business to Mohamed and what he has learned from him.

Fig. 22.7. Hatem Ali, Tour Operator for Quest Travel, 2012.

Akram Farouk worked as our escort on my last trip in 2014 and he is a tireless, sweet, kind, funny, and gentle man who is entirely dedicated to his work and to doing the best job possible. He took care of all the details with precision and kindness. He has become a good friend and I am grateful of his wonderful care.

I loved hearing stories about his daughters and seeing how hard he is willing to work in order to make a good life for his children. He impressed me with his impeccable attention to the details, and his continuous optimism, kindness, and humor.

Fig. 22.8. Akram Farouk, Tour Operator.

These loyal individuals are members of the incredible staff who made my journeys to Egypt so lovely. They do their jobs with kindness and warmth and a sense of humor that is infectious. I have to pay special tribute to the bus drivers that Mohamed hires. There is Hasson, who almost always picks me up or drives me to the airport, day or night, and is always a delight to see. There are also various bus drivers in Cairo, Alexandria, Luxor, and Aswan who manage to get us to our destinations despite the narrow streets in the Khan for instance or the nearly impossible-to-navigate areas—all while remaining kind, helpful, and compassionate. Indeed Mohamed is blessed by his workers.

His Business Associates

The business relationships Mohamed cultivates are invaluable to his business. Much of his success is built upon the associations he developed many years ago and maintains to this day with his loyalty and dependability. He has developed warm and personal relationships with people within the government and its various agencies, as well as people within the tour industry: restaurant owners, hotel managers, boat company owners, and their employees. All of the employees at the Mena House love Mohamed, and Mohamed considers them part of his extended family. He has helped many of them personally when they were in a time of need.

From government officials and security officers to street vendors, wherever we traveled in Egypt, people seemed to recognize Mohamed. He is friendly and kind to people at every level of Egyptian society. He is well known in Egypt and people are happy to do business with him.

He counts among his friends and business associates important Egyptologists such as Mark Lehner, Kent Weeks, and Zahi Hawass. I will talk more about Lehner and Hawass in the next two chapters. Dr. Kent Weeks is a leading Egyptologist and is the director of the Theban Mapping Project based at the American University of Cairo. Dr. Weeks has been working on the excavation of KV5, the tomb of Ramses II's sons, one of the largest tombs in the Valley of the Kings. These men often speak for Mohamed's groups as guest lecturers.

Chapter 23: Zahi Hawass: World-Renowned Egyptian Egyptologist

Fig. 23.1. At the pyramids. Photograph courtesy of the Quest Travel website.

Times have changed since I first interviewed Mr. Nazmy for this book and talked to him about Zahi Hawass. In 2010, Hawass was the Secretary General of the Supreme Council of Antiquities. Nazmy's friendship with Zahi Hawass was helpful to Mohamed, allowing him to achieve the high quality of service he offered his clients. The legal policies that were developed and established under Hawass' tenure, and which Nazmy was instrumental in creating, continue to allow Quest Travel as well as other travel companies to provide their groups with private times at the sites.

Zahi Hawass is a world-renowned archaeologist who has directed excavations at Giza, Sakkara, and the Valley of the Kings. He is also a well-known television personality connected with ancient Egypt. He received his PhD in 1987 from the University of Pennsylvania, where he was a Fulbright Fellow. More than his scholarly articles, books, awards, and honors, Hawass is known for his charisma and ability to reach the public. He was profiled as one the world's 100 most influential people by Time magazine in 2006. His latest book *Ancient African Kingdoms on the Nile: Nubia* was released in 2012.

Hawass has raised awareness of archaeology and the preservation of Egypt's precious heritage, utilizing contagious enthusiasm. He has helped to institute a systemic program for the preservation and restoration of Egypt's antiquities, and to train young Egyptian archaeologists to improve their expertise. The LA Times once called him "the living face of ancient Egypt, an ambassador for long-dead Pharoahs who uses his high-wattage personality, telegenic showmanship and knack for wading confidently into controversy to preserve both their star power and the monuments that hordes of laborers built at their command."

The flamboyant Hawass has always been a controversial character known for his passion and drive, but also for his domineering style, strong opinions, and his overreaching use of power. However, since the 2011 Revolution, there have been many dramatic political changes in Egypt, and these changes continue as Egypt struggles with its own set of challenges. With the fall of Mubarak came the fall of Hawass. He is no longer the Chairman of the Antiquities Department, and his ties to the Mubarak administration have caused him strife.

In 2010 when we discussed Hawass, Mohamed explained that he had known Hawass for roughly twenty-five years, ever since Hawass was the inspector of the Giza Plateau and the pyramids. At the time, Mohamed was a manager at Sphinx Travel. Both had similar backgrounds, living and studying in the States. "Our careers started to grow," Mohamed told me, "and we both established great success while keeping our friendship. We do this because there is equality in our relationship."

When Hawass became responsible for the Antiquities Department, Mohamed wanted to make sure not to jeopardize their relationship by taking advantage of Hawass' position. "We developed a good legal process for allowing visitors to have private time in the sites," Mohamed said. That process involved lots of official paperwork and fees. This system allowed all groups to legally have alone time at the temples and sites so that participants can experience the energies of these various places, away from the throngs of tourists. This private time can be the cornerstone of a trip, because we use the private time for quiet reflection or ceremony creating a very powerful experience.

For Mohamed, his relationship with Hawass was a practice in separating business and friendship. He never asked Hawass for special favors, nor did he ever ask for any illegal shortcuts. Mohamed, as the consummate professional, honors his business relationships with integrity. So when Mohamed needed something from the antiquities department, he always followed the official policy, submitting a letter with his proposal, which he still does to this day. Thankfully the protocols Mohamed helped set in motion are still in effect today.

Mohamed said of his friend, "When I was in his office I was in the office of Dr. Hawass, the Chairman of the Antiquities Department. On the other hand, in the evening, if we would go out to dinner, I would call him Zahi." Because many of Mohamed's friends are also ambassadors, security officials, and "higher-ups" who help him with his business, he is clear to draw a line between social time and work. Mohamed and his business partners and friends all follow this policy. Outside the office, they are on a first name basis. At Quest Travel, Mohamed is addressed as Mr. Nazmy. Outside the office, he is Mohamed.

After the Revolution of 2011, Hawass became a target of anger among young protesters who helped depose President Hosni Mubarak, as well as many others who resented his overreaching use of authority. After Mubarak was ousted, Hawass left office under a cloud of unproved corruption allegations. These allegations reportedly included allowing antiquities to travel out of the country illegally, wasting public funds, and abusing his position inappropriately to aid a charity run by the wife of Mubarak. He was banned from travelling outside Egypt while he was under investigation. Hawass always vehemently denied such accusations. After two years of investigations into the complaints, the First Attorney-General for Public Funds Prosecution dismissed the allegations.

Mohamed continues to be friends with Hawass. Since 2011 everyone in Egypt has had to adjust to the profound shifts in the political landscape. I am confident Mohamed will continue to thrive, thanks, to his reputation and broad based relationships founded on good will, integrity and loyalty. Mohamed believes that people will continue to travel to visit Egypt no matter who is in office, and he is there to continue to host them and to carry out his vision.

As for Hawass, since the overthrow of Morsi in July 2013, he has been traveling in the States and all over the world, eager to convince travelers to return to Egypt. I have read that he would like to continue to help in the building of the new Egyptian Museums, help train young archaeologists, and aid in returning Egyptian artifacts that are now abroad. He is also leading groups and lecturing for tours that are visiting Egypt.

Hawass reminds me of a cat with nine lives. He has such a big personality and has done so much to promote global interest in Egypt that his work will never be complete. He has such relentless passion for Egyptian archaeology and Egyptology, and is really responsible for creating *far-reaching* interest in the sites, monuments, and new discoveries. Mohamed is grateful to Hawass for all that he has done to stimulate interest in Egypt and her treasures, and for implementing the private visits protocol, which insures that tour companies may book and receive official permission for private visits, serving travelers to this day.

Chapter 24: Mark Lehner: Director of the Giza Mapping Project and the AERA

Fig. 24.1. Mark Lehner PhD. Courtesy of Mark Lehner.

Mohamed and Mark Lehner, a world-renowned Egyptologist, have a win-win relationship. Besides their treasured friendship, Mohamed is able to provide tours for Mark's associates who are interested in Egyptology, archaeology, study and education, while Mark brings Mohamed much-appreciated business.

Lehner has more than thirty years of experience excavating sites in Egypt, having first visited as a student in the '70s. He was intrigued by the mysteries of the "Sleeping Prophet," Edgar Cayce, and Lehner found that his initial assumptions about the ancient civilization along the Nile just didn't stand up to the archaeological facts. He turned to the scientific method of scientific discovery in order to improve his understanding of the culture, eventually completing his doctorate degree at Yale University. As director of the Ancient Egypt Research Associates (AERA), it has been Lehner's job to conduct interdisciplinary archaeological investigations. His international team currently runs the Giza Plateau Mapping Project. The goal is to excavate and map the ancient city of the builders of the Giza pyramid complex, which dates to the fourth dynasty of Egypt.

The AERA has conducted a number of archaeological field schools for Egyptian antiquities inspectors under the auspices of Egypt's Supreme Council of Antiquities. This organization has also run basic and advanced courses at Giza, as well as courses in salvage archaeology along the Avenue of Sphinxes in Luxor. Through the AERA, Lehner seeks to help young Egyptians conduct field work and become Egyptologists, an endeavor wholeheartedly supported by Mohamed. This is one of their biggest shared visions—for Egypt to have many of its *own* archaeologists. Lehner said, "These young people are some of our best field school students."

Lehner is a visiting assistant professor of Egyptian archaeology at the Oriental Institute of the University of Chicago, and has produced the only known scale maps of the Giza Sphinx. His book, *The Complete Pyramids*, is an exhaustive catalogue of Egypt's many pyramid sites. He has appeared on many television programs about Ancient Egypt and has assisted in the production of several documentaries regularly aired on the National Geographic Channel. He also acts as a liaison to prominent figures in universities and museums in the United States who sponsor archaeology and field work in Egypt. It is through these associations that Lehner has brought groups to Egypt and Mohamed has acted as their land carrier.

Mark and Mohamed have mutual respect and admiration for each other, and promote and support one another. Both are interested in the welfare of the Egyptian people, the education of its youth, the preservation of its sites, and the documentation of its archaeology so that Egypt's ancient past can be shared with the whole world. Today, Mark has a villa in Giza and works just down the street from Mohamed. He remembers meeting Mohamed in the '90s and being skeptical of the work Mohamed did with "new age" groups. In spite of this, Mark found that Mohamed and his company organized outstanding trips and conventions, and so Mark hired him to work with his archaeological groups. In 2004, Mohamed worked closely with Mark to arrange a tour for members of the board of Mark's organization, the AERA, and for the board of the American University in Cairo. Mohamed has also organized tours for the American Research Center in Egypt (ARCE), a consortium of American museums and universities that Mark is involved in. It was clear that good relations with orthodox Egyptologists, archaeologists, scholars, museums, universities, and donors who promote and sponsor research in Egypt were just as important to Mohamed as spiritual groups.

I was able to meet Mark when he spoke in Seattle for an ARCE program. He was a kind, genuine man who spoke slowly and apologized to me for not being able to give me a longer interview when we first met—he has such a demanding schedule. Mark sees Mohamed as a natural ambassador for Egypt. "He is full of love and is gifted with graciousness," he told me. "He is charming and a part of Egypt." Mark said Mohamed is special because he represents many points of view: religious, spiritual, academic, etc. Mark said he has grown more tolerant because of his relationship with Mohamed—he has become more thoughtful about where the true meaning in his life lies.

When it comes to Mark's efforts to foster the skills of young Egyptian Egyptologists through the AERA, Mohamed has always lent a hand. He organizes visits for major donors, hosts dinners, and invites the organization's biggest supporters over for some genuine Egyptian hospitality. Mohamed believes the education of the youth of his country is essential. He also knows that the preservation of Egypt's ancient sites will one day be in the hands of these young people. As far as he is concerned, the more they know, the better.

Mark told me about a dramatic experience in April of 2011, when a radical group broke off from demonstrations in Tahrir and protested in front of the AERA villa in Giza. The demonstrators mistakenly believed the villa belonged to Zahi Hawass, whom they opposed because of his association with Mubarak. Mohamed, who lives a short distance away, came and sat inside the AERA villa garden, keeping guard late into the night as the group continued demonstrating outside the gate. As the group became louder and more threatening, they pounded at the gate meaning to break in. "At one point," Mark said, "Mohamed stood before them and spoke to them with passion, telling them he thought they were making a very big mistake." They did not continue to try to break through the gate.

This story demonstrates Mohamed's deep loyalty to his friend and his ability to protect and help others. I know that he is very pleased with Mark's dedication to the education of many young Egyptians in Egyptology, and also for all he is doing to study ancient Egypt, documenting it for the world. Mohamed put himself on the line and in the path of potential danger to protect his friend. Mark is extremely grateful. To Mohamed friendship is everything.

Part Seven: An Award Winning Travel Company

Fig. Part Seven.1. The Quest Travel office.

Do What You Love and Have Passion For

Chapter 25: Quest Travel Rises to Success

Fig. 25.1. The Peace Bus.

Mohamed described his job at Quest Travel as that of a master chef. "There is all this wonderful food on the table—cooked just so, and prepared for the best flavor," he told me. "Egypt is the same." Mohamed is a talented, creative individual, and he must have an outlet for his intuition and spontaneity. His work is a wonderful way to channel these qualities. It takes Mohamed about eight to ten hours to design a tour, and the end result is what Mohamed would call "a most amazing meal."

When I traveled to Egypt to interview Mohamed for this book, he would typically call my apartment in the morning to let me know he was in the office and ready to talk more. "Sharlyyynnn," he'd say, purposefully dragging out the last syllable of my name. "Where are you?" I would grab my tape recorder and hurry over to spend some time with him before the office became so busy that it would be impossible to continue the interview.

One day, we planned to talk about his travel business. Mohamed smiled at me from behind his desk, and I sat across from him with a cup of tea his receptionist had kindly delivered.

"Drink," he said, pointing to my tea. When I took a sip of the hot, aromatic brew, he nodded in approval. Not surprisingly, he began talking about how important human connection is in his work, and the interview was obviously underway. "I cannot do what I call 'dry business,'" he said. "I use my intuition to design a tour." Mohamed explained that he can't design a tour unless he has spoken to his clients in person, on the phone, or through Skype. He needs to gain an understanding of the client before he starts the planning phase. "Otherwise, I don't know how to sincerely be of service and plan the most incredible and excellent trip," he said.

He raised his eyebrows as he continued. "You know what I am saying? I am looking at it from the angle of making a perfect spiritual trip, not just travel. You have to have an aim—a target. It really does change people's lives, so you do everything to the maximum in order to do that."

No matter what Mohamed has planned by collaborating with the tour leaders before the group arrives, things always change. When a group finally sets foot in Egypt and Mohamed develops his connection with them, he alters the itinerary as he follows his intuition. "I hear what I hear through their hearts," he said. "Nobody tells me. I intuit that it is important for them to experience this place." Between Mohamed's many connections and daring personality, he can usually arrange it for them with a phone call in a matter of minutes.

"How fun is that?" I asked him.

He answered with a smile.

I asked him if he was following his intuition when he arranged for my group to go to the pyramid of Unas in 2010 which proved to be one of the spiritual highlights of my life. He nodded.

Success

The success of Mohamed's business has grown each year because of its reputation for providing unique spiritual journeys and because of the employees' genuine concern and care for their clients. This care and attention to detail has become the foundation on which his company continues to thrive.

Quest Travel is now at the top in its field, and the company has won many awards from Egypt's Minister of Tourism. Two world-renowned luxury hotel and resort companies have bestowed Quest Travel with highly prestigious awards. The Sonesta Group named Quest Travel number one among 2,200 travel companies, and it received the Oberoi Hotel Award for being among the top ten travel companies in Egypt. Mohamed continues to win awards and receive letters of recommendation. Quest Travel's mission is still to introduce the many aspects of Egypt to its clients in unique and personal ways, while ensuring the preservation and protection of the sites. Quest Travel strives to assure that each person who travels to Egypt, goes home changed in a positive way.

Chapter 26: The Trips Mohamed Creates and a Sample Itinerary

If you love Egypt and want to experience her mysteries on the deepest level possible, Quest Travel's tours are simply the best. Quest offers tours that are more comprehensive than other Egyptian tour companies, and therefore has little competition. For most tours, they are able to arrange special permission for private visits, access areas not normally open to tourists, and provide lectures by world-renowned personalities, authors, and Egyptologists. Quest Travel has established excellent contacts and a remarkable reputation that allows its groups to experience all that Egypt has to offer.

Jane Bell, who has taken tours to Egypt for years with Quest, can attest to how Mohamed has changed the travel industry in Egypt. When she first started leading tour groups in the '90s, the environment was something akin to the wild-west. She explained how in addition to difficulties with the White Brotherhood, travel was challenging. Bags were lost, travelers were left stranded without transportation, and it was hard to get the help one needed. "It is really Mohamed who revolutionized the travel business in Egypt," she told me. "He has changed the name of the game, and now he is able to provide first class trips for all his guests." He attends to every detail, which makes traveling in Egypt a pleasure for his clients. From the moment tourists arrive at the airport until they depart, everything is taken care of.

Today, Quest Travel gladly customizes tours to suit the specific needs of businesses, organizations, families, tour groups, and individuals. As I spoke about in the Introduction, Quest specializes in metaphysical and spiritual tours, archaeological tours, tours for educational institutions, and independent travel programs. Mohamed has arranged tours for diplomats, leading businesspeople, humanitarians, and celebrities—and the list continues to grow. And then of course there are the many spiritual teachers, leaders, scholars, and authors who work through Mohamed, many you will hear about in the upcoming Part Ten of this book.

Some of the specialized tours Quest Travel offers are entitled The Holy Family in Egypt, Safari Trips, and The Return to Egypt Trip—any of which can incorporate add-on excursions to the Sinai, the Delta, and the Siwa Oasis. Quest Travel also offers the following extensions to Abu Simbel, St. Catherine's Monastery, Alexandria, and the Red Sea. They have recently added a trip to Jordan to visit Petra.

Mohamed develops itineraries very carefully, spending hours preparing for each group, whether the focus is spiritual, archeological, or academic. He works with small groups and large groups that come for conventions and conferences, always providing quality service and detailed attention to meet needs and exceed expectations. A typical itinerary and accommodation list for a fifteen-day metaphysical tour might include the following:

o All scheduled travel in Egypt as described in the itinerary
o 5 star hotel accommodation at the Great Pyramids and throughout Egypt
o Deluxe 5-day (or longer) cruise on private sailing yacht to visit the temples along the Nile
o Most gratuities and tips included in the itinerary
o All sight-seeing outlined in itinerary including entrance fees
o World-renowned Egyptologist to explain the history, culture, and art of Egypt and the sacred sites
o Exclusive private visits to selected sacred sites, including sacred initiations, ceremonies and mediations which are led by the tour leaders
o Private visit in the Great Pyramid

o   American breakfast daily, 8 lunches and 9 dinners
o   Camel or horse ride in the desert

The Itinerary:

Day 1: Depart for Cairo from JFK airport in New York City at 6:30 P.M on an overnight flight.

Day 2: Arrive in Cairo in the late morning. Representatives of Quest Travel and tour leaders meet the group. Check into the luxurious Mena House Oberoi Hotel in Giza. Relax and acclimate. Walk to a local restaurant for dinner and opening circle.

Day 3: Sunrise tour of the Giza pyramid complex. The tour begins with our private path of initiation at the paws of the Sphinx— guardian of the mysteries—and culminates in a camel ride up to the pyramids on the Giza plateau. Afternoon visit to the Cairo Museum. Shopping at the Khan Khalili Bazaar. Evening flight or overnight train ride to Aswan.

Day 4: Arrive in Aswan. Check into our private sailing yacht. Afternoon sail to Elephantine Island for an initiation at the Temple of Knum.

Day 5: Sunrise initiation to Isis at her island temple at Philae. Afternoon circle on deck as we sail to Kom Ombo—the temple of Sobek and Horus—where we'll work with the forces of dark and light. Sail on to Edfu, the temple of Horus.

Day 6: Early morning at Edfu, the temple dedicated to Horus the hawk, for a powerful experience of the heart. Continue sailing toward Luxor, the ancient city of Thebes, which was once the capital of Egypt. Circle held on deck.

Day 7: Continue sailing on our private ship and stopping at a small village. Visiting the Knum Temple at Esna and shopping in Esna.

Day 8: Arrive in Luxor. Evening visit to Luxor Temple.

Day 9: Drive by bus through the beautiful countryside of Egypt to Abydos, where we'll visit the Temple of Seti I, and the ancient Osireion dedicated to Osiris, to see the most beautiful reliefs in Egypt. Here, we'll also see the *Flower of Life* symbol tattooed on the temple column. Then we'll travel to visit the exquisite Temple of Dendera dedicated to Hathor, the goddess of love and joy.

Day 10: Early morning visit to the magnificent Karnak Temple and receive Sekhmet (the lion goddess) initiation at her chapel.

Day 11: Visit the necropolis of Thebes, known as the West Bank and explore the tombs of the pharaohs in the Valley of the Kings. Travel to the Valley of the Queens and Deir-El-Bahari (the temple of Queen Hatshepsut) and the mortuary temples at Medinet Habu (the temple of Ramses III).

Day 12: Afternoon flight to Cairo. Check into the Mena House in Giza.

Day 13: Morning visit to the Step Pyramid at Sakkara, a huge temple complex from the Old Kingdom. The pyramids here hold the oldest ancient religious writing in the world called the Pyramid Texts. Then lunch at beautiful garden restaurant. Time to rest and relax at the hotel.

Day 14: Private visit to the Great Pyramid culminating in an initiation in the King's Chamber. Visit to old Cairo and the Christian churches and the Jewish synagogue. Free time for last-minute shopping before our closing circle. Farewell dinner at a local restaurant and entertainment by a local Sufi group of musicians and dancers.

Day 15: Farewell to Egypt. Morning flight departs from Cairo for New York and arrives at JFK at 3:25 P.M.

Although this trip clearly offers time for rest, relaxation, and introspection, the pace is fairly intense. The leaders participate in setting this pace because they have their own agendas and teachings to share as they move their groups through the temples and sites. The leaders are also responsible for the ceremonies, initiations, and rituals involved, including the circles where participants come together to share their experiences.

When most people step onto the Giza Plateau and stand in front of the Sphinx or the Great Pyramids, they are blown away. But then, they head to Sakkara or another lesser-known temple, and are blown away again. Destination after destination fosters one amazing experience after the next, and the accumulation of emotion matches the rapid pace. In addition to the powerful energy, add the incredible food, lovely people, luxurious accommodations, and the flurry of the markets in Aswan, Luxor, and Cairo. There are also special visits to the carpet store, the scented oil store, the papyrus store, the alabaster store and the jewelry store. The experience can be described as nothing else but "over the top," in nearly every sense of the phrase.

A Window into a Tour

When I first toured Egypt with Quest Travel in 2007, representatives from Quest Travel picked us up from the airport and escorted us to our hotel in Giza, making our entry into Egypt effortless. We stayed at the luxurious Mena House, which sits at the bottom of a short hill just below the Giza Plateau and the pyramids.

The Mena House is a famous, historic hotel, initially built as a hunting palace in 1869 for the Egyptian King Isma'il Pasha. The king sold the lodge to an English couple, Frederick and Jessie Head, who came across it on their honeymoon and used it as a private residence. In 1885, it was sold to another English couple, the Kocke-Kings, who immediately began construction to create a hotel. They preserved much of the Arabic influence of the facility, enhancing it with fine Mashrabia work—finely carved wooden doors, intricate blue-tile mosaics, and medieval brass-embossed embellishments. The Mena House opened to the public in 1886. In 1890, the hotel opened Egypt's first swimming pool.

Fig. 26.1. The Mena House. Photograph Courtesy of Tarek Lotfy.

The hotel is named after the founding father of the First Dynasty, Mena, or King Menes of Memphis, who founded the great city of Memphis and unified Upper and Lower Egypt. During World War I the hotel was requisitioned by Australian troops and was occupied again by the Australians in World War II when it was converted to a hospital. By 1971, the hotel was already nationalized but an agreement was made with Rai Bahadur Mohan Singh Oberoi to manage it. Mr. Oberoi was an Indian hotelier, the founder and chairman of Oberoi Hotels and Resorts, India's second-largest hotel company. P.R.S. Oberoi, Mr. Oberoi's son and The Oberoi Group managed the hotel and renovated it. As of 2012, the hotel is under the management of the Egyptian General Company of Tourism and Hotels.

The hotel is full of history; in 1979 representatives from Egypt, Israel, America and the United Nations sat down in the Mena House in a quest for peace. This Mena House Conference followed up the 1978 Camp David Accords and signing of the peace agreement between Israel and Egypt.

President Carter, President Sadat, and President Begin met in the Al Rubayat room which was the Pasha's original dining room. In fact at my last farewell dinner on my most recent tour, Mohamed arranged for our dinner to be served in this very room. I was deeply touched by his gesture and I knew he was honoring me for writing this book.

Many celebrities have stayed at the Mena House, including Richard Nixon, Agatha Christi, Omar Sharif, Roger Moore, Cecil B. DeMille, Charlton Heston, Frank Sinatra, and Charlie Chaplin. Field Marshal Montgomery also stayed there during World War II and has a suite dedicated to him. Winston Churchill stayed there many times and the most famous was when he met with Roosevelt and Chang-Kai-shek for The Cairo Conference in 1943. There is a suite dedicated to Churchill's memory.

The Mena House today has an exquisite Moroccan feel. The ceiling of the foyer is embellished with wide beams of dark wood, while the hallways boast marble arches. From the café, one can look up and see the pyramids through the windows. The grounds of the hotel are lush and full of palm trees and flowers—a true oasis at the edge of the desert. There are multiple restaurants within the complex, and there is a newly built lounge and bar area with beautiful reflective pools and fountains. It really is exquisite. Everyone at the Mena House knows Mohamed well and they are like family to him. Because they knew we were with Quest Travel they took special care of us because of their affection for him.

Fig. 26.2. The Mena House garden.

Fig. 26.3. The Sphinx.

The Great Pyramids and the Sphinx

After arriving and settling into our luxury hotel, our tour began with a dinner at a local restaurant where we met each member of the tour and talked about the itinerary.

The next morning began with a private sunrise visit to the Great Pyramids and the Sphinx on the Giza Plateau. Standing between the paws of the Sphinx, watching the sun peak over the horizon, is something indescribable and surreal. Typically, tourists are not allowed to stand so close to the Sphinx, but Mohamed had special arrangements. I could not find words to express those first few moments of standing at the base and staring up at the Sphinx looming a couple stories above. We held a brief ceremony in which we connected to the land of Egypt and gave our gratitude. This monument has stood guard and watched every sunrise since the beginning of civilization. There is something deeply moving about this watchful sentinel.

After further exploration—and lots of picture-taking—we were herded up a broad staircase to the road above, where we were greeted by a herd of camels. Their masters wore dusty blue galabeyas and white turbans. We were told to pick our camels, and the leader touched a long stick to the side of the camel to let it know it was time to kneel down so that we could climb on. The process of riding a camel is as riotous and noisy as riding a donkey which I will describe later on in the book. Some camels simply don't want to be ridden, and have a loud way of expressing their displeasure. When they move from the ground back up to their standing position, it's more than a challenge to stay on for the inexperienced rider. We held on tight to the saddle horns to keep from falling, and finally, we were up on our standing camels. The leaders held the reins and escorted us up a long hill onto the plateau for our up-close encounter with the pyramids. It seemed like a dream.

Fig. 26.4 The Cairo Museum. Photograph courtesy of Ron Werner.

The Cairo Museum

That afternoon, we visited the Cairo Museum, which is housed in a two-story neo-classical building. It is painted a rather unexpected pink coral color, with a huge Moroccan arch over the entrance. The complex is surrounded by a wrought iron gate and is close to the infamous Tahrir Square, where the Revolution of 2011 took place. The museum's front garden patio is strewn with statues. It feels like the most crowded place on earth, besides the market. People from all over the world stand in line to enter, and as one traverses the museum, there are guides speaking every language imaginable. The museum was founded in 1935 and its collections exceed 120,000 pieces, spanning the pre-historic era to the Greco-Roman period.

With no air conditioning, we fanned ourselves and guzzled water from our bottles. When we first entered the museum, the central area of the first floor was full of gigantic statues. They looked familiar; I had studied many of them in books, and here they were, right in front of me. We started on the first floor, which has rooms dedicated to artifacts from the earliest dynasties. Emil began to share his knowledge of Egyptology, and it was far more than I could take in. I could have spent weeks in Cairo, visiting the museum every day to truly appreciate all its wonders.

In Egypt, every experience is an adventure. The ancients infused statues with energies of the gods and goddesses, and the funerary statues of pharaohs were infused with the energy of their Ka, or etheric doubles. For a sensitive or psychic person, this can be an energetic overload. And since the statues have been moved from their original homes, they are not particularly happy. It's not unusual for people to leave for a while in order to get their bearings. Others have visions of the ancient past or recall past lives. I was feeling overwhelmed and was in desperate need of a bathroom break. Unfortunately, I found myself haggling with a bathroom attendant who thought my tip was too small.

Eventually, we climbed the stairs to the second floor, which contains the King Tutankhamen exhibit. There is a large statue of Anubis, who protected the boy king for ages in his undiscovered tomb. An air-conditioned room houses the jewelry of the boy king, and although this display is breathtaking, it is also crowded. I avoided the mummy room, which is now home to the mummies found in the Valley of the Kings. Something felt wrong about it. The mummies are no longer in their original resting places, and throngs of people view their bodies. It felt sacrilegious: like an invasion, so I stayed away.

The Khan Khalili Bazaar

That evening, we visited another one of the most crowded places on earth, the bazaar. It is so hot during the day that people do their shopping at night. The Khan El Khalili Bazaar, better known as the "Khan", is full of narrow, cobbled alleyways broken into tall cubbies and stalls. Brightly colored blankets, scarves, dresses, shirts, and belly-dancing costumes hang at the top of the stalls, and swing above shoppers' heads as they walk by. A plethora of goods are displayed on low tables outside of the shops. Merchandise is stuffed onto every shelf and cranny: jewelry, copper plates, galabeyas (long traditional dresses), inlaid wood boxes, small statues, and touristy trinkets like mugs painted with "I Love Egypt."

Among the small, cluttered stalls are fine stores with expensive jewelry and authentic antiques. The alleys are swarming with shoppers from near and far, and there are almost as many vendors as buyers. The vendors stand at the entrance of their shops, hoping to entice customers to enter. Vendors yell from their spots, "Hey beautiful lady, come in here!" or "You are Nefertiti. Come look, I have a deal for you." The din and the jostling can be overwhelming. The cobblestones are uneven, and customers must keep their wits about them as they weave around oncoming foot traffic to avoid collisions, all while trying to decipher a sea of possible purchases.

Emil took us upstairs to a second-story shop that sold only scarves; I'd never seen so many in one place. Emil, of course, struck a deal for us, and we took our time choosing. We stopped at a coffee stand and sat on an assortment of metal lawn chairs drinking thick, strong Turkish coffee. A woman in her hijab (a traditional scarf that covers the women's hair) with a baby in her arms swiftly came up and placed the baby on my friend's lap, asking for some money, a little "baksheesh." The guide shooed her away. Everything happened at double the speed.

Over Night Train Ride

Since the revolution of 2010, we usually fly from Cairo to Aswan, but on my first trip to Egypt we traveled by train. In the late evening and after our adventure at the bazaar, we left Cairo on the overnight train ride to Aswan. When it was time to sleep, an attendant came by and folded up our couches that became upper and lower berths. There are even tiny personal sinks that came down from the walls. As the train traveled south, I was lulled to sleep by the wheels clacking along the track and the car jiggling back and forth. Although the train ride is uncomfortable for some, it has its pros. The train moves parallel to the river, and in the morning, I could pull open my shade and see a glimpse of life along the Nile. There were small villages, and farmers working in the countryside as we passed. It's like stepping into ancient times. The satellite dishes, conspicuously placed on the top of mud brick houses, were the only reminders that we were still in present modern time.

Aswan

Immediately upon arriving in Aswan which is in the far south of Egypt, we took a bus from the train station and then were ferried across the Nile. We used to stay at a hotel for a few days and then move on to a large ship for our sail. However, since 2010 we have traveled on Mohamed's special boat.

Upon our arrival, our luxurious dahabeya, our sailing yacht the Afandina, which means *Our King*, awaited us. We were greeted with a cold juice drink and a refreshing wash cloth along with warm greetings from the crew and then we were escorted to our lovely cabins. We had the afternoon to acclimate and settle into our beautiful accommodations.

It is usually very hot in Aswan so the air conditioning on the boat was greatly appreciated. It wasn't long before we were unpacked and called out onto the deck for lunch where we checked out the scenery. This is a peaceful place so unlike the noise and chaos of Cairo. Our little bit of heaven was moored on the west bank of the river and looming above us were high hills of sand full of ancient tombs. As we looked out to the east over the river, we could see the big boulders that mark Elephantine Island. This little island sits right between the two banks of the river. Beyond the island we could see the laid back town of Aswan. The famous Aswan dam sits just to the south of the town.

Fig. 26.5. The bank of the Nile from the Afandina.

In the late afternoon we boarded a small motor boat that took us to the southern end of Elephantine Island and the Temple of Satet. Since the beginning of ancient Egypt, this island has had layers and layers of temples built upon its ground. This place honors Knum, the ram headed god and his wife Satet and his daughter Anket. To the ancient Egyptians they were the triad in charge of allowing the flow of the Nile each year as the inundation approached. The flooding ensured renewal for all of Egypt as the river over flowed her banks all the way to Cairo and then to the delta and out to the Mediterranean Sea. In keeping with the theme of the waters, we asked for permission to enter the south in a sacred way and to give gratitude for the waters of the planet. We walked through the huge doorway that looks out over the Nile and claimed our new potential. As we walked through the threshold we let go of that which no longer served us and opened to new beginnings and a new better story of our life.

Fig. 26.6. Gateway on Elephantine Island.

The next morning we traveled to the island of Philae for a private sunrise visit, getting up at 3:45 A.M. in order to get there on time and it was well worth it. Here sits the beautiful temple of Isis. The goddess Isis is the all-encompassing mother goddess and she is all about forgiveness, nurturance, love, kindness, and magic. The opportunity for a private visit within the holy of hollies, the altar room within her temple complex, is a blessing beyond words. Her energy there is palpable and no one leaves her sanctuary untouched. After the ceremony we were led out into the courtyard where we could watch the huge golden Egyptian sun raise its sleepy head to greet the new day. We watched the darkened sky turn to a brilliant turquoise as the awakening rays of the rising sun illuminated it. It was a truly holy moment to sit quietly and feel the peace of Philae.

Fig. 26.7. Philae Island.

After returning to the Afandina via a short motor boat ride and bus trip, we took some time to catch up on sleep before we ventured out for some serious shopping. We visited the colorful Aswan market and came home with scarves, galabeyas, blankets, jewelry, and other various souvenirs. The Nubians also sell their jewelry and wood and bone carved souvenirs on the small boats that transported us to Philae and Elephantine Island, so there was shopping coming and going. All the while they sang us a song and played their drums for us. They even got us to sing along!

The Sail Begins

Then we began our serious sail down the Nile and visited various temples along the way. We sailed all day and eventually came to Kom Ombo. This temple is dedicated to Horus the elder and Sobek the crocodile god. Its teaching is about the acceptance of opposition and duality. It is an impressive temple that sits right on the bank of the Nile. This was a healing center in ancient times and on the back wall there are inscriptions showing sponges, scissors, and medical tools used for operations not unlike our modern ones. The temple is divided into two sides and right in the middle between the two is a niche carved into the stone that we each sat upon. We call this the seat of neutrality. Here you can sit and experience what it is to accept the light and the dark, when there is no charge or preference. There is a strong sense of acceptance and understanding that the yin and the yang together make up the whole, and both are necessary.

Fig. 26.8. Kom Ombo Temple.

The next day we sailed to the town of Edfu and after a rather short chaotic horse and buggy ride we arrived at Edfu Temple which is dedicated to Horus the hawk, son of Osiris and Isis. It was Horus who avenged the murder of his father and fought his uncle Set for eighty years. He finally overcame Set although he was not able to kill him. Here we embrace the activating male principle of Hours as well as the mastery of light over dark, of good over evil. Here we received an activation of the heart. The edifices of Edfu tower high above and its size alone is enough to fill one with awe. Here we connected to the soaring spiritual aspect of Horus and the use of power when it is properly mediated through the dictates of the intelligent heart.

Fig. 26.9. Edfu Temple.

After Edfu, we continued to sail for the rest of the day and so we just relaxed and visited with one another. This was a great time for a circle in which we shared our experiences. This was the time to really let down and I caught up on my journal writing and enjoyed the Nile and the peaceful life along her banks.

The next day, Mohamed arranged a visit for us to a small village which gave us a taste of rural life. We met the people and saw how they live. This was a very heartwarming experience. Then we came to Esna Temple dedicated to Knum and we also toured the town of Esna which is very old. Most of this temple actually sits underneath the town itself, and is not assessable. The front part of the temple is full of colonnades and interesting paintings. They were beginning to clean the high walls and the colors were still very vibrant.

Fig. 26.10. The Temple of Esna.

The next morning after mooring in Esna, our boat traveled through the locks. It took some maneuvering by out captain to make sure that the Afandina was tied up correctly and was safely moved through to the lower waters below Esna. While we worked our way through the locks, local vendors threw blankets, bedspreads, table cloths, and dresses down or over to the boat deck. If we liked something, we threw money back in a can, if not we threw the merchandise back!

Luxor

Our final destination for the sail was modern day Luxor, known in ancient days as Thebes. We arrived there in the afternoon. Docking on the western side of the Nile, we sat on deck to look out at the view of Luxor across the river. We would travel each day from our Afandina home via a small motor boat and across the river to the east bank, Luxor, and our awaiting bus. There were many exciting adventures ahead of us. Each of these sites has special teachings and special gifts to share with us, and they are all breathtaking and beautiful.

We visited Luxor Temple that night and it is in the heart of Luxor. It is dedicated to Amun, the sun god in his fertility aspect, his wife, Mut and son, Khonsu. It is a jewel of a temple and it is bathed in golden hues due to the spectacular job they do of lighting it up at night—that make it so magical. It is often referred to as the temple of man as it reflects the human body; as you enter you are at the feet and as you move further on and back into the temple you are finally into the holy of holies and the head. It is a healing temple and we made prayers for the healing of the parts of our bodies that we had concerns about. We made prayers for the healing of our planet and for our loved ones and friends. Luxor is also a cosmic temple and reminds us that we are multidimensional beings and that we are star seeded. When we take photos of this temple at night our shots are full of orbs. The spirits are alive and well here.

The next day we visited Karnak Temple which is a huge temple complex with the remains of temples built from the oldest dynasties up until Roman times. It is here that we visited the lion goddess Sekhmet, one of the rare statues housed in her original home. She provided each of us with an activation of healing, love, and empowerment. She is the awakener par excellence.

Fig. 26.11. Karnak Temple with its row of Sphinxes.

Fig. 26.12. Hatshepsut's Obelisk at Karnak.

Fig. 26.13. The Sekhmet statue at Karnak.

On the next day we drove three hours to visit Abydos Temple which was built by Seti I and completed by his son Ramses II. It was one of the most sacred sites in ancient Egypt and it houses beautiful paintings of Seti, and the gods and goddesses. When we stood in the shafts of light that come from the little square windows cut into the ceiling, we received activations of light. Many of us were downloaded with spiritual information and bliss.

Fig. 26.14. Abydos Temple.

This temple is dedicated to Osiris It also houses the Osireion which is a much older structure, and very mysterious. There is no answer to how it was built given the huge blocks in its structure. Here we find the Flower of Life symbols tattooed into one of its supporting pillars. Some say this is the most healing place on earth.

Fig. 26.15. The Osireion.

Fig. 26.16. The Flower of Life symbol.

Then we drove on to Dendera Temple which is dedicated to Hathor, the goddess of love, bliss, ecstasy, and healing. The colorful decorations on the wall are exquisite here. They have cleaned the ceiling and walls and the blues, turquoise, and reds and gold colors look as if they were painted just yesterday. This was a place of joy, music, dance, and song. I could almost hear the drums and sistrums, the ancient rattles used by the priestesses. There was also a healing center here and dream work was an important part of the process. As we climbed up the stairs to the roof, we discovered what is called the Zodiac of Dendera on the ceiling in one of the rooms, and also a beautiful little outside chapel. It was here that we danced to feel the joy of the place. I always feel so happy here.

Fig. 26.17. Dendera Temple.

Fig. 26.18. Hathor.

The next day we woke early and visited sites on the west side of the river which is called the West Bank. This is where we find the mortuary temples and tombs. We took a short bus ride in the wee hours of the morning so that we could be there for the sunrise as we visited Deir el Bahari, the stunning mortuary temple of Queen Hatshepsut that sits high up and into the western mountain. To me this is one of the most peaceful places that I know. From the temple you can look back out over the West Bank, the Nile, and Luxor. There is a lovely little chapel dedicated to Hathor on the left side of the temple as you approach it, and another one dedicated to Anubis on the right side. This is one of my favorite places in all of Egypt.

Fig. 26.19. Deir el Bahari.

Then we went to Medinet Habu, the mortuary temple of Ramses III which is known for its deeply carved hieroglyphs and wall decorations. There were rooms here in which we toned and made sounds, and I swear, I heard sounds come from the wall themselves. It felt like the spirits were singing with us.

Fig. 26.20. Medinet Habu.

In the afternoon we visited the Valley of the Kings where the pharaohs of the New Kingdom are buried. It was here that I had a most amazing experience on that first visit when Mohamed arranged for us to have private time in Seti I's tomb which is usually closed to the public. I write about this in Chapter 30. The ancients understood something about death that we have lost. They looked forward to entering the afterlife and they saw it as an even better experience than their earthly one. They saw it as a returning to the light. They also believed that communicating with their dead relatives and friends was essential to living a good life while one was on earth. Here we always take time to thank the ancestors and remember our own friends, family, and animals that have passed over.

We also did a lot of shopping in Luxor. We visited not only the market, but also the alabaster store, Radwan's jewelry store, the papyrus store, and finally the scented oils store— we were unstoppable.

The Afandina continued to be our home away from home. Every time we went out on another excursion and returned home to rest and take a meal, our crew was there ready to greet us with their warmth and hospitality. It was hard to leave them when it was time to return to Cairo for the last few days of our trip. I always cry when I say goodbye to my family on the Afandina.

Returning to Cairo

Flying back to Cairo meant returning to the employees at the Mena House, as well as our friends from Quest Travel. Those we had come to know on the first days of our trip greeted us and made us feel welcomed and comfortable. One would imagine that we had come to the end of our tour. However there was much more adventure ahead packed into those last few days in Cairo. There was still so much incredible experience ahead of us according to our itinerary. Our tour would take us to Sakkara and the famous Step Pyramid that is really a cemetery for the Old Dynasties of Egypt. Here we would have ceremony in Teti's tomb where we would see the famous Pyramid Texts, the oldest spiritual writing in the world. This is also where I was able to visit the Tomb of Unas on another journey that I write about chapter 31. Near Sakkara we stopped at the carpet store, and many in the group made a purchase.

Fig. 26.21. The Step Pyramid at Sakkara.

We were scheduled to visit Old Cairo and its famous churches and synagogue. These would prove to be sites of profound spiritual energy. Here stand the oldest Coptic churches in Cairo, and Christians from all over the world come here on pilgrimages. St. Sergius which was built in the fourth or fifth century is thought to stand upon the place where the Holy Family rested during their flight into Egypt. Very close to this church stands the Hanging Church, the Church of St. Barbara, and the Church of the Virgin. All are beautiful and alive with spiritual presence. The synagogue of Ben Ezra stands close to these Coptic churches. According to tradition, there has been a Jewish community here since the time of Moses. Some interesting documents are housed here including a copy of the Torah dating to the fifth century. This also proved to be a very poignant place to visit.

Fig. 26.22. Old Cairo.

And finally we had our private visit and initiation in The Great Pyramid ahead of us. This meant that we had the Great Pyramid to ourselves for two hours. Here we would have our culminating ceremony in the King's Chamber and then we would have time to explore the Queen's Chamber and the chamber underneath the pyramid called the Pit. When we entered the chamber, the lights were turned off and candles lit the darkened space. There sits the basalt sarcophagus. Each participant lies in the large stone structure with the intention of integrating the spiritual experiences they have encountered. The group toned for us and after our allotted time, we each arose up and stepped out renewed and regenerated. We were reborn to our new perspectives and understandings. It is an incredible privilege to have this experience. I get goose bumps just thinking of it.

Fig. 26.23 The Great Pyramid of Cheops.

It was bittersweet as we met for our last dinner together at the very restaurant that I described in the introduction of this book. Here we were entertained by Sufi musicians and dancers, which proved to be yet another spiritual high. Here we reminisced about our trip and shared our final stories and experiences. We had become a family under Emil and Mohamed's support and care. And it was here that I heard Mohamed talk to us about becoming his Peace Ambassadors. It was a glorious ending to a perfect spiritual pilgrimage. It was very hard to say goodbye, and that is why so many return to Egypt. This is why I have returned over and over.

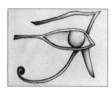

Chapter 27: The Afandina: Mohamed's Special Sailing Boat

Fig. 27.1. The Afandina. Photograph courtesy of Tarek Lotfy.

The Afandina actually became our home away from home during our sail in Egypt and she has a special place in the heart of every traveler who is so privileged to sail on her. She has quite a story. I remember when I was interviewing Mohamed for this book and after days of talking with him that I asked him, "What else do we need in this book?" His face lit up. "My heart is with the Afandina," he said. He became so animated when he began the story, I couldn't help but become enthused. It was as if he was talking about the birth of one of his own children.

Mohamed had the Afandina built especially for his metaphysical and spiritual visitors. The boat has ten cabins and has room for twenty: sixteen travelers, two tour leaders, an Egyptologist, and an escort. The captain and crew have their quarters in the rear of the boat. Mohamed wanted traveling on the boat to be a small, intimate experience, so the dahabeya, the name for a sailing boat on the Nile, is like traveling in your own private sailing yacht. Groups can sail down the Nile and visit places off the beaten path—places most tourists never see. Meals are prepared by an excellent chef, and the food rivals any gourmet restaurant. The crew— almost one crew member for each guest—are eager to please and spoil the travelers. One can't help but feel like Cleopatra or Mark Anthony, sailing the Nile in utter luxury.

Mohamed had the Afandina built in order to fulfill a dream he had of providing something special for spiritual leaders. Previously, tour groups traveled in large boats with more than sixty cabins and one hundred guests. "My desire was to create a more private and intimate experience for my guests," he told me as we sat in his office. "I wanted the energy to be different." In Mohamed's mind, having a small, private boat with ten cabins creates a feeling of one group, one energy, and one purpose: a community and a family. "I really have had this vision for a long time," he said.

The idea for the Afandina came to Mohamed one day when he was having lunch in Alexandria. His voice rose as he described it, tapping his forehead. "It came to me; the dahabeya," he said. "I saw it in my mind!" As he ate, he found he was paying less and less attention to his food, and more and more attention to the visions of sailing on a boat with friends and travelers. Soon, the Afandina was much more than a vision. "Once my heart connects with my mind, I move forward," he said.

When he returned to Cairo that night, he called the owner of a shipyard that he knew, and told him he wanted to meet. When Mohamed arrived, he had the money only to begin building the boat in his pocket, and his pen was poised to sign a contract. Although Mohamed was eager to move forward, the process was no quick deal. Where was he going to get the money to complete his dream?

The story of how the money came to Mohamed is quite an interesting one. It seems that he had an American friend who told him about an Italian businessman who had traveled to Egypt and was quite unhappy with his experiences. The Italian had decided not to do further work in Egypt. Upon hearing this, Mohamed made up his mind to see if he could change this man's mind. He was quite sure that he could provide the man with the experiences that would alter his opinion. When Mohamed sets his mind to something, he is truly determined. He invited the man to Cairo and set up some rather amazing experiences for him. He set up a dinner for two at the foot of the Great Pyramid. And at another dinner he asked his friends, the well-known Zahi Hawass and head of the Antiquities Department, and Omar Sharif, the famous actor, to have a seat with them. This impressed the Italian businessman enough for him to ask Mohamed to run a conference for him in Egypt.

This was Mohamed's plan all along. He knew this man had the potential to be a big business partner, and Mohamed was also adamant about changing his experience of Egypt. So the man hired him to take charge of a large conference and Mohamed took care of every detail. He even arranged fireworks at the Pyramids, which was no small order, and a big dinner for all of the 1500 participants at the foot of the pyramids with a performance from the Opera Aida provided by the Egyptian Opera House, as the evening's entertainment. This made quite a spectacular impression on the Italian businessman.

As it worked out, the man made a great deal of money, and even though they had never signed an agreement, he handed over to Mohamed a check of one million dollars! Thus Mohamed was able to complete his boat, and also make seven others, all of which he sold except for the Afandina.

Building the Afandina

Mohamed explained that it usually takes about eight months to build a ship, but his took a year and a half. He raised his hand high above his head, palm parallel to his crown. "The reason it took so long," he explained, "was because there were many times when something about the design didn't feel right, and I thought, 'What will Sharlyn, Jane, Nicki, or John say? Will the leaders like it?'" Mohamed continued making changes, trying to make it match his vision. Eventually, he was satisfied. Before the Revolution, sails on the Afandina were booked a year in advance, with just a few dates available.

"It has been a blessing for me," Mohamed said, "and now my friends have a boat." Mohamed placed his hand on his heart. "This boat is their boat. This boat is made for them and by them." Since it was first built, people like Bill Gates, the prime minister of Canada, and other celebrities have also stayed on the Afandina.

There is no doubt that the Afandina is something truly special, both for the heart that went into it and the accommodations. The staterooms below either have two twin beds or a queen size bed with bathroom and a shower. There is closet space, a bureau for clothes, a mini- refrigerator, a safe for valuables, and air conditioning. The beds are comfortable, with the best of linens, and each room has a broad window so travelers can rest in bed and watch the scenery pass. A narrow hall leads to either to the living area above or to the deck at the bow.

On the floor above is a lounge and dining room. The walls are paneled with wood and the ceiling is decorated with wood beams cut into squares. It is furnished with long, wooden tables for dining and soft couches and chairs, purposefully grouped to encourage small, intimate conversations. Thickly woven rugs carpet the gleaming hardwood floors. There is a big-screen television, a sound system, and plenty of space for meeting and socialization. At the dining area bar, travelers can grab tea, coffee, water, or soft drinks whenever needed.

The living area leads to a covered deck near the front of the boat that provides shade during the day, where we would often just sit together and enjoy each other's company before meals were announced. Evening meals were typically indoors, and we would serve ourselves buffet-style. Occasionally, though, we would eat by candlelight outside. The evening air was always balmy and the night so romantic when we dined this way. We could see the stars out over the darkened horizon and hear the lapping of the river as it met the boats sides as we enjoyed our food. Our voices were low and our intimate conversations were marked by the clinking sounds of the china or our glasses. I felt like I was in a movie.

Breakfast is always served on the deck, and the chef makes the eggs the way each person wants them. Each morning, I would think to myself, 'what a way to wake up.' The deck has tables, couches, chairs, and a hot tub. It is here that people can relax—reading, talking, or just being with the river. There is plenty of space, and lots of room for alone time if travelers so desire.

A flight of stairs leads to the top deck that offers a panoramic view of the Nile, as well as the captain's cabin and a square, tent-like structure with drapes to block the sun. It was here that we often did yoga in the mornings. At night, the cooling breeze on this deck was magnificent as we stargazed, feeling very close to heaven and a glorious full moon.

Being on the Afandina means being in the lap of luxury. But even more importantly, as we traveled, we became friends with the crew and began to develop relationships with the Egyptian people. There were many hours spent on the Afandina playing music, listening to drums, singing, dancing, and enjoying their company. When we travelers return, the crew remember each one of us and are glad to welcome us home.

I give my gratitude to the chef Salah and his helper Omar, to the stewards of our cabins, Hassen and Sayed, who decorate our bed with towel art every day and freshen up our rooms, and to Taha and Tiger who serve our meals and attend to our needs. I am also grateful to our crew who sail the Afandina and keep us safe: the Captain Alwald, the engineer Korashi, and Mohamed Ali, Masry, Bakar, and Abdel Fatah. There are a few more but they stay either in the kitchen or on the tug boat that moves our ship along and so I wasn't able to get to know them personally, but I am still very grateful for all that they do.

Fig. 27.2. The lounge on the Afandina. Photographs courtesy of Tarek Lotfy.

Fig. 27.3. Set up for dinner on the deck at sunset.

Fig. 27.4. The upstairs deck under the tent.

Fig. 27.5. The crew of the Afandina become our friends.

Fig. 27.6. The chef Salah, Taha, former worker, the engineer Korashi, Emil, Sharlyn, and Tiger.

Fig. 27.7. Tiger and Sharlyn's husband Ricardo.

Fig. 27.8. Taha and Sharlyn.

Fig. 27.9. The Captain Alwald, Masry, and Emil.

Fig. 27.10. Bakar.

Fig. 27.11. Mohamed Ali.

Fig. 27.12. Abdel Fatah.

Chapter 28: Testimonials

Websites of tour leaders and travel companies are chock-full of testimonials about Mohamed and Quest Travel. The following is a small sample of testimonials that demonstrate the experiences Mohamed helps create:

Courtesy of Nicki Scully's website Shamanic Journeys:

> In 1992, we met Mohamed Nazmy, who was the land agent on our tour to Egypt. At that time, he was the sales manager for Sphinx Tours. What was clear from the start was that no one could ever pay Mohamed enough to serve the people in the very special, over-the-top way that he did. No requests were too little or too great for him, and no participant was ever left out of his net of care, because serving people on the tour was his greatest happiness. Whether arranging a midnight camel ride or special entry into a sacred site when it is not open to the public, or just making sure that everyone feels seen and loved, Mohamed makes tourism a sacred spiritual practice.
>
> —Nicki Scully and Jane Bell

Courtesy of Sharlyn Hidalgo's website Alchemical Healing Arts:

Wow, a testimonial! Where to start or end to describe the trip of a lifetime? Briefly, it was beyond my imagination or dreams—so well organized, first class treatment throughout, and an incredible view/introduction to Egypt and its many facets. From pyramids, to temples, to market places, to farms, the town of Esna for a step back in time, the incredible Nile River and it's amazing scenery, and so much more to mention. The Afandina experience still amazes me, the beautifully scripted ceremonies you held at the temples, Emil's in depth knowledge of history and Egypt, all memorable and incredible. I would do it again in an instant, and with Quest Travel with Mohamed at the helm is a gem unto its own. Everyone in the organization is first class. Thank you so much.
—*Eddie Hidalgo, June 25, 2012*

Courtesy of Mohamed Nazmy and Quest Travel:

This is a client testimonial sent by email to Quest Travel in July 9, 2005. It was great to see that I wasn't the only one who was deeply affected by Mohamed's speech about Anwar Sadat:

Dear Mohamed,

Your hospitality on our recent trip to Egypt was very much appreciated. I have traveled to many different parts of the world and have never been treated with the kindness and the warmth that that you, your staff and the Egyptian people showed towards my wife and I. Going to Egypt was the fulfillment of a desire I have had since childhood, I have always been fascinated with Egyptian history and while in college minored in Archaeology. To be honest I had put that desire aside because of all the conflicts in recent years in the Middle East and a perception that Americans were not welcomed in your part of the world. I am very happy that I went and that my perception was wrong when it comes to Egypt. Many friends have asked me about our trip to Egypt, all having indicating their desire to see your country, all having the same concerns I had about going. They were all surprised when I told them it was by far the most enjoyable and interesting trip I had ever taken in my life. They all followed up with "didn't you feel as if you were in danger, that the people in the country hated you", and again they were surprised at my response that I felt not only safe but I felt that the people truly cared about my well-being and wanted my journey to be the best it could be. I guess we owe much of this perception to the way the media only portrays a small incomplete part of every story. Mohamed many of the trips experiences will always be in my heart and mind, but one of the most memorable ones was the stop we made at the memorial and tomb of Anwar el-Sadat, certainly the memorial was a beautiful tribute to a great man, but it was your words and your emotion as you spoke about him to us that made a lasting impression on me and a desire to learn more about his life. When I returned to the States I went to purchase his autobiography "In Search of Identity", only to find that it is not in print any longer in the US. I fortunately was able to find a book dealer selling a copy that was in perfect condition on line. I found the book very interesting and it clearly showed that Sadat was a man of peace. Two beliefs that Sadat maintained were significant to his ability to always seek peace:

"There is no happiness for people at the expense of other people."

"There can be hope only for a society which acts as one big family, not as many separate ones."

It is unfortunate that his life was cut short by a violent act; your part of the world may have been saved much of the turmoil it is experiencing today if he had lived to become the great peacemaker of the region.

One other item that I reflected on after I read the book was the warmth that we received from all of your staff. Anwar in writing to our President Nixon late in 1970 wrote "As it is the law of nature for each action to have a reaction, a good move by you will be met by dozen good moves by us, and vice versa." You, Emil, Fath, and Hatem showed this philosophy many times by reacting to our positive reactions with many more positive reactions. I thank you and all of your staff for the wonderful and lasting experiences your trip provided us and hope someday to visit with all of you again. If you or any of your staff are ever in our part of the world please give us a call, Monica and I would love to see you and return the hospitality you have shown us. You live in a truly wonderful country with a tremendous history. I wish you and all your people health, happiness and peace.

—You're Friend, Mike Prat

Part Eight: Egypt and Her People

Fig. Part Eight.1. The crew on the Afandina, 2012.

We Create Peace When We Become Friends

Chapter 29: The Mystery and Magic of Egypt

There is simply no place in the world like Egypt. Not only is Egypt home to one of the world's most ancient, mysterious, and intriguing civilizations, but it also houses important religious sites of Christianity, Judaism, and Islam. Mohamed firmly believes that the treasures of Egypt belong to the entire world, and he wants people to experience these powerful roots of civilization. At its most basic, he wants people to love Egypt the way he loves it. He has developed his business so that his travelers can experience aspects of his country they may not encounter on other tours, whether it's a rare visit to a site or an interaction with someone they might not otherwise have met. Mohamed always says Egypt's people are its greatest asset. Clients have said it is the alchemy between Egypt and Mohamed that makes what he has to offer so amazing and rare.

I've heard many people who have traveled to Egypt say they have had a long fascination with everything Egyptian, and that was certainly true for me. I had been fascinated with Egypt ever since I saw my first mummy in a museum in Washington State at the age of seven. My parents were hard-pressed to separate me from that mummy that I was so fascinated with—in love with, in a way. I didn't want to leave. I was taken with the Sphinx, the tombs in the Valley of the Kings, and the temples. Before I went to Egypt in 2007, I read all I could about the Old, Middle, and New Kingdoms, as well as the sites attached to each period. People often have the experience of "coming home" when they get off the tarmac at the Cairo airport, and indeed, this was my experience as well.

Visiting Egypt is such a drastic cultural change, and as tourists, we have no choice but to let go of control. As the kindness of the Egyptian people and the mysteries of Egypt begin to work their magic, we find it easier to be open and relaxed. When I traveled to Egypt, this was enhanced by Emil, Mohamed, and the employees at Quest Travel, who are so gracious and attentive. They are big-hearted, full of warmth, love, and effortless smiles. Humor is a big factor in all of this, and the laughter is healing.

Although Egypt is known for drawing those fascinated by history, archaeology, and spirituality, it's also a beautiful vacation spot—a wonderful environment to rest and relax. Every year, tourists visit from Europe to enjoy the warm climate and scuba dive or snorkel along the coast of the Red Sea and Alexandria. I found my relaxation as we drifted slowly down the Nile in Mohamed's yacht. As we journeyed down the river, I was able to slow down and contemplate my life in ways that are not possible when I am home. As one sails along, one sees that rural life for the Egyptians has not changed much since ancient times. Families tend to crops and work the land by hand with the help of animals: donkeys, water buffalo, and even camels. The houses are made of mud bricks and are shaded by date palms. There are no signs of modern conveniences. Life moves slowly.

This passage through time was food for my soul and reminded me that modern life is not necessarily better. Though the people were poor, they seemed happy and full of love. I remembered a story of a fellow traveler who wanted to take a picture of a man fishing along the river with his young son. She didn't want to intrude on their time together, but when she saw them flash their wide smiles, wave, and nod their permission, she snapped the perfect reminder of their kindness. They were happy to participate and share their lives, and, in a strange way, she felt they cared about her happiness, even if from afar.

Spiritual Sites—Both Old and New

The sacred sites of Egypt resonate. Emil would say, "They activate you." There are intense, palpable energies within them. The array of energetic experience as one moves from site to site along the Nile, culminating in a private visit to the Great Pyramid, is unbelievably powerful. I experienced the temples and tombs as huge, stereo speakers that transmit spiritual energy and a vibration of love, forgiveness, kindness, and unity. Within those walls, it is easy to recognize that one is a spiritual being with incredible potential. Beliefs that we are separate from one another, fall away. Jane Bell once told me, "Egypt is where the light is."

Every ancient Egyptian temple is dedicated to a different god or goddess, and each one represents a facet or principle of the divine and has its own teachings. In that sense the Egyptians worshipped one creator God. And yet this God expressed itself in many different ways. For instance, the Temple at Philae is home to Isis, the great mother goddess of love and acceptance. Dendera Temple is dedicated to Hathor, the goddess of joy and bliss. It is indeed a privilege to be able to have private time for ceremonies and meditations in these beautiful places.

I agree with the words of Olivia Temple—an artist, writer, and coauthor of *The Sphinx Mystery: The Forgotten Origins of the Sanctuary of Anubis*. In the Introduction she writes:

> I am not alone in dividing my life into two, an equivalent to BC and AD, which in my case were Before Egypt and After Egypt. Most people who spend time among the ancient places there find it becomes harder subsequently to visualize how life was before...
>
> Since my first trip to Egypt many years ago, the meaning of life has become clearer. Questions and doubts, fears and shadows, have become mysteriously clarified as if I have suddenly found the key to a complicated coded message (1).
>
> ...Everyone who knows this place [speaking of the Giza Plateau specifically], who spends more than a casual amount of time in the sacred places of the ancient Egyptians, experiences a defining moment, an alchemical change that creeps into your psyche like a drug (2).

Egypt is rich with spiritual history. The newer religious sites attract busloads of pilgrims from around the world to see the synagogues, the early Christian churches, and the beautiful mosques in Old Cairo. Egypt is where the Nag Hammadi manuscripts were found. There are ancient Christian sites all over Egypt, including St. Catherine's Monastery in the Sinai. All these sites are powerful, housing spiritual energy and conveying the sacred. These sites are sacred to Muslims, Christians, and Jews. Add this to the thousands of years of ancient Egyptian spiritual history reflected in the monuments, temples, tombs, and sites and you have magnificence available to you.

Danielle Rama Hoffman, who helped lead both of the first two tours I took to Egypt, writes on her website Egyptiscalling.com:

> Egypt is one of the most magical destinations on the planet. Being in Egypt immerses you in the realm of infinite possibilities. The veils are thinner. Your connection to your full potential is accessible, and your heart opens more easily. Your pilgrimage through Egypt is a process of conscious evolution, one that can be classified as an ascension spiral into the open heart. As you, the initiate, journey through the sacred sites in Egypt, you unlock and access energy, consciousness, and wisdom which align you with your soul, your inner being, your divine self, your full potential. You and your life are forever changed for the better. This process is one of renewal, transformation, personal growth and expansion. (Danielle, Hoffman. "Home Page." Egyptiscalling.com. Web. 28 Mar. 2012.)

When I am in Egypt, my heart sings. I am filled with love and joy. I have come to a greater understanding of myself as a spiritual being and I understand more about my own potential and possibility. I no longer feel a strong sense of limitation. I feel compelled to help others—to be of service. Mostly, I feel happy. I feel close to Spirit. In Egypt, love feels like my true state of being.

Chapter 30: Inside Seti's Tomb in the Valley of the Kings

As I envisioned stepping inside Seti's tomb in 2007, visions of the film *The Mummy's Curse* flashed through my mind. I imagined Lon Chaney: wrapped in mummy cloth, arms outstretched, clumsily stalking his soon-to-be victims who had intruded upon his tomb. Would the mummy's curse descend upon me for entering the pharaoh's last resting place? Would I feel the icy fingers of death as I entered this cold, lonely chamber? Would I be haunted by memories of being buried alive, or experience nauseating claustrophobia?

We were told that the tomb of Seti the First had not been open to tourists for twenty years. The government had limited access to protect it from deterioration at the hands (and cameras) of visitors. Not surprisingly, Mohamed arranged for our group to have a two-hour, private visit. We were warned to be very respectful while we were in the tomb.

We went in the afternoon, and it was scorching hot in The Valley of the Kings. With no shade, the sun was difficult to endure. Slowly but surely, we walked away from throngs of tourists and travelers and found ourselves trekking up a distant lane to a set of stairs. As we stood above the entrance, we bristled with anticipation. We watched as Danielle, our tour leader, was given the key and walked down the steep stairs to the iron-gated door that marked the entrance. At first, Danielle couldn't get the gate open, and we worried that "fate" wouldn't allow us to enter. She jiggled the key a bit, and it finally opened. We began our silent descent down a dark, sloping corridor that led to the tomb.

What we saw took my breath away. Life-sized paintings of the pharaoh and Egyptian deities lined the walls along the stone corridor. Although they were painted more than three thousand years ago, the colors were vibrant; the images were captivating. This place was deeply alive. Rather than the grief, heaviness, or sense of "haunting" I expected to feel, I felt happiness, peace and joy. I felt blessed in this sacred space.

As we reached the bottom, a sense of relief washed over us as coolness touched our skin. It was dim and chilly, a welcome contrast to the hundred-degree heat and glaring sun in the valley above. As we entered the main gallery, I could have sworn I heard a voice greet me as "the tree lady." I've done healing work with trees for many years, but I'd never thought of myself as "the tree lady," and this was the last place I expected to hear such a greeting. I was thrilled to have been recognized by the energies of the tomb, but caught off guard. I chalked it up to heat, excitement, and a vivid imagination. I'll never know, but I was certainly feeling happy, and more relaxed with each passing moment.

We noticed small rooms on either side of us as we moved into the large open gallery, where tall rows of pillars appeared to hold up the ceiling. Here, too, there were colorful, larger-than-life paintings of Anubis, Pharaoh Seti, Hathor, and Osiris. We walked through the last two pillars, then down a few steps to a room with a curved, vaulted ceiling. It was painted a beautiful lapis blue and studded with golden stars. Nut, the sky goddess, arched across the ceiling-sky, and on either side of her, Isis and Nephthys served as guardians and protectors. Paintings of the gods and goddesses of Egypt lined the back wall, and beneath them, a large, rectangular hole was cut into the floor. This had once housed Seti the First's sarcophagus, which now lies in a museum in London. We were in the tomb although it felt more like a holy temple, and its beauty was beyond words.

As we settled in to do our ceremony, I sat on the porch-like stairs and leaned against one of the supporting pillars. Then, the assistive lights were turned off and we were enveloped in total darkness. I ignored my instinct to feel fear or panic. Peter Sterling, who was traveling with us, began playing his hand-held harp, and with the angelic music, I became calm and receptive. We toned together (making the sound of ohm) and then Danielle and Friedemann, our leaders, began to take us on a guided meditation. During that meditation, these were the words that came to me on my inner voyage:

This is a place and not a place. This is not a tomb as you know it. This is a hall of peace and transformation. Here is a sacred intelligence. Here I am form and the formless. I am the duat [a region that lies midway between earthly and spiritual worlds]. I am the territory of the inner life. I am the end and the beginning. This is not a place of death. This place holds a blueprint for how one is able to live a conscious life—a life of love and grace. This place tells the story of how one is to go through transition in life, and transition even in death—as all things change, but there is no end. Open to your evolution and allow the vibration of this sacred place to expand you and break all limitation. The truth is that you have always been free. Walk with us now and embrace your own divinity. As you hold our hands know that we are the gods and goddesses of nature, the principles of divinity and universal consciousness. We are the pharaohs as fully realized human beings. This is your destiny, as well. We are alive in other dimensions, always available to you. Be open to all possibilities. Experience and remember this holy vibration. When you remember this place you will remember this expanse, this light, this bliss, and this love. Let this sacred white light re-form you.

At that moment, I was standing in pure white light and nothing else. I lost track of time and space. I stood in joy, peace, and oneness. Who would believe that visiting an Egyptian pharaoh's dark tomb could be an experience of light? I awoke from my reverie when the meditation concluded and the lights came back on. I wasn't sure how long we'd been journeying, but I *do* know that I felt tremendous joy and ecstasy. I had the strange sensation that I was very, very tall.

As we explored the rest of the tomb and took in the exquisite art upon the walls, I tried to ground myself and get back into my body. I was blown away and shaken by this unexpected experience of light and regeneration. When they announced it was time to leave, I was seven years old again, begging my parents not to make me leave the museum. This place felt like home. I felt safe here. I was free from worry or mind-chatter. I was changed. It was hard to gather up my backpack and water bottle and begin to ascend the passages that led back up to the entrance of the tomb and out into the blazing sun of the Valley of the Kings.

There was little time to reflect on my experience as we were immediately escorted back to our bus and we were driven straight from the Valley of the Kings down a long winding road that eventually led us just past the Colossi of Memnon, two huge famous statues that sit at what used to be the entrance of the great temple belonging to the pharaoh Amenhotep III. The temple no longer exists as it has been reclaimed by thousands of years of the flooding of the Nile. The two statues now sit as sentinels to an empty field.

Fig. 30.1. The Colossi of Memnon.

Our bus pulled over to the side of the road and we were asked to depart so that we could receive a surprise. There along the roadside we saw a herd of donkeys which we were scheduled to ride! It was a raucous romp through the countryside: the last thing one would expect to do after an enlightening spiritual experience. It was utter hilarity watching each of the thirty group members attempt to mount their reluctant donkeys. It was pure chaos, full of dust, loud braying, and shouting from the attendants and little boys who were supposed to lead each donkey but failing miserably to get some obedience. The donkeys were in charge, they didn't want people on their backs, and they certainly didn't want to take these people in the same direction at the same time.

Luckily, this dose of humor helped with my "grounding." It was the perfect end to my expanded reverie. The ride was unruly, noisy, and fun. Through it all, I sat on my donkey, my feet just inches from the ground, moving through the land as the ancient people used to and still do today. When the donkeys got too close they began to kick each other, and it took all my concentration to keep my donkey from running into the one in front of me. By the time we reached our little village where lunch was scheduled, I was sweating and my arms hurt from pulling back on the reins. I was exhausted and ready for a meal. And yes, I was well-grounded.

The fact that Quest Travel made it possible for us to not only enter, but also have private time in Seti's tomb was incredible. Because of Mohamed, I had one of the most awesome and wonderful spiritual awakenings of my life. For me, having the opportunity for meditation in a place that was created for communication with divinity is beyond words. I was able to experience how a tomb can be a place of power and consciousness. Spirit comes to life here during ceremony. This sacred space truly opened and shared its high vibrational essence. I can say truthfully that I had an experience of 'standing in the light', and it was a precious and elevating event. With good faith, I can say that spiritual awakening awaits you in Egypt. I would also suggest a good donkey ride. If your spiritual experience takes you too far into the ethers, you can be sure that a ride on a little donkey will bring you smack down to earth.

I will never forget Seti the First's tomb and the experience I had there. I continue to connect to the higher realm of consciousness that was shared with me in the tomb. If I forget this state of being, all I have to do is return to the memory of standing in that special place and absorbing that incredible energy. I can hear the words again, and I become one with the art, with the sacred, and with the ancient wisdom. Whenever I question myself or the reality of spirit, I remember this tomb and this experience, and the presence of that intelligence and love fills me once again. I reopen to my full potential as a spiritual being on the planet, with work to do as a light-bearer. I remember that I want to share this light that was shared with me.

It was at the end of this trip that I first heard Mohamed talk about world peace, and this is when he asked us to become his Peace Ambassadors. I didn't need convincing. Egypt, Mohamed, and the experiences of the tour had worked their magic. I was a wholehearted member of the peace team. I also knew I had to return to Egypt.

Chapter 31: Our Adventure in the Pyramid of Unas

When Danielle and Friedemann began arranging another tour for May of 2010, I initially decided not to return to Egypt for a number of reasons. Gradually, however, things changed. As a practicing astrologer, I read the yearly solar return charts of two friends who were going on the trip, and all signs pointed to an absolutely incredible tour. At the last moment, I heard Mohamed would be traveling with the group, and I just *knew* I needed to go. I was in luck: someone had just canceled—there was one spot left for me. It was a good omen.

There was another reason I wanted to go. I had a keen and insistent desire to get into a very special site called the Pyramid of Unas, which sits outside the walls of the Sakkara complex and the Step Pyramid. This tomb is 4,350 years old, created during the Old Kingdom. However, it is younger than the Great Pyramids by about one-hundred years, according to orthodox Egyptologists. The walls of this tomb are inscribed with the *Pyramid Texts*, which are considered one of the oldest spiritual writings in the world and are indeed one of Egypt's great national treasures. I had read extensively about this pyramid and its writings, and I had been utterly fascinated by this site for a long time. It seemed to me that this tomb was a place where something big could happen.

When Mohamed hears that someone on one of his tours has a special desire to see a certain site, he'll work wonders to make it happen. As usual, it was the master magician Nazmy parting the sea for a rare and sacred opportunity. My intuition told me this was the trip on which he would make it happen, and that this was the perfect time and perfect group of people to share the experience with. Reliably, Mohamed ended up arranging for us to have private time in the Pyramid of Unas. He loves to see the smile and surprise on the face of someone who gets what they wish for, and I duly delivered both.

The Tomb of Unas

It was on one of the very last days of our tour that we were able to enter the Pyramid of Unas. I was itching to see the Pyramid Texts. In his book, *The Valley of the King: Exploring the Tombs of the Pharaohs*, John Romer writes, "They deal with themes of ritual and resurrection and are the oldest surviving body of religious writing in the world" (21). These mystical texts are classics of world literature. The Coffin Texts and The Book of the Dead texts that we find in the later Middle and New Dynasties are renditions of this original canon.

It's quite possible that these texts also describe experiences meant for the living. In his book *Shamanic Wisdom in the Pyramid Texts*, Jeremy Naydler writes, "What the texts describe are direct encounters with a spiritual dimension of existence" (310). In my mind, these hieroglyphs offer us a description of how to contact the spiritual realm. The texts are a roadmap for how to enter heaven and the enlightenment of consciousness; they describe an ascension process. Spiritual experiences occur when the boundary between the worlds is consciously crossed. I believe this tomb is one of the places on earth where this can happen—that it was created in part, for the purpose of spiritual initiation.

It was my belief that the Pyramid of Unas offered my group a direct experience with the spirit world. I knew that here was a place where one could more easily communicate with one's higher self and with universal consciousness. I believed it was possible to experience a rebirth and a powerful regeneration here. I felt that it was possible to create a channel in which the power of all that is could reestablish itself upon the Earth plane. I believed that the goal was not simply to enter into relationship with the divine, but also to bring the divine into relationship with the earthly. There are no more kings to unite these realms. It was my feeling that the group that I traveled with—these eighteen daring souls—were drawn to the Pyramid of Unas to participate in this "sacred technology" together. In creating their sacred sites, the ancient Egyptians took into consideration where they built the structures, how they oriented their temples in terms of directionality, what stone would hold the desired vibration they were creating, and what the teachings of the god and goddesses of that site were imparting. In this way they created a technology that would hold and sustain the vibration they were working with.

The day we visited the tomb, we first entered the Sakkara complex itself, which is surrounded on three sides by a wall. On the fourth side is the Step Pyramid, built by King Zoser of the Third Dynasty. This area was selected as the necropolis for the dead because it stands on the west side of the Nile, across from Memphis, which was the ancient capital at that time. All of the mortuary temples, burial sites, and tombs are built on the west side of the river. Sakkara was built by Zoser's brilliant architect, Imhotep.

First, we passed through a doorway built into a towering edifice and walked down a corridor with a row of massive pillars on either side. As we walked through this corridor, it was as though we were about to enter another dimension. It felt like we were walking through a deep forest of tall trees. We emerged into bright sunlight and stood on the vast rectangular Sakkara courtyard, which was like a football field or a landing pad for alien spaceships. At the far end, the huge Step Pyramid loomed above us. Everything there was the color of golden sand, standing out against the expansive turquoise sky. On the walls you could still see remnants of temple entrances, pillars, chapels, and rooms. The place was originally built for the Jubilee celebration, the ancient Sed Festival of the pharaohs.

The desert beyond the walls stretched out forever in all directions, and heat waves danced above the sand. Emaciated dogs panted in the heat, tongues hanging out. Alas, there was no shade and no water. They reminded me of Anubis, the jackal god of embalming who serves as a guide for souls making their way to the afterlife. I was reminded of the power and magic of this site and its purpose of guiding the deceased into their new life. As we explored the sandy Sakkara plateau, I grew anxious to enter Una's chamber. I was hot and restless, and could hardly stand waiting another minute to arrive. I hid my growing frustration because I didn't understand it myself, but our Egyptologist Emil was content to take his time. He strolled to a wall that had small windows cut into it, which he called healing windows. There, we could place our heads in the windows and make sound with the intention of sending healing to ourselves or loved ones.

We walked across the courtyard to a wall, where Emil pointed out multiple upright cobras that sat along the top. The raised cobra, called the Uraeus, symbolizes protection. You will often find them on pharaoh's headdresses, ready to spit their venom at an approaching enemy. Emil talked more, and I grew agitated. Usually, I find Emil's Egyptology lectures fascinating, but that day was different. I couldn't stop thinking about Una's chamber, and I wasn't myself. Emil noticed something was off and asked me if I was too hot. Inside, I screamed, "No, I just want you to shut up and take me to the tomb!" Outside, I simply shook my head.

Finally, we walked up rock-hewn stairs to the top of a wall, then down another stairway that took us outside of the enclosure. We moved as a group toward the tomb—the Pyramid of Unas. My heart pounded. Chains blocked off the stairs that led down to the entrance. As the guard pulled the rattling chains away, I could barely contain myself. We descended the stairs, then crouched to make our way through a low causeway. We arrived in the middle of a dark room, where we could stand up again under a vaulted ceiling. In the dark, cool interior, lit only by a few dim floor lights, we waited quietly. We felt and heard—the sacred silence of thousands of years. We looked at the blue hieroglyphs that stood out against the white walls and gazed at the lapis blue ceiling, studded with gold stars.

Back to crouching, we pushed through another entryway to the room with the sarcophagus, where we formed a circle. Like the first room, the ceiling was painted blue and embellished with stars. Each of the four stone walls was covered in raised hieroglyphs from bottom to top. The little chamber was like a book, a permanent text that had withstood time, unlike the many scrolls of papyrus and vellum that had crumbled and disintegrated away with age.

There they were: the famous Pyramid Texts. These texts of such immense power took my breath away. They tell a story of how the pharaoh traveled to the stars, visited with the gods, consumed their powers, and returned to share knowledge and inspiration with his people. The Pyramid Texts are also known as the "cannibal texts" because the powers and wisdom of the neteru are eaten. Utterances 273 and 274 are called the Cannibal Hymn because they describe the king hunting and eating the gods. The eating of the neteru reminds me of the communion in Christianity, in which believers symbolically ingest the spiritual blood and body of Christ. Is this the origin of this practice? It is interesting that the word cannibal is used in reference to the texts, but not to communion. I think they describe the same thing; the ingesting of the spiritual essence of God.

On the floor opposite the entrance stood the large, black sarcophagus. It took up the entire west side of the room. We could barely see, but over time our eyes adjusted and we used our flashlights to see the details. The sarcophagus was made of solid black granite and was empty with no lid. Décor on the wall behind it had designs that looked like lotus plants and stripes.

The guard at the entrance eventually turned the lights off, and we chanted together and made our prayers. This place felt holy and sacred to me. Strangely enough, it felt like home. Many believe that this place was not just a burial chamber, but that it was a place where one could achieve inspiration and elevated consciousness. As Danielle and Friedemann led us on a guided journey, I felt myself traveling to my higher self and an inner world of spirit. I felt empowered and supported to continue my work of healing and helping raise the consciousness of those I work with. I better understood myself as a co-creator with spirit and I gained greater understanding and compassion. For a brief moment, I became fused with all of creation in a field of unity and love. It was a true moment of enlightenment.

I wrote about the experience as soon as I could:

We became the modern ones who stepped into the pyramid of Unas, and through our ritual and intention, and the power of the pyramid and the ancient texts, we traveled through our meditation to the realm of the neteru [the gods and goddesses of Egypt who represent principles of the divine oneness]. We left our physical bodies and traveled in our light bodies to the realm of the stars to meet the gods and goddesses. We journeyed to the formless world of light. We stood in the dimension of ascended souls, and they fed us with love and light and information and power.

Here we united with the heavens and the stars from which we are seeded. We plugged into a direct line to star connections and frequencies. Galaxies and star systems downloaded us; gifting us with messages and purpose and directives and missions. Each person in our group now had access to this communication. It was their choice what they might do with this. The main directive given to us was to help establish harmony on the planet.

Then, coming out of the meditation, we slowly returned to our bodies. As we stood together in a circle within the pyramid, we grounded, as best we could, what we had taken into ourselves. Like the ancient kings, we'd reestablished a link and strengthened and widened the connection between the worlds. We escorted in Maat or universal harmony for the planet at this time in history. Each of us held our individual key, and yet, coming together, we formed one unique key that granted us access into the spirit world where we were able to dance with the cosmic fabric of creation. We were able to reopen that portal, inviting in this energy. We established Maat or cosmic harmony on Earth once again.

After the meditation, they turned on the lights. Suddenly, it was time to return from the meditation to the chamber. I remember trying to ground the energy down through my body and into the earth while still feeling spacey and strange. We were given some time afterward to simply be in the chamber and explore the texts and decorations, using our flashlights to soak in every detail. In this time, we were able to feel the energies of this sacred ancient site. Mohamed and Emil say this is the best part. I slowly acclimated and became aware of my senses in the present.

Soon, it was time to ascend the stairs and return to the crowds of tourists and the grueling heat of the plateau. I remember exiting the stairway and feeling like I slammed into the sun. It shocked me to be back in real-time. As we sat outside for a moment, blinking helplessly as we leaned against the wall along the side of the pyramid's rubble, I remember hearing someone talk about football. Like my unique donkey adventure, there is nothing like reality to bring you back to planet Earth. Except, something miraculous had happened and we were changed.

Special and privileged ancient Egyptians, and I believe those of us in that tomb that day, ingested the neteru, the gods and goddesses that make up the Egyptian pantheon and represent the principles of nature. We took into ourselves the qualities of the ascended ones. We absorbed into ourselves the power of divinity, so that we could become fully realized humans. We were invited to embody the Sahu, the golden light of the spiritually awakened. We were made over by our coming to this place and consciously doing ceremony together. We grew tall, we expanded, we encountered our higher selves, and we experienced a union with the first cause and its expression in dimensions and worlds that are of a higher vibration than our own. We were seeded with the universal life force of eternity. We became Khepera, the Egyptian scarab beetle god, representing the awakening of our becoming. We were radiated by god-stuff, and we had now become the living Horus of light. The hieroglyphs had infused us with their knowledge and power. We read them through our bodies as we ate their messages. We entrained to their instructions and codes. We "knew" without books or intellectual understanding. We absorbed the process for becoming a star and returning with the energy of the cosmos.

We had become generators of peace, order, and harmony. All eighteen of us were offered a sacred opportunity. We were now set in motion to do something with what we had received, if we so chose. My friend Keith said it best. "I expect great things from each of us," he announced. I believe we were each challenged to reveal the mystical content of the Pyramid Texts by demonstrating spiritual revelation in our own lives and sharing it. Although each of us is a seeker on our own pilgrimage, and we seek our own spiritual passion and path and enfoldment, perhaps we are also tied as a group to a unique challenge and interpretation. This stellar influence of specific symbolism and guidance was infused into each of us, and I knew it would be interesting to see what each person chose to do with it.

A large part of my choice was writing this book, as well as leading my own Egypt tour in 2012 and 2014. It was like shedding a skin and stepping into a bright spotlight. It is my personal addition to the pot of soup called peacemaking, and everyone on this earth has something to add. I will be forever grateful to Mohamed for paving the way for us to have time in this powerful site. Over and over in Egypt, we would think we had had the greatest experience of our lives, only to have another one, and yet another. In Egypt, I remember my true nature and my own power. I know I will always continue to return, because it is my soul's home—a place that feeds my spirit.

Chapter 32: The Peaceful Nature of the Egyptian People

It means quite a lot that despite the historic and magical sites of Egypt, Mohamed says the *people* of Egypt are its main attraction. He believes they are special people with a unique level of kindness and open-heartedness, and he wants Westerners to see it. On each tour, he ensures visitors can have exchanges with the people of Egypt. In this way, he promotes peace by building relationships between nations, one person at a time.

I was fortunate to be in Egypt twice during Ramadan, a month-long period of fasting and prayers. From sunup to sundown, a majority of the people, neither eat nor drink, although pregnant women, the elderly, and the ill are not required to fast. Imagine abstaining from liquid in a climate so very hot and dry. Hatem Ali, who works for Mohamed as a tour manager, explained to me that fasting is a way to become closer to God, understand that others go without food and drink, and feel compassion and empathy. The Egyptians are deeply religious people, and when they break their fast at sundown, they place their tables outside and invite anyone to their table who needs a meal.

Many people in Egypt make pilgrimages to Cairo at this time. To accommodate them, the citizens of Cairo set up tables in the marketplace. Everyone sits and eats together, and there is a vast sea of people joining and giving thanks to Allah. Both Mohamed and Emil wanted me to experience this moment, so I could witness the peace and the joy that abounds when people come together to share. Emil drove my friend Kelly and me to the Khan, where we could view the meal at sunset. Seeing so many people sit together at long tables in the outdoor square, sharing a moment of peace and grace while they broke their fast in celebration, was touching.

These people walk their talk. These people are there for each other. These people help each other, and it is all part of their Muslim religion. Mohamed said it took him some time to adjust to America, where people are not as open to strangers. In Egypt, even in a bustling city like Cairo, you can trust most anyone to help you. If you are lost or in distress, you can always ask someone to lend a hand. At one point, I lost my camera while we were in a large pavilion before going into the Valley of the Kings. I assumed someone had stolen it, and was ready to accept that it was gone forever. I asked a female attendant at a bathroom about it, and she promptly led me outside to a friendly-faced, little old man in a soiled blue galabeya and a white turban. He smiled at me with a toothless grin, gently took my hand, and led me to my camera. I was embarrassed by my own assumption that someone had taken it.

On another evening on my trip to interview Mohamed, Emil took Kelly and me to the Khan Kahlili Bazaar to go shopping. Emil has a way of knowing what experiences will be valuable for each individual, and he surprised us by leading us to the beautiful mosque that is located right next to the bazaar. Without much explanation he literally shoved us into the mosque and left us abruptly with the words, "You will like it."

He left us at the entrance to the woman's side of the mosque, where Kelly and I stood in a state of some confusion. A woman there gestured that we should take off our shoes and that we could rent two scarves from a little cubby there. And so we took off our shoes and rented our scarves. Two women chuckled at how we had thrown our scarves haphazardly over our hair, and proceeded to rearrange and tie them neatly as they shook their heads. One of them took our hands and escorted us to the shrine within the mosque. All around us, the women smiled and laughed, and teenage girls snapped photos. Certainly, they were amused, but we were amazed by their friendliness and inclusiveness. They seemed amazed that foreigners wanted to be there.

Outside of the shop women, the hotel staff, and Mohamed's family, this was one of the few moments I had contact with Egyptian women, and it was very meaningful for me. It changed my perspective and opened my heart. It also broke any link I still unconsciously formed between the words "Muslim" and "terrorist." I am now more likely to equate the word "Muslim" to the word "kindness." It was eye-opening to find myself in a huge room full of women who held a religion I had stigmatized, then have them treat me with love and respect. I saw only expression of joy and happiness that I was there with them. Not one face showed anger or hatred. When we were complete at the mosque, there was Emil waiting to pick us up with a big smile on his face.

After Cairo, the usual tour takes a plane down to the very south of Egypt to the city of Aswan. On my first trip to Egypt, we stayed at a hotel on Elephantine Island which is in Aswan. I met a young man who worked at the hotel there who was about the same age as my son at the time, twenty-six. Each morning when I sat in the garden terrace of the hotel, he brought my morning coffee to me. I was able to have many brief talks with this young man. He told me about his family, his life, and his dream of going to America. We talked about politics, religion, and spirituality. We developed a sweet friendship, and I was touched by his humility and kindness. When I went back the second time, I looked for him at the hotel, but he was gone. I've thought about him many times since then. I wish I had asked for his contact information. It is strange how you can feel so close to someone so fast and think about them for the rest of your life.

When I first went to Egypt, I was scared stiff of everything. I was afraid of strangers, foreigners, Muslims, Arabs, and "third-world" people. I especially feared the shop keepers, because I believed that they would try to scam me. It's funny to think of being overcharged when the price of something is only five dollars! In one shop, a lovely young woman helped me through the buying process that I found so intimidating. I told her about my fears, and she worked with me to purchase what I wanted at a reasonable price. It was a small kindness, but my sense of relief was huge. She was very kind, and we laughed a lot. I'll never forget her. When I went back to Egypt the second time, they were remodeling the area where her shop had once stood. She was gone, just like the boy at the hotel. I was disappointed not to find her. I remember that her name was Nancy and I wish that I had also asked for her contact information.

Shopping is an event in Egypt. On my second trip I discovered what fun it could be. The merchants, usually young men, would tell me how much they were charging for a shawl or a bracelet.

"20 pounds!" they'd call out.

I'd say, "No, too much."

"Oh, ok, then 50 pounds!" They'd respond. That would get me laughing, and they'd laugh right along. Sometimes, as I passed by, they'd yell, "Come to my shop and I will rip you off big time," with a sheepish grin. Everything is done with a sense of humor.

One time, when we were sitting in the tour bus, a young man circled the bus, trying to sell scarves to those of us inside. After settling on a price, I stuck my arm out the window to hand the man my money. I didn't have the correct amount, and assumed he'd take off with the extra money without returning my change. To my surprise, he returned with the money, which I then gave to him to show I appreciated his good faith. We laughed, smiled, and shared a moment of friendship. By the end of this trip, I had a whole new outlook on bartering; it was now a fun way to connect. Money was not the most important thing.

I had three new experiences to add to my feelings about the people in Egypt that occurred on my trip there in May of 2014. One had to do with a vendor who gave me a ride on his horse from the Step Pyramid to the bus, just really a short jaunt down the way. The vendors had become very aggressive due to the fact that so few visitors were coming to the sites. Emil specifically asked them to wait until we had seen Sakkara before they approached us, and if they would do so, we would buy from them or use their services. They waited, but when we completed our visit, no one in our group would get on a horse or a donkey for a two dollar ride. No one seemed to realize that those few dollars would go to feed the men's families. When I got on the horse, others finally got on the waiting horses and donkeys, and we proceeded down to the bus. The owner of my horse was so kind, and so grateful, that I asked him to wait for a moment. I went to the bus to get him a larger tip. I said this is for you and for your family. He got tears in his eyes and touched his hand to his heart in gratitude.

Another time, a man at the temple of Dendera hassled me to buy a shawl as I walked down the cause way that led to the bus. I don't wear shawls. He said it was a hard time in Egypt and would I buy a shawl. I said no. He looked down cast. I asked him to wait a minute. I went to the bus and got some money to give him, not for a shawl, but just to express my care for his family and for this hard time in Egypt. He said I would always be his American friend. On my most recent trip there in September of 2014 in which I hosted my second tour, I visited Dendera again, and ran into my friend. He was just coming into the parking lot on his motor scooter, and I was walking back to the bus with my group. He said, I remember you, you are my friend. And I answered, yes I remember you! We smiled and shook hands and I was glad for the experience. He remembered me just as he said he would and this time no money was mentioned. We had made an impact on each other.

At the Mena house I always tip those who do a service for me. I tip the drivers who may give me a ride from the hotel to the lobby in their little carts. Not all the tourists bother to do this. The last time I was there, and I was ready to leave, the bell captain came to me, and said that they saw how I appreciated their help, and that I was now a member of their family. He touched his hand to his heart, and his eyes shared his feeling. I was touched and glad that these small amounts that I shared were helpful and that they could see my intention behind them. These experiences continue to enlighten me and show me how I can grow relationships one person at a time.

Any hesitations or prejudices I had when I first traveled to Egypt were rooted in fear and I am glad that I am far less fearful and more generous. And although it is true that my heart has opened and no matter how many wonderful experiences I had in Egypt, I acknowledge there are risks involved in travel. However, there are risks no matter where one goes in this world. It has taken years for the Egyptian economy to improve after terrorism took its toll, and now the political chaos and polarization has made it difficult for tourists to return. During these challenging times, it is the Egyptian people themselves who suffer in a struggling economic system, fighting to make a living and feed their families.

Mohamed believes that tourism and peace are intertwined, and that travel is the antidote to terrorism. Thanks to the personal relationships Mohamed has formed with his tour leaders, he has weathered the storm of terrorism as well as financial and political turmoil. They know Mohamed will take care of them and ensure their safety, and they maintain that Egypt is a safe place despite the one-sided perspective we often see in the media. It is this strong foundation with key American tour leaders that has helped bring business back from the United States. People like Greg Roach and Halle Eavelyn, Nicki Scully, Jane Bell, Normandi Ellis, Aluna Joy Yaxkin, and John Anthony West continue to travel, and their initiative has helped others follow suit. And there are others from Europe and Australia who continue to come and bring large groups. And many individuals continue to come back to visit as often as they can.

I remember George Faddoul's comment about the people of Egypt. He said, "Here is Egypt with its ninety million people crowded along the Nile, and here is George coming from twenty million people in a huge country and even still the Australian people feel they need more. It is a miracle how so many people crowded together have learned to get along. They have much to teach us."

Part Nine: The Creative Alchemist: I Am Here to Serve

Fig. Part Nine.1. Mohamed working at the office, 2014. Photograph courtesy of Mohamed Nazmy.

The Impossible is Always Possible

Chapter 33: Gratitude and Giving Back

I learned about Mohamed's generosity from his friends, colleagues, and employees. Although he "loves to blow people's minds with his surprises," as Jane Bell put it, he doesn't like to boast. Mohamed is not likely to mention, for example, that he once paid for a young boy's medical testing and treatment because the boy's father couldn't afford it. (The father was a friend of the cousin of a friend of Mohamed's, someone Mohamed didn't even know.) Today the boy is alive and thriving but he probably would not have survived without the treatment. That story, I heard from Greg Roach. Mohamed probably also won't tell you that he once purchased an array of fishing gear for a couple on his tour, simply because they mentioned their love of fishing. That one I heard from Jane Bell. Or how he initiated the hunt for the "best wedding dress in Cairo," when a member of his tour was getting married. You might recall the story of Emil, and how if household guests admire his possessions too long, he is more than likely to offer them as gifts. Mohamed is the same way: If you express your needs or desires in front of him, you may well end up having them fulfilled.

That said, Mohamed has a capable group of helpers he can rely on to help him fulfill the promises he makes. Employees and team members may well likely end up sharing the burden—or blessing—of carrying out one of Mohamed's beautiful surprises. When Mohamed asks someone if they want to visit Alexandria, you'll notice Emil cringe in the background. Emil knows he is probably the one who will actually *take* the person to

Alexandria. Of course, in the end, the Quest team is dedicated to making clients happy and helping Mohamed in any way they can.

Because of the countless acts of generosity Mohamed has performed, he is well-known throughout Egypt. Greg Roach called Mohamed's name a "significant calling card," because everyone seems to be familiar with it. Greg said he would never hesitate to drop Mohamed's name in Egypt, especially if he found himself in a tight situation. When he mentions Mohamed, Greg said, people always respond, "Give my very best to Mr. Mohamed." He explained that even those who have only met Mohamed once hold him in high regard, and often, it is because he has already done something to change their world in a positive way.

On my most recent trip to Egypt in September of 2014, a woman who worked at the Mena House, the luxury hotel we stayed at, told me how much she cared for Mohamed who had helped her brother out financially. She said he has helped many people when they have a need. I saw how the workers at the Mena House value Mohamed. Every time he goes there they all take the opportunity to say hello and wish him well. And he takes a moment to greet them. There is much love given and reciprocated. It always touches my heart to see this love and affection that is shared.

Charity Work

Always grateful for the success he has had in his own life, Mohamed enjoys being able to give back and share his prosperity. One of the tenets of Islam is to help those who are less fortunate, and Mohamed follows this principle faithfully. He is very involved in charity work in Egypt. For example, to show the great love and respect they have for their parents, Mohamed and his siblings decided to create something that would have a lasting effect on the people of Egypt. Together, they created the Mercy Association.

One day, as we sat together in his office, Mohamed began to speak about this charity work, but not before one of the business interruptions I grew so accustomed to. Before we began, Mohamed turned his head toward the computer screen, held up his finger, and said, "Just a moment please." He typed a quick response to an email with the index finger of his left hand. Then, turning back to me, he smiled and shrugged his shoulders as if to say that he was at the beck and call of his business and that he was doing the best he could to give me his time. He smiled and said, "Let me tell you about my family's organization." The Mercy Association does not accept outside donations or funds, rather, the money is generated by Mohamed and his siblings. Each year, they save and put money together, and spend it on worthy causes. For instance, there was a village in northern Egypt that did not have an ambulance, and the Association bought one for them. They've helped people finance their education, pay for marriage ceremonies, and more. Mohamed said the association has about 1,500 people who are under its care.

Mohamed reached up and stretched for a moment, then said, "I am telling you the truth—we don't collect money from anybody." He added, however, that when people hear about what the association does, they want to get involved. In the past, Mohamed has had people ask what they can do to help, and he tells them. In some cases, that means buying a helpful item for a family in need. However, Mohamed always wants the gift-giver to visit the gift-receiver. "We help that person bring it, so they can see the happiness their gift brings," he said. The association has been facilitating this for more than eight years.

For each person who comes to Egypt through his company, Mohamed puts aside one dollar a day from the business for each day they stay. If a group of fifty come for a fifteen-day tour, Mohamed will have put aside $750. At the end of each year, he's accrues a hefty amount to put toward people in need. Mohamed takes money from the profits he makes on his business—he doesn't charge extra in order to be able to put aside money for charity. "Even though travelers would be happy to pay to help others," he said, "I don't want people to feel like I'm taking money. I take it from my profits." When Mohamed delivers a gift, however, he tells the recipients that American travelers made it possible. Those people then begin to see tourists differently, Mohamed said. Indirectly, this facilitated "exchange" helps bring peace and understanding.

In America, we often give money to charity, but rarely, if ever, connect with those who benefit. Mohamed's approach seems like a wise and wonderful way to bridge gaps by providing direct connection. The way Mohamed has developed his charity work seems like a most intelligent way to build trust amongst communities and societies while helping others. He brings those giving together with those receiving.

The Peace Council

Nearly ten years ago, Mohamed was invited to an awards evening at the Mena House. It was a large, formal dinner, full of ambassadors and ministers. Mohamed, by chance, sat next to the Egyptian Ambassador to the United States. Because they had both lived in the States, they got along and understood each other well.

Their getting-to-know-each-other was interrupted, however, when Mohamed's name was announced. He had won an award for excellent achievement for his travel company. Startled, he rose from his seat and walked to the front of the room. When Mohamed returned to his seat, the ambassador leaned over and said, "You are good Mohamed. You are good at attracting people and good at bringing people together. You have a gift." Promptly, he told Mohamed he was recommending him for a position on the Egyptian Peace Council of the President and the Prime Minister.

The Peace Council is an organization of the Egyptian government that works with other countries when diplomacy and peace-making are in order. Within three weeks of meeting the ambassador, an official letter came in the mail, saying he had been accepted into the Peace Council. As we spoke, Mohamed held his palm up in the air and said, "I swear to you, Sharlyn, this was such an honor for me and it was a big step in my life. I am always concerned with how to connect, and this had been a vision of mine since I was five years old. As I grew up, I could see how everything happening in my life was leading to the same avenue and same target— always the same target in different ways."

Mohamed explained that when problems with other countries arose, the council was called to help, seeking to resolve issues through personal relationships on the ground. "They would hope that we could make the gap in understanding each other smaller and smaller and smaller," Mohamed said. He leaned forward and held his hand to his heart for a few seconds, telling me how proud he is to serve on the council. "Being a member of this council has really helped me a lot," he said. "I have been involved in making peace between countries. I have learned how to help other people. I have learned how to help my country by going to other countries and talking about Egypt, so that people can see Egypt in a different way." People who attend a speech by Mohamed might come in imagining Egypt as the sum of camels, pyramids, and the Sphinx. When they leave, they understand it in a deeper way, whether it's more knowledge about the economy or Mohamed's quest for peace.

Public Speaking

Mohamed gives lectures all over Egypt, other countries, and even the States with the goal of enlightening humanity and improving international relations. He has been on various television shows, including Good Morning Arizona and Good Morning America in New York, where he discussed peace and human relations. He does frequent presentations and TV shows in Egypt. He doesn't use notes; what he says comes straight from his heart in the moment. As he told me about his lectures, he tapped his desk a few times and said, "You have no idea what it means to me to do something for humanity. The satisfaction that comes from doing this work means more to me than money. This is a service of great value not only to my family, but to people all over the world."

And to me he offered, "You are enriching humanity by writing this book. We are grateful and thank God for this opportunity. I want to help the people you know and you are helping to let them know about what we are doing here in Egypt."

Chapter 34: Love is My Religion

Jean Houston, described Mohamed as a man who has "profoundly done his human homework." He walks his talk when it comes to love, understanding, and acceptance. In Mohamed's mind, Egypt is a mystery, and we're all attempting to make sense out of it. This common effort is what unifies us, and Mohamed is more focused on that unity than on what pulls us apart. To him, diversity isn't a barrier, it's enriching. Mohamed looks at the whole—each piece is important, but it's not the whole picture, and he relishes this. No one has the market on the truth, but everyone *adds* to the truth, so he sees no need for fighting.

Mohamed has many friends, and though they have an array of views and perspectives, he's able to love them all equally without taking sides. He believes that despite our cultural, religious, or philosophical differences, if we come to know each other personally, we can bridge our gaps through lasting and loving relationships.

This tolerant approach is fundamental to Mohamed's business, because group leaders often feel that their perspective is perhaps the most correct. It's quite natural for Mohamed to work with people who have varying or conflicting ways of viewing Egypt and interpreting its past. Mohamed actually seems to enjoy the fact that there are many approaches to his country, and he always manages to identify with a group's purpose and discover the importance of it. He will sit down with people of opposing beliefs with no hesitation.

Mohamed tries to find something in common with each person he meets, no matter how different their background or culture. On my second tour, I watched him find common ground and form bonds with each person in the group. When I asked him if it was hard sometimes, he said yes, but in his experience, he can always find at least *one* thing in common—and that's all it takes. Jean Houston told me that even when there are "royal pills" on trips, Mohamed makes them feel special, honored, seen, loved, and cared for. Mohamed uses Quest Travel to create understanding, one relationship at a time. Each encounter with each person is considered an important relationship, and Mohamed lends himself to those relationships wholeheartedly. He emanates such infectious joy and such a strong aura of love that it's healing simply to be in his presence. And royal pills tend to chill out eventually.

Even among Mohamed's friends, there are opposing camps of thought and belief. There are orthodox Egyptologists such as Dr. Zahi Hawass and Mark Lehner, and researchers and writers who have conflicting views, such as Graham Hancock, Robert Temple, and John Anthony West. These people have formed strong opinions based on their own research. They disagree about the age of the Sphinx and the Great Pyramids, as well as the purposes of these wonders. The fact that these people come together in Mohamed's humble office is remarkable. Mohamed asks them to respect each other in spite of their differences, and they follow suit.

Mark Lehner, spoke of becoming more open-minded through his relationship with Mohamed. Mark said, "Mohamed has helped me be more tolerant of New Age ideas. I am more tolerant of people who believe in alternative histories of ancient Egypt. Whereas I think many New Age and Egypt-related ideas, like those about Atlantis and an older Sphinx (older than Egypt's Old Kingdom, about 2,500 BCE), have a very low degree of probability, Mohamed helps me see that there is a place for people to pursue these ideas. If the alternative views lead to something, fine, if not, they will always have a place in some minds."

Ambassadors of Peace

When Mohamed was working for Sphinx Travel in the '80s, only three or four spiritual groups would visit each year. Today, there are many spiritual tours, and people come from all over the world to experience Egypt through Mohamed. As Mohamed recruited more and more Ambassadors for Peace, as he calls them, more and more came for tours. Tourists were eager to tell those at home about the open-hearted, loving Egyptian people, breaking down fears and encouraging travel. To Mohamed, this increase in spiritual tourism is evidence that more people believe in spiritual revelation and the positive change that comes when the heart opens through love and understanding. He is optimistic about peace, and his voice carried that undeterred enthusiasm when he told me, "We can change the world for sure!"

Mohamed acts as what he calls a "lie buster." He makes a point to ask his tour members to go home and tell the truth about Egypt and its people. He has seen it over and over: When Westerners have the opportunity to interact with Egyptians and discover the reality of what Egypt has to offer, they're no longer afraid. He dispels the myths of fear that so many Westerners carry about foreign countries. More specifically, he hopes to foster understanding about Muslims and the Islamic religion. Increasing tolerance and understanding through awareness is his ultimate mission and purpose.

Mohamed strikes me as a cross between a spiritual teacher, a rock star, a CEO, and a teddy bear. When he walks the streets, it is as if he is the Godfather, only he hasn't used force or fear to build the respect he garners. Instead, he has used love and concern. Warmth and humor. Joy and altruism. He somehow makes time to greet everyone with a warm hug or a kiss, giving his full attention even if it is only for a short exchange. From the humblest man on the street to the most important visitors, he does not hold back.

And always, Emil is there, showing blasé indifference as Mohamed greets people one by one. I can still picture Emil in his orange polo and tan pants, rubbing his balding head and rolling his eyes as he waits for Mohamed to finish saying hello—to everyone. As he leans against the car door, Emil's gaze is on his watch and his mind is on the next place they're supposed to be. Deep down, though, Emil loves being there for Mohamed. The routine is always the same.

Emil is used to Mohamed's whims and knows he can change course on a dime. Ideas, plans, and insights bubble out of him, and he follows his heart. Still, Emil is there by his side.

Chapter 35: The Mohamed Phenomenon: Making Magic Happen

"Be who you are," Mohamed told me one late afternoon in his office. He pointed at his chest. "I am not afraid of anyone. I say what is on my mind. I do what I want. Do not be afraid of anyone. You are your own authority. Just be yourself and don't be afraid anymore." He could tell that I was struggling with issues of claiming my own authority without me even saying so. His words were like lightning, strengthening my spine and bringing to light the next steps I had to take to claim my life as my own. I looked at what I was avoiding out of fear and how I was giving my power away.

Mohamed encouraged me to bring my own group to Egypt in 2012. I had thought that it was "those other people" who brought groups to Egypt. I had never really thought that I could lead a tour or that I was ready to take on the responsibility and the leadership role. Although this was a big step for me and not entirely in my comfort zone, I received more in return than I could have ever imagined. It was a huge thing for me to grow into this leadership position and to lead the ceremonies and rituals within the sites that would be worthy of my group and the ancient spiritual technology. With Mohamed's encouragement, my dream to return to Egypt often and share it with others is now a reality. Here was a way to put all of my study into practice and lead people through their own alchemical changes. What an honor! How does he do that? How does he instill such strength and affect such change?

Mohamed is a catalyst. He has a special ability to see where people are on their journeys in life and push them further down their path. He looks at them deeply, sees their potential, and offers them a step up, whether that is a business opportunity or simple mentorship. He might tell them they should lead their own group, suggest they open a travel agency, share his knowledge about the business, or simply encourage people to write their books and follow their dreams. In anecdote after anecdote, when people take him seriously and follow his advice, their lives change for the better. This is what I call the "Mohamed Phenomenon."

Mohamed will sometimes discover a spiritual person who he believes will return to Egypt and bring just the right people. Mohamed intuited that my friend, Tania Maria, was one of them. The following is a letter he sent her:

> *I am so grateful for your love and friendship. I was sure from the first time we met that we are members of ONE family, and I also know and reconfirm that you will be coming back "Home" to Egypt many, many times on future trips. I honestly believe that your soul belongs here and that you do have a lot of work to start and to continue here in Egypt. I will always be here for you, and trust me, I will spare no efforts to make every journey of yours a unique experience for those who are meant to join you and with whom you can share your love for Egypt. I have always trusted the Universe with our tomorrow, and I know that we have a BIG role to play in this lifetime for the best interest of our Global family. So let us join each other hand in hand, to bring peace on our planet.*

Clearly, Mohamed has persuasive skills, but what is so lovely about this letter is that every word is sincere. It's his greatest desire to create a global family, and he does this one relationship at a time. This is how he begins to create new tours, welcome new leaders, and bring more people to Egypt. How can one refuse such attention? This is how it began for George Faddoul and also for Greg Roach and Halle Eavelyn.

In 2001, Greg Roach was invited to a conference in Alexandria. His initial spiritual trip to Egypt in 1998 had affected his life dramatically, and he was thrilled to be returning. After the conference, he visited Mohamed in Cairo. Mohamed encouraged Greg to get some of his friends together and bring them to Egypt. Sure enough, Greg brought eighteen family members back on his next trip. Mohamed told Greg he had a knack for leading spiritual tours. "You should do this," he said. Today, Greg has his own company called Spirit Quest Tours. For Greg, Mohamed became a role model and teacher as he navigated his new travel business.

Greg said Mohamed has an uncanny ability to see into people and open their hearts. He will even offer opportunities to those he knows won't be able to use his help. This speaks to his generous nature and his desire to encourage the dreams and the potential of the people he meets. "Once," Greg told me, "Mohamed offered to help a man in business, in spite of the obvious fact that this person had a lot of issues. Mohamed offered him an opportunity. This person didn't follow up and missed out." Halle Eavelyn, the co-owner of Spirit Quest Tours, also sees Mohamed as a mentor in the spiritual travel business. "He sees clearly," she said. "He can see into people." Halle has learned a lot from Mohamed, such as how to be two steps ahead of the travel guests, anticipating their needs. Mohamed has also been a force of guiding encouragement for Danielle Hoffman and Dr. Friedemann Schaub, as well as Maureen St. Germain.

Mohamed inspired Maureen to write her first book. Mohamed had heard Maureen talk about her ideas, and one day, he sat her down and told her "I want you to tell me what you are going to do differently to make sure your book is written." Right then and there, she came up with a plan. Maureen wrote that book, and has written many since then. "He inspired me and lit a fire," she told me. In her book, *Beyond the Flower of Life,* Maureen writes, "Mohamed has done much to advance the opportunities for spiritual teachers, and we all owe him a debt of gratitude. I love him very much" (42).

When I asked Nicki Scully what she'd learned from Mohamed, she told me it's hard to quantify it. "It has crossed every aspect of my life," she said. Nicki's work has its roots in Egypt, and her growth as a business person has been intricately tied to that foundation. "I have learned so much about service and how to treat people," she continued, "how to bring people together and how to see the challenges as opportunities."

Greg Roach described Mohamed as "the joke pasha," "big king," and "big boss," while he described himself as an "outsider," "Westerner," and "interloper." Yet Mohamed never made Greg feel like an outsider, but rather treated him like a member of his family. Greg's travel business evolved as he learned through observation and through Mohamed's explanations of how and why he did things. Greg said he has tried to treat his own clients as Emil and Mohamed treat theirs: with a deep, profound, and honest openness. It hit him that there was a beautiful lesson in simply being present, which he learned by watching Mohamed interact with clients. From Mohamed, Greg learned how to open his heart over and over again.

He Always Lands on his Feet

When I spoke to Nicki, she said, "The most important thing I can tell you about Mohamed is how he can extricate victory from the claws of defeat." Mohamed demonstrates how to take risks, follow one's heart, and trust in the universe. He is a man of great faith, but he is also a man of courage who believes in himself. It does seem true that luck is always on his side, as if there is an ever-present angel on his shoulder. He is bold and he dives in head-first, and it is this audaciousness that has led to his success. Whether he is working in a French restaurant or simply planning a tour, Mohamed always seems to come out on top.

Jane Bell remembered a time when Mohamed and Emil were with her in San Francisco. The three of them decided to return a rental car they didn't need, but they also had to get Jane to a radio interview. Mohamed insisted that he drive Jane's car while Emil and Jane returned the rental car to the airport. Jane told Mohamed to pick them up at the National Rental Car office, but Mohamed thought she meant the National Terminal at the airport. So Jane and Emil were waiting at the office knowing that Mohamed had no money and no phone. Apparently this was before cell phones.

Jane and Emil were able to go up on the roof of the building of the car rental office. They actually could see Mohamed driving around, looking all over for them, but they had no way to contact him. All they could do was scream at the top of their lungs. Luckily, the car window was open and Mohamed was able to hear them. He pulled over and got out so that he could locate where they were, and he let them know that he has spotted them on the roof.

Jane ended up calling the radio station and holding her interview from the car rental office. And Mohamed picked them up as they'd planned—just a little late.

"With Mohamed it always works out," Jane said. "It can be a wild ride, but he always ends up on his feet!"

He is the Star of the Show

Mohamed has a way of taking over and creating what we in the '60s called "happenings." He is the master magician, and he steals the show wherever he is due to his magnetism and dynamic personality. Jane described a tour of the sea caves in Oregon with Emil and Mohamed, during which Mohamed took over and began showing the caves and making everyone laugh as if he had been leading cave tours his whole life. "He just can't help it," Jane said. "His love of life is always pouring over into the environments in which he finds himself." Jane explained how Mohamed simply has a certain energy people like to be around. There is a kind of momentum, excitement, and drive to his energy field. It helps that he has a big heart, a big sense of humor, and a way of making people feel seen. "He affects the field wherever he is," Jane said. "and whatever situation he is in. He raises the bar."

He Makes the Impossible Possible

Between his good luck, audacity, and energy, Mohamed makes things happen which at first seem impossible. Back when Gregg Braden began taking tours to Egypt, he desperately wanted to take his group to Abydos. However, as Nicki explained, militants were taking potshots at passing buses and boats, and certain sites—including Abydos—were shut down. Mohamed took Gregg's group anyway. He put the group on a train, and they unloaded near Abydos. He knew that because no one was expecting them, they would be safe. Tourists did not use those particular trains at that time. According to Nicki, Mohamed has lots of tricks up his sleeves—some he can only use once before site guards catch on.

If there's a problem, Mohamed is always ready with a creative, if not mischievous, solution. When John's plane was delayed due to a sandstorm, Mohamed presented the travelers as important journalists so they could get on the first plane out. From then on, they received quite spectacular treatment, finding themselves in first class. "There are loads of stories like that," John said.

Today Mohamed is so well known that he doesn't have to be so creative in order to manifest the experiences he wants to provide. He merely asks and receives the help he needs.

Jean Houston told me about times she would get radical ideas of things she wanted to do in the temples that she thought would be off the table. Mohamed's answer was always: "Done. We will make it happen." Danielle and Friedemann also spoke about the way Mohamed creates magic. "One of the reasons people go back to Egypt is because of what he creates for them," Friedemann said. Whether it's catering a dinner right in front of Luxor Temple after it is closed to the public or bringing tourists together with the people of Egypt, Mohamed handcrafts experiences for each group. It is healing to be cared for in this way, from the very moment one arrives. Friedemann explained that while Egyptology is very scientific and perhaps leaves out the "magic" that is Egypt, Mohamed has never turned his back on it and in fact he reveres it, feels it, and embraces it.

Chapter 36: Humor and His Joie de Vivre

The first time Mohamed and Emil traveled to the States together, Emil was in desperate need of a cigarette by the time they got off the plane, so Mohamed decided to play a practical joke on him. He told him to go into one of the bathrooms for a smoke, then had Emil paged by the airport staff. When Emil heard his name called over the loudspeakers, he dashed from the bathroom in a frenzy, terrified that the U.S. police were coming after him. Mohamed laughed his head off, knowing Emil was probably already at work plotting his revenge.

Emil, who is a Coptic Christian, has an easy way of getting back at Mohamed for these kinds of mischievous schemes: During the month of Ramadan, he relentlessly (and quite purposefully) eats and drinks in front of Mohamed. As a Muslim, Mohamed fasts during this month and chooses not to eat or drink anything from sunup to sunset. Watching Emil and Mohamed joke and tease each other reminds me of growing up with my three brothers. There are times when their humor seems a bit harsh, but it is a part of their relationship they appear to revel in.

As I spent more time with Mohamed in the office and on the boat traveling, the role that humor plays in Mohamed's life became clear. When things become stressful or boring, his solution is simple—he just has some fun. Waves of people come and go, and the laughter rises and falls with them. The constant barrage of funny stories and jokes makes for a day filled with delight and joy. It seems they follow a philosophy that life is not worth living if you are not enjoying yourself, so they ensure even the most tedious duties are peppered with laughter and countless funny stories. During tours, they often say no to someone's request just to set up a surprise and join in the delight when the request is answered.

Emil and Mohamed are practical jokers who play off each other spontaneously. I will never forget the night in which Mohamed and Emil wisecracked about their belly-dancing mothers—their version of a "your mom" joke. We were sitting on a rooftop terrace underneath the stars, and apple tobacco from a nearby hookah scented the air. As Kelly and I looked on, a bit bewildered, Mohamed and Emil began to entertain us with their teasing.

Mohamed turned to Kelly and me in a serious manner and told us that his mother was very beautiful (which is probably true), and that she was a belly dancer (which is probably not true). Then Emil jumped in and said that his mother taught Mohamed's mother how to belly dance. Then the teasing began in earnest: Mohamed said that Emil's mother was very ugly and only had one eye. Kelly and I didn't quite know what was going on, but Mohamed and Emil were laughing their heads off, and we couldn't help laughing with them. In America, you can't make jokes about your friend's mother, but from listening to Mohamed and Emil, I would guess that the same is not true in Egypt. Your mother is a very funny topic—especially when she belly dances, is ugly, and only has one eye! We all laughed uproariously as they went back and forth. Life is never dull with these two.

Mohamed and Emil have been to the States many times and often stay with Jane Bell. They both mean everything to her; and she thinks of them as her brothers. Their families go on vacations together and are very close. In the early '90s, the three of them drove from her home in San Francisco up to Oregon to visit Nicki Scully in Eugene. Jane said she thoroughly enjoyed her road trip with these two men who liked nothing better than to joke and laugh. On the same trip, when they got to Eugene, Nicki took them to the Oregon Country Fair. Nicki explained that the fair can be quite overwhelming, with thousands of people attending. Mohamed and Emil decided to "take a break," then disappeared for the rest of the day. They were completely MIA, and Nicki couldn't devote much time to finding them because she was preparing for her own show. She assumed they were okay and went about her business.

Twice a day, a marching band led by the Flying Karamazov Brothers would parade to the stage, gathering crowds as they proceeded. It is quite a spectacle, with torches, giant puppets on stilts, and an elaborate procession of costumed participants. That night, as Nicki prepared for her performance, the band came through as usual. She looked up, and there was Mohamed and Emil, donning robes and big hats, leading the band with the torches. "You should have seen the look on my face," Nicki said.

It is just one more valuable lesson I've learned from my dear friends Mohamed and Emil: enjoy the moment and laugh when you can. In a world where we often choose to take things quite seriously, dwell in the past or worry about the future, it means a lot to realize how much fun there is in the now. How can we create a moment of joy, or make our friends or loved ones laugh? It's true that laughter lightens our hearts, harmonizes the path, and is the best medicine in the world. How can *we* lead the parade?

Chapter 37: Alchemy and Writing a Book

Mohamed has said, "Each person houses a seed within their soul that, when nourished, helps them grow toward their life's meaning and purpose." Egypt is a place that awakens that seed. Emil would say people are "activated" when they come to Egypt. Egypt offers visitors the opportunity to experience the ancient spiritual energy that still emanates from sacred sites. Jane Bell, said that spending time on a tour in Egypt is worth "twenty years of therapy." By traveling to Egypt, I've learned that interacting with its mysteries and magic offers the possibility of what I call an "alchemical change in consciousness." Egypt changes us. We come home feeling less afraid, more open, kind, and caring. This is what I call "transformative high Egyptian alchemy."

While there is much to learn from ancient Egypt, there's also much to learn from the modern Islamic world. I've gained a greater appreciation and respect for the big three religions by visiting important Jewish, Christian, and Islamic sites. All of these sites house Spirit, and Mohamed and Emil know this. The tour leaders and authors who bring groups to Egypt know this as well, and together they offer the treasures of ancient *and* modern Egypt to their clients. This alchemy is the subject of the anthology that Mohamed and George Faddoul put together entitled *The Modern Day Alchemist from the Land of the Pharaohs: Secrets of Manifestation Revealed to Awaken the Alchemist Within.*

During one tour, not long after Mohamed suffered his stroke, George decided to spend some time in Cairo. He had an opportunity, as I did, to spend a number of days with Mohamed in his office. For the first time, George looked up at Mohamed's large wall of books about Egypt. Many of them were about alternative theories about the age of the pyramids and the Sphinx. Others were metaphysical books and books about healing. Others were about Ancient Egypt and spirituality. He noticed that all the books were signed by the authors especially for Mohamed, and an idea struck him. Why not get all these people together to tell their stories in one book? Why not collaborate to spread the word about the magic of Egypt? George had been involved in a book like this before, and Mohamed wholeheartedly agreed to the project.

George and Mohamed's book is an awesome compilation if you're interested in the experiences people have had in Egypt and how their visits to Egypt have affected them and influenced their teaching. Many of these people have been mentioned in this book. Truly, Egypt offers the opportunity for alchemical changes in one's consciousness. In *The Modern Day Alchemist*, you'll read about how Egypt changed these people and acted as a catharsis in their lives as they created their own work, teaching, and writings. They in turn, have affected the consciousness of people all over the world.

George said that it was quite beautiful to create the book with Mohamed. He especially likes that it is a way of showing what is going on in Egypt and with Quest Travel. I loved reading this book, and I wholeheartedly suggest that you add it to your library. You can buy it from the websites of George, Nicki, Normandi, or Danielle listed at the end of the book or at Amazon.

Part Ten: The Tour Leaders: Clients Become Friends and Family

Fig. Part Ten.1. Halle, Mohamed, Greg, and Emil. Courtesy of Spirit Quest Tours.

World Peace is Built One Relationship at a Time

Chapter 38: The Interviews

When I spoke with Mohamed in his office, I, like George, looked up and saw the wall filled with books, written by teachers and leaders from all over the world and signed for Mohamed with great affection. Those books represent the global web of friendship and collaboration Mohamed has created. The authors have influenced thousands of individuals, including Mohamed, through their teachings, workshops, books, and tours. They, in turn, have been influenced by Egypt and the consciousness of Mohamed. This reciprocity and synergy is ever-present. Thousands of conversations held within the walls of Mohamed's office have invigorated and expanded what is possible in this world. That space has bred a cross-pollination of ideas, teachings and investigations melded with open-heartedness and desire to allow the wisdom of love and Spirit to infiltrate lives. I often think of Mohamed's office as a "consciousness hub."

As I became more familiar with Mohamed and what he does in Egypt, I became aware of what I refer to as a "synergy of consciousness." This activating synergy is created right there in Mohamed's office when tour leaders from the West sit in front of his desk to plan and converse. It starts a few days before a tour, as he and the tour leader sit face-to-face pouring over the itinerary and fine tuning the final details. And once it is created, it never ends.

Mohamed's clients always become his friends, and his friends always become his family. When I asked Mohamed if he is familiar with all the ideas and theories his tour leaders ascribe to, he nodded. He likes keeping up with what his friends are doing and exploring, so he catches up with them via Skype, email, or phone, always seeking meaningful discussions. There is a purposeful and powerful communication and creativity at work in the lives of all involved.

The people who lead tours and bring their groups to Egypt do amazing things. These friends of Mohamed are among the most open-minded people on the planet—searching for truth and sharing their insights. As the land carrier for groups led by these very influential teachers, Mohamed has had the primary responsibility for tours led by these new thought leaders and teachers.

From the moment I began interviewing people for this book, it was clear that Mohamed is dearly loved and that others understand how special he is. The more people I interviewed, the more I felt the large web of love, care, and laughter that Mohamed has built. No one talks about him without warmth, joy, laughter and fun. Everyone I spoke with has been positively affected by his or her relationship with Mr. Nazmy.

I felt honored to interview his friends and coworkers. My world has been vastly expanded because of this project, starting with simply gathering the courage to contact those who know him. I soon discovered that Mohamed's friends are full of love and peace. We are all joined in the purpose of opening the minds and hearts of our readers, students, and travelers, and we all want to spread the message that we live on a precious planet, that we can become a global community, and that we can live in peace and work together to solve our problems.

I was amazed by how quickly and eagerly Mohamed's clients, coworkers, employees, friends, and family responded when I reached out to them. They were more than ready to be part of what I wanted to create, and I felt blessed by the support and the encouragement. Maureen St. Germain, who has traveled with Mohamed many times, said she hoped this project would become part of Mohamed's legacy. "I am totally thrilled for you, and that you can be there for him. He gets to be the main event! Mohamed has always made his groups the main event. It is so exciting to see that he is the main event in this book. Part of the movie *Hidalgo* was shot in Egypt which suggests great fortune to you!" I was glad to receive her blessing and encouragement. Halle Eavelyn, co-owner of Spirit Quest Tours, told me she was happy to see someone acknowledge all that Mohamed has done for those around him. "It is nice to see that something is being done for him," she said. "He is all about doing things for others." Kathianne Lewis, minister of the Center for Spiritual Living in Seattle wrote, "Sharlyn, I'm praying your book on Mohamed is going well. Thank you so much for honoring our dear friend in this way."

The constant confirmation that Mohamed's story is one that needs to be told kept me going. Whether it was a phone call or a simple letter, those who have been influenced by Mohamed rallied around him to help create this book, and their personal stories are sprinkled throughout the pages to illustrate Mohamed's special qualities and how he has influenced those around him.

It is my intention to show through the words of these people how very much Mohamed is loved and respected, and how he has earned the trust and friendship of all of them. Together, he and his friends have created incredible, unique experiences, and I believe there is no one who can do what Mohamed does. He is a role model for all of us, and a wonderful example of how an individual can create peace on the planet one relation at a time.

By the time I had finished interviewing Mohamed's friends and clients, I really had a comprehensive understanding of the scope and orbit of influence he has developed. It is truly amazing to witness the web of consciousness, research and study, and spiritual teaching that is coming forth from these people. We are all bound together through great love and appreciation for Mohamed and his work. It has been impressive to see just how much one Muslim businessman who lives in Cairo can affect individuals, and just how much he, in combination with the country that he loves, is affecting the consciousness of our planet.

Chapter 39: Jane Bell

"I often have said that there is the Dalai Lama and there is Mohamed Nazmy."

Photograph courtesy of Jane Bell.

When Jane Bell brings travelers to Egypt, she tells them she is taking them to her "beloved." It was in Egypt that "mind moved over for the heart" and she fell in love with Spirit. Mohamed and Emil were a big part of that discovery, recognizing her special connection to Egypt. She described them as her Egyptian brothers—the ones who "brought her home." When speaking of Mohamed, Jane said, "I often have said that there is the Dalai Lama and there is Mohamed Nazmy. He is a man of great proportion and with the alchemy of Egypt there is nothing like it. He comes from such a heart place. You realize that under Mohamed you see the best. He protects you." Jane believes traveling to the sacred sites of Egypt not only transforms lives, but also works on a global scale to transform world consciousness. Jane co-led tours with Nicki Scully for nine years before she began leading tours on her own in 2003.

Jane now lives in San Francisco and has been taking spiritual tours to Egypt through Mohamed for almost twenty years. She is a spiritual teacher and counselor who is constantly working to better serve Spirit and mankind through her business, Presence of Heart. Mohamed's book, *The Modern Day Alchemist from the Land of the Pharaohs* describes Jane's work:

> Jane is a certified Focusing Trainer, employing a psychological process of inquiry that allows the client to access deep knowledge through the body's felt experiences. Her expertise in this arena opened a related body of work in manifestation and life transformation. She is a graduate of the Corelight Teacher Training program, conceived by Leslie Temple Thurston to help people break through limiting dualistic beliefs so they can live in a unified state of consciousness. For the past six years [more now] she has also been studying the Diamond Logos, a psycho-spiritual approach to uncover the Essential Self with Faisal Muqqadon (165).

Jane's work with Corelight has taken her to South Africa, where she and her husband built a home and are doing humanitarian work in support of orphans affected by AIDS. In 2008, they built thirty-six low and middle-income housing units in their town.

Like Mohamed, Jane is on this planet to serve and collaborate with others. "I am grateful to those who know that we are all part of a larger community, sharing the same hopes and dreams for our future on this planet," she told me. Mohamed, Emil, those who work for Quest Travel, the people of Egypt, and her clients are all part of this community.

Jane has a special connection with the lion goddess Sekhmet, which Mohamed and Emil recognized immediately. During Jane's first visit to Egypt, it was the statue of Sekhmet at Karnak Temple who communicated to Jane that she was to bring people back to Egypt. The ancient Egyptian's documented their ability to invite the energy of a deity into a statue so that its power, teaching, and love could be transferred to those who spent time in its presence. In this sense, the statue of Sekhmet is alive and shares herself. Mohamed and Emil are well aware of the effect this statue has on people, and so they make sure private visits are possible. To be in the presence of this three-thousand-year-old, ten-foot tall, lion-headed goddess with the body of a woman is a healing and moving experience.

Sekhmet sits in her original site in one of three chambers, which is unusual because most statues are now in museums or moved from their original sites. Another chamber houses a small headless statue of her husband, Ptah. The third chamber now stands empty, but once held a statue of Sekhmet's child, Nerfertum. The entire complex sits off the beaten path within Karnak Temple in Luxor. When participants have private time with the statue of Sekhmet, they come face-to-face with the loving, unconditional presence of the divine feminine. She is a ferocious ally. An interaction with Sekhmet can change your life, firmly setting you upon your spiritual path, and holding you accountable for following it. She is a great awakener and activator.

Between Jane's spiritual awakening in Egypt and her experiences with Mohamed, she is dedicated to bringing more people to Egypt so they can experience its mysteries and magic. She is really another bodhisattva on the planet, dedicated to alleviating suffering, and devoted to helping others and to the work she shares with Mohamed. She is also deeply concerned for the people of Egypt and wants them to prosper. She hopes people will begin to travel to Egypt again.

She feels a special affinity for Mohamed and Emil and the work that they are doing in Egypt. It is her honor to share with them this "alchemy of magic and love" that Egypt offers.

Although her travels to Egypt are mostly spiritual, she won't deny that she enjoys the shopping opportunities. When I mentioned shopping in Egypt, she lit up. "It's great fun," she said. And I have to agree.

She often travels to Egypt just to spend time with Mohamed. Jane and her family have become great friends with Mohamed and Emil and their families, and they see each other often. It's clear that she holds these two deeply in her heart, and is ever grateful for everything they've brought into her life.

Chapter 40: Halle Eavelyn and Greg Roach of Spirit Quest Tours

"If Mohamed Nazmy blesses something it prospers." (Halle)

"He truly is an ambassador of peace. He represents the best potential for both cultures. This is why he is so important." (Greg)

Photograph courtesy of Richard Fero.

In 1998, Halle Eavelyn and Greg Roach came to Egypt for the first time as part of a Rosicrucian tour that Mohamed and Emil led when they worked for Sphinx Travel. This group was one of the first to travel to

Egypt after the massacre at Hatshepsut's Temple at Dier El-Bahri. Greg refers to this trip as the "long cruise," because it sailed the length of the Nile River from Aswan in the south all the way to Cairo in the north. This is the only river in the world that flows from the south to the north. Typically, travelers go from Aswan to Luxor by boat, and then take a plane to Cairo. The area in between Luxor and Cairo didn't have the infrastructure for tourism, and was deemed unsafe at the time, because it was considered a stronghold for extremists.

When their well-guarded boat arrived in Luxor, Halle and Greg were offered an upgrade to the ship's presidential suite. After weeks of intense work with their high tech company, Hyperbole, they were thrilled for a relaxing getaway in the beautiful suite, which was across the hall from Emil and Mohamed's quarters. As they put it, their living rooms became "party central," and the four of them spent many hours getting to know each other, bonding, and becoming friends.

After the massacre, the government provided heavy security for tourist groups. Although the boat had sailed safely from Aswan to Luxor, they still hadn't received permission to travel on to Cairo. As few as five minutes before their ship left, the group didn't know if they were going to be able to continue the cruise. Needless to say, Mohamed was immediately on the phone—straight to Mubarak's office, and eventually they received clearance from the highest level. When Greg's group finally sailed, their cruise ship was surrounded by four zodiac boats meant to patrol and offer protection. Some of the patrol members boarded the ship and positioned Gatlin guns on the rails at the back. As Greg described it, "The extreme measures were totally unnecessary, but the government was in the midst of their crackdown against extremists. They were terrified that if anything happened to our group, it would be the death knell for Egyptian tourism, so they overcompensated."

It was on this trip that Greg named Mohamed and Emil "the surgeon and the magician," nicknames that have stuck with them for years. Despite the circumstances, Mohamed and Emil did everything necessary to make sure it was an enriching experience. "Mohamed and Emil are the masters of what they do," Greg said. "I watched as Mohamed threaded the needle to provide our spiritual group the access and space that we needed to engage with the spiritual energies of Egypt; holding the political and military forces at bay just enough so we could do what we wanted to do. And then Emil stepped in and worked his magic so that we were assured alone time at the sites without interference."

Greg

For Greg—this was a transformative tour. He had a radical and utterly unexpected spiritual awakening, something that is not uncommon for those who visit Egypt, as I quickly realized during my interviews. Greg said that it has actually taken him years to integrate this experience. He described it as "a descending spiral into a dark night of the soul." Greg told me he relived a vivid and disturbing past-life event that left him feeling very alone, but Mohamed and Emil were there for him, helping support and guide him. "Emil came to me after the experience and said, 'you are channeling your higher self. Just relax, and don't fight it,'" Greg said. Everyday Emil was there to reassure him with comforting words. "This was healing water for my troubled soul." The experience was radical and unsettling, and he is forever grateful that Mohamed and Emil were there for him as spiritual support and friends.

After this first trip, Greg traveled back to Egypt for a convention and arranged to visit with Mohamed. It was at this time that Mohamed invited Greg to return and bring a group with him. Greg did, then continued to bring groups as a hobby until he made it official and began his own travel company called Spirit Quest Tours. As Greg traveled more to Egypt, he became better friends with Mohamed. The two of them love to go on adventures around Cairo. "We make quite the sight," Greg said. They travel to the upscale shops in Cairo in Mohamed's Mercedes—Mohamed wears an Armani suit, while Greg wears his galabeya. "Mohamed looks like an American in his elegant suit, trimmed hair, and sunglasses, and I look like a white guy dressed like an Egyptian temple-keeper," he added.

When I asked Greg what he wanted the readers to know about Mohamed, he confirmed what I often say: that Mohamed is an ambassador of peace. He also emphasized that Mohamed represents the best of both Western and Islamic cultures. He is steeped in the values of Islam, but doesn't hesitate to rebuke unhealthy aspects of any religion or ideology. "He rejects any portion of a worldview that is xenophobic, insular, or paranoid," Greg said. "In fact, he directly works to counter those by sharing himself and showing who he is."

Who he is, as Greg said, is someone who is forward-thinking, compassionate, funny, intelligent, and well-spoken. "He breaks down the images that we might have." In a culture that often judges Egypt based on stereotypes and fear-based beliefs, Mohamed helps bring the truth into the world. "There is so much idiocy that is going on in this country [the United States.] All you have to do is walk down the streets of Egypt, and you see that this country has value." Now, Greg has made it part of his purpose to break down stereotypes and fears about Egypt and her people. "I feel blessed," he said. "Egypt changes you. My experience provides me the opportunity to say to Americans that I spend a lot of time in Egypt and to say that the stereotypes are not true." In this ambassadorship, Mohamed and Greg share the same mission.

Halle

Halle, for her part, affectionately calls Mohamed "Momo." She describes their initial meeting as "a rather positive synchronicity" that led to a true friendship. "Mohamed has a great understanding of the spiritual power of the ancient Egyptian sites," she said. She believes there is no one better in Egypt when it comes to travel—that no one has better connections or is more capable. She explained that because of his love for both Egypt and America, he can offer tourists something unique.

"He stays in Egypt because he loves Egypt," Halle said, "but he works with Americans because he loves America so much." Halle spoke of how impressed she was that Mohamed continued his business in the face of the financial disaster caused by 9/11, and how he helps his country prosper. When a hotel at Sharm El Sheikh on the Red Sea was having financial difficulties, Mohamed invested in it and brought business until it began to recover. Now, the hotel is so popular it's nearly impossible to book a room. "If Mohamed blesses something it prospers," Halle said.

Clearly, Halle is deeply connected to Mohamed. She described him as an unusual man who opened her heart. "His encouragement means so much," she said. "He sees me, and I can just relax and feel that I am a valuable human being. Emil makes me feel the same. I have the same bond with both of them. When I am home I don't feel the same way. It is just so palpable there." She also spoke of Mohamed's generosity, telling me stories about how he would send back hand-blown glasses for a tour leader in the States or spontaneously buy all the flowers for a wedding ceremony of his friend. "This is pretty typical," she said.

Halle has also had her share of entertaining adventures with Mohamed. At one point, he enticed Greg and her to sneak off from the Cairo Museum to go to the barber with him. Unfortunately, the barber only knew how to cut men's hair. Her words for the experience? "Not good."

Halle and Greg are business partners and own a travel company called Spirit Quest Tours. Greg is a designer, writer, creative director, and inventor. He is the founder and creative director at Spirit Quest World, which explores the convergence of spirituality, travel, and mobile media. Halle is an editor, screen writer, and author, and has a book out called *Red Goddess Rising*, which is a wonderful travel memoir that contains stories about Egypt, Mohamed and Emil, as well her own revelations and experiences.

Chapter 41: Normandi Ellis

"In Quest Travel, which specialized in the spiritual tourist, Mohamed has created an empire of devoted followers around the world."

Photograph courtesy of Normandi Ellis.

In *The Modern Day Alchemist from the Land of the Pharaohs,* there is a description of Normandi Ellis:

> Normandi Ellis is a poet with a deep sense of the mystical. In her books about ancient Egypt; *Awakening Osiris: The Egyptian Book of the Dead* (translations from the hieroglyphs of The Egyptian Book of the Dead); *Dreams of Isis;* and *Feasts of Light: Celebrations for the Seasons of Life*, she resurrects the myths of ancient Egypt with the grace and

skill of the storyteller. She captures and savors the splendid, fecund world of which she writes. As a facilitator of workshops on creativity, spiritual autobiography, and hieroglyphic and symbolic thinking and as a leader of sacred travel in Egypt with Shamanic Journeys, Normandi brings her participants to the brink of a new understanding—of not only ancient Egypt—but of what it means to be fully human.

She is the author of 6 books [now many more] of poetry, fiction, and nonfiction, an ordained priestess of Isis, and a certified, applied poetry facilitator through the National Association of Poetry Therapy. She has received the Bumbershoot literary prize, and numerous awards and fellowships from such places as the Kentucky Foundation for Women and YMCA Writer's Voice. In addition to her community work, she has taught at the Open Center in New York, the Women of Wisdom Foundation in Seattle, at NAPT [the National Association of Poetry Therapy] conferences, and the Association of Expanded Learning Practices (146).

She has also published in more than 50 national publications. Recently, she created the PenHouse Retreat Center at her home in Kentucky, where she offers retreats and classes for writers and spiritual seekers.

Normandi understands the heart of Egypt. Not surprisingly, it was Mohamed and Emil who helped her to visit its sacred sites and develop her deep relationship with its mysteries. Normandi initially traveled to Egypt by herself in 1989. A few years later she learned that Jean Houston had been asked to read her book, *Awakening Osiris,* on tape as the audio rights had been licensed. After that she made arrangements to attend Jean's Mystery School at Estes Park where they met one weekend a month for eight months. She also discovered that Jean had been using her text while leading initiations into the Egyptian Mysteries. They struck up a friendship and mutual admiration club. She traveled back to Egypt with Jean in 1992.

Jean Houston feels that Normandi has brought ancient Egypt's profound teachings into the light. "Normandi is one of the greatest living interpreters and writers of Ancient Egypt who has ever lived," Jean told me. "She is very important to the re-emergence of Ancient Egyptian knowledge and genius." Normandi is just as enthusiastic about Jean Houston, crediting her, along with Nicki Scully, for helping her get her work into the world.

Now, Normandi takes groups to Egypt with and through Nicki Scully and Shamanic Journeys, Ltd. Normandi has worked closely with Nicki and often comes to Eugene to help her present her Egyptian Mysteries Retreats. She has spent years following her passion of discovering the deeper meanings of the hieroglyphics and the original sources of the myths, history, and spirituality of ancient Egypt.

Normandi has continued traveling to Egypt and was able to visit in March of 2011 after the Revolution. Normandi's tour was a big help to Mohamed because travelers saw, once again, that they could safely travel to Egypt despite the political turmoil. In the May 6, 2011 edition of the *State Journal Newspaper* of Frankfort, Kentucky, Charlie Pearl wrote an article about Normandi entitled, *Egypt: Land of Inspiration,* which reads:

> Her [Normandi's] March visit was one of the best trips, she said, "because everybody was committed to being there. Tourists had overcome obstacles themselves to get there—family objections, delays, lost passports.
>
> "Everybody felt a sense of being alive in a moment of history."
>
> The Egyptians the tour group talked with "were optimistic and nervous, just as you would expect," Normandi said.
>
> The trip wasn't just about "going to see all these beautiful places. It was almost an ambassadorship to say to the people there, 'We're proud of you (A1).'"

Normandi is adamant that it is through good faith, good will, and compassion, that we can overcome hatred and fear. "The world we live in must never be dictated by hatred and fear," she said. "Mohamed is right, as John Lennon was right…all we need is love!" Normandi had the chance to see how people are sticking up for their rights and beliefs closer to home in Kentucky, when she attended a rally to garner support against mining mountain tops for coal. In Charlie' Pearl's article he wrote:

Normandi said at the Feb.14 "I Love Mountains" rally in Frankfort to protest mountaintop removal coal mining, she saw an elderly woman in a wheelchair holding a sign saying if Egypt can do it, we can do it here.

"It was great to be able to go to Egypt one month later and tell the people you've made a difference all around the world. People are standing up for things they wouldn't have stood up for before (A7)."

The Egyptian Revolution seems to have renewed people's belief in their ability to affect change. We have been encouraged to stand up for our rights, and to support causes that we believe in.

In 2011, Normandi published a new book, *Invoking the Scribes of Ancient Egypt: The Initiatory Path of Spiritual Journaling,* co-authored by Gloria Taylor Brown. Gloria is a university lecturer, Alchemical Healing teacher, and a recognized mystic and visionary who often works with Normandi and with Nicki Scully. Normandi described their book as offering "a fresh look at memoir and travel writing" (*"Egypt: Land of Inspiration,"*A7). This book is really spiritual biography at its best, and it involves a trip that Mohamed provided for Shamanic Journeys, Ltd.

As the group traveled through the sacred sites, they used meditations and creative writing exercises to explore the powerful themes of death and rebirth. They explored the hieroglyphic texts of ancient Egypt and *The Egyptian Book of the Dead* as a means of getting to the root of the spiritual technology of ancient Egypt. They immersed themselves in the spiritually transformative power of writing. The book is a travel log, and a dynamic example of how spiritual autobiography can be so powerful and transformative for both the writer and for the reader.

In this book, Normandi and Gloria write about Mohamed in their Acknowledgments:

We are indebted to the people at Quest Travel in Giza, Egypt, who made our tour possible, particularly Mr. Mohamed Nazmy, its president. Given that he was educated in the United States, Mohamed has superb command of the English language, as well as the ability to understand what pleases foreigners who visit Egypt. In

Quest Travel, which specialized in the spiritual tourist, Mohamed has created an empire of devoted followers around the world.

In addition to providing exemplary accommodations and arranging all aspects of our travel, Mohamed also provided us with the sacred boat, his beloved and beautiful Afandina, which allowed us to work together fluidly and luxuriously as we traveled. His was a gift given in love and rendered with exquisite detail.

Emil Shaker is the chief Egyptologist of Mohamed's Quest travel, guide extraordinaire, and all around great character. He accompanied us on the tour, providing knowledge and humor in equal measure. Emil is a master storyteller, and in his company all of Egypt comes alive. We owe him a deep bow of gratitude for bringing so much of his own magic to our trip (xi).

The networking among those fascinated by Egypt is a story within itself. Normandi's translation of *The Egyptian Book of the Dead* led her to Jean Houston. Normandi studied and traveled to Egypt with Jean and was encouraged to offer more of her understanding of ancient Egypt to the world through her writing, which, in turn, brought Normandi to Nicki Scully's attention. The two women formed a friendship and shared mutual love for the mysteries of ancient Egypt. As a result, Normandi spent more time in Egypt, exploring and studying, which led to more books and new teachings. Normandi also developed her own friendship with Mohamed, Emil, and Quest Travel. She also developed close ties with John Anthony West, who is also a great friend of Mohamed's and knows much about Egypt. As Normandi writes in her acknowledgments in the *Feast of Light*, he is one of the people who is "always part of every book I write on Egypt."

As the seeds of her destiny were nourished from her own passions and purpose, and with the help of her mentors, Normandi grew and developed her gifts, and the flower she is today has many beautiful petals that she shares with us. She has helped spread the power and the poetry, literally the word of ancient Egypt, and the spiritual technology embedded in those words. She also conveys her love of the Egyptian people, and this is just what Mohamed had hoped for. She is, indeed, one of Mohamed's Ambassadors of Peace. Many tour leaders use her book *Awakening Osiris* as they do ceremony and ritual at the sites in Egypt. Her book entitled *Imagining the World into Existence* came out in 2012. It is really a culmination of nearly 30 years of work with the mysteries of Egypt. On the back cover it reads, "Revealing the initiatory secrets of the Osirian mystery school, Ellis provides the essential teachings and shamanic tools needed to return to Zep Tepi—the creative source—as we face the transitional time of radical change currently at hand."

Mohamed Nazmy Shows Us the Colossi

When I spoke to Normandi about Mohamed, she chose to share a story about Mohamed and Emil from the old days:

On this particular trip—maybe 2000—Quest Travel owner Mohamed Nazmy joined our group on the bus. It was unusual to have him on any trip because Mohamed so often stayed behind in Cairo to attend to the business matters of his many trips. From behind his desk, I used to think, he waved a magic wand and just like an Egyptian sorcerer of old—poof! Magic happened for his tour groups. For this particular trip, however, he decided to come along. I'm not sure if he was concerned for the safety of his bus with these particular participants, or if he just wanted to see for himself what the group was like. While Mohamed and Nicki go way back, this was one of the first times I met Mohamed.

The perennial red tie had come off and he wore a tan flight jacket and a New York Giants baseball cap covering his thick dark hair and its shock of white that streaked up from his forehead. The bus lurched along and he hung onto the overhead racks. No problem for his tall, commanding presence. He grinned at us and his eyes glittered and his white teeth gleamed. His smile was infectious. I think I fell in love with him then and there, but, of course, it was his business to be charming.

Emil sat in the seat next to him, smaller in stature, a little more wiry. His Coptic blue eyes darted from one person on the bus to another. He was a puckish fellow, a little excitable, a great storyteller, easy to laugh. And laughter was the key to understanding Mohamed and Emil. The two of them sang under their breath. Unfortunately, they each sang separate songs at the same time. It was a little hard to concentrate on the lyrics. Mohamed kept up John Lennon's "All we are saying is "Give peace a chance," while Emile hummed a little song until he got to a chorus he remembered, "Om Namah Shivaye..." They were quite a pair.

We rode along the bus in Luxor. Emil had given us the spiel about where we were, what was out the window, where we were going, what we were to see, why he had to stay together. "As one" became the operative key phrase. We jostled along in the Quest mobile admiring the scenery, the sugar cane fields on the western bank of Thebes as we rode along the road to Hatshepsut's Temple of Deir el Bahari. The sun had just come up and the steep cliffs ahead of us had turned peach colored in the early morning light. I looked up to see one of my favorite sites—one I had seen only once before in real life, the Colossi of Memnon (Amenhotep).

Perhaps to other people the two enormous statues out in the middle of a cornfield did not seem like a big tourists draw, but I was fascinated with the legend of how the Colossus on the right had once been heard to sing at dawn. Apparently, the moisture from the river fog collected in the fissures of the stone at night and iced up. In the dawn light, the ice expanded within the rocks causing the statue to appear to sing. The Greek ruler was so fascinated by this that he decided to fix up the statue, which had fallen into disrepair after an earthquake. But his tribute failed; the Colossi of Memnon stopped singing.

"Now really," I told Mohamed, "that is a fascinating legend. It had everything to do with how we try in vain to fix and modernize the world in which we live and destroy it." I wanted to stop there.

Beside me, Nicki Scully, the tour leader, said, "But it's not really an important site for what we are doing."

"Of course, it's important," I said. "The only reason it doesn't seem important is that the world rushes by in a bus because all it sees is a field with corn and such."

Emil stopped signing and started talking to Mohamed very animatedly. He said my name in the middle of all his Arabic run on sentences. I thought maybe he was mad at me.

"But couldn't we just stop and say hello?" I asked.

"Normandi, my dear," Mohamed said, kissing the top of my head. "I know you want to see it. And I understand. You can wave to it out the window. We have a schedule to keep."

"Okay," I said, sitting back in my seat, a little defeated.

Emil jumped forward in his seat and began talking wildly again. He shook his hands and stamped his feet. Mohamed leaned forward and laughed, looked at me with a bit of pity and laughed again. Gee whiz, I hate being the butt of a joke.

The day in Deir el Bahari and the Valley of the Kings, of course, turned out to be stupendous. We toured Medinet Habu, drank sodas and ate in a little restaurant listened to a rababa player, bought great stuff, and then went to the alabaster shop. What a full day, and I was not disappointed.

We got back in the bus and on the way "home" to our boat, we drove past the Colossi again as the sun was setting. We kept on going, almost as if we were driving in circles. Leaning on the head rest, I was halfway asleep, trying to think about the day's events when suddenly, the bus slowed down. I looked out the window. The bus stopped. A man and his workers appeared to have driven this herd of donkeys straight into the road. The animals were milling about and the man was shouting, holding up sugar cane. Wagons full of sugar cane had stopped in the middle of a field. Children gnawing on sugar cane watched us. Those children had beautiful eyes.

The bus driver opened the door with a sigh and Mohamed stuck his head out. The man with the stick and the donkeys said something. Mohamed said something back. Emil jumped in and leaned out the window yelling, his eyes flashing. Mohamed looked stern, let his jaw slide open, then he turned and addressed all of us on the bus. "Well, I guess we will have to get off now. There's no way around it. We will have to walk into town. We've missed our dinner on the boat now," he said shaking his head and looking down at his shoes.

"Maybe we can get something to eat in town," Emil chimed in.

Disembarking from the bus, it suddenly became clear when the bus driver took off that it had all been a ruse. The donkeys were lined up, and blankets thrown across their backs. All 45 of us were loaded onto the back of a donkey and given the reins. In that way, we processed through the edge of the sugar cane field toward town. I had never ridden a donkey before and had no idea how to control it. Donkeys know that about their riders. My donkey took it into his head to follow, not the other donkeys, but the man driving the wagon loaded with sugar cane. He started trotting off down the street trying to grab the cane off the wagon with his teeth. "Help! My donkey's out of control," I screamed.

Mohamed and Emil were laughing hysterically at me. In the middle of the donkey run through the cane field, I caught out of the corner of my eye, the two enormous statues of Amenhotep, somewhat illuminated by orange floodlights. They were even more impressive looking at them from this angle, as if they were giants looming up from a green sea of cane.

It really was Mohamed magic. I have never forgotten how tenderly he kissed me head on the bus and told me not to worry. I never worry when I travel with Mohamed and his groups. I know everything will not only be okay, it is sure to be one of the most incredible experiences of a lifetime.

—Normandi Ellis

Chapter 42: George Faddoul

"Mohamed's desire is to leave the door open to the individuals who travel to the ancient sites so that they can come to their own unique experiences."

George Faddoul has known Mohamed for almost fifteen years. When they first met, there was an immediate kinship; Mohamed felt like a brother. George was teaching seminars on Neuro-Linguistic Programming (NLP), which is an approach to communication, personal development, and psychotherapy, so he was used to manifesting win-win situations. This was definitely a win-win connection. "There was just no strain," George said. "That was the beauty." He loved the laughter that Mohamed would bring to every situation, even when things weren't that funny. Through Mohamed, he quickly learned how nice the people of Egypt were. "Mohamed has faith in human beings," George said.

I was able to meet George in the summer of 2010 in Egypt and see for myself the great mutual love and respect Mohamed and George have for each other. George was actually born in Alexandria, Egypt, and now lives in Australia with his wife, Nitsa. They have four grown daughters. George owns Quantum Change Seminars and facilitates trainings in Neuro-Linguistic Programming (NLP). He has authored three bestselling books, and he owns a travel company that his daughter Roberta runs. He is a kind, fun, and heart-centered man.

George never thought he would lead groups to Egypt, but thanks to Mohamed, he has brought a group every year since the two met—about thirty people each time. As he explained it, "Mohamed came up with a vision that travel brings people together. He has a great passion for making sure that when people travel, there is more to it than just looking at sites. That is what distinguishes him from a travel agent. Mohamed uses words like 'the quest', the 'search for truth', and 'unity'. Every step is a prayer in his travel relations." According to George, people form strong bonds on these trips. "One couple proposed on the cruise and bought their rings in Luxor. People make friendships here and the connections do not end at the end of the tour. People from the States and Australia and England come together and remain friends," he said.

George stressed that these trips to Egypt change travelers' perspectives. "They change their view of Egypt and they change their views about the world," he said. "You can't really go to the pyramids and stay in the King's Chamber and not feel some change; some little effect." In addition to opening their minds about other cultures and other places, people have spiritual revelations. He explained that Mohamed wants to leave the door open for those who travel to the ancient sites of Egypt so they can have their own unique experiences. "People say that when they go to the Sphinx that this is worth the whole trip and that they are complete. But then there is so much more to come. As they sail down the Nile things slow down, and they see life along the banks as it was in biblical times."

That got me thinking about my own cruises down the Nile. Most tourists travel down the Nile on large cruise ships. On my first trip, we too traveled this way, but it felt impersonal, and I felt it impeded the group from becoming more closely connected. However, the trip down the Nile on the Afandina, which only has room for twenty, was beyond words. I felt like Cleopatra on the Nile. My heart opened and I fell in love with the group I was with. I fell in love with Mohamed, Emil, and all the workers that took care of us. We became a family.

The Nile is the only river in the world that flows south to north, and it was amazing to experience life on the banks of the river as we sailed. Tall rushes, reeds, and lush, green foliage swayed slightly as we passed. An occasional water buffalo stopped for a drink at the river's edge, while egrets and pelicans hunted for fish and preened themselves in the shallows of the dark green waters. Women washed their clothes or carried water jugs on their heads, children drove donkeys with loads of palm fronds or sugar cane, and men in white turbans and their traditional galabeyas farmed the land with hand tools. There is no modern equipment. Palm trees and small mud houses fill the countryside. It looks like a patchwork quilt of lush fields, separated into small, workable areas of different textures and color. One can slow down, calm down, and breathe deeply. The love seeps in and it is easy to enter a state of quiet and rest.

Of course, as you travel down the Nile, you have the opportunity to stop at many sacred sites. People prefer to visit different temples because they might resonate more with the energies of one or another, but the trips are always full of once in a lifetime experiences and spiritual awakenings. "I get goose bumps just talking about it," George said.

George explained that over time, Mohamed's understanding of the sites has evolved. He has made it his business to study the business of travel as his life pursuit, and as he started to visit the sites, he also started to build his relationships. "It is a puzzle and each piece fits to make it a seamless journey. All parts are valuable."

Around the time George first came to Egypt with Christian Bernard, and the Rosicrucians, Nicki Scully and a few others had already been leading tours, but Mohamed encouraged George to lead his own. George said he wasn't in the travel business, but Mohamed was more than convincing, getting George private tours of museums and showing him the possibilities. George said there is something powerful about Mohamed. "Once you are in his aura, it zaps you," he said. George often talks about Emil and how Emil uses the word "activation" to describe what Egypt does to a person. In NLP, one uses the metaphor of recharging a battery. To George, that activation or recharge often offers a new connection that leads you toward your destiny. And this is exactly what happened for George who eventually opened his own travel business.

George expressed many hopes for a book about Mohamed: He wanted people to understand what happens to people when they travel with Mohamed in a spiritual way. He wanted people to hear about Mohamed's childhood. He wanted people to know how Anwar Sadat influenced Mohamed. He wanted people to understand how well-connected Mohamed is, and how these connections enable him to provide incredible experiences. Most importantly, he wanted me to press Mohamed on his vision for the future.

In reference to this book George said, "It is a noble task. I take my hat off to you." When I said I had been pushed and led by spirit his last words were, "Well done!" I appreciated his love for Mohamed and his great vibes! I was touched by the genuine level of love and friendship that Mohamed and George have, and I found George to be very eloquent at summing up exactly what Mohamed and Emil and Egypt offer us.

Chapter 43: Danielle Rama Hoffman and Dr. Friedemann Schaub M.D. PhD.

"Mohamed really models aspects of open-heartedness that we talk about in our work." (Danielle)

"He has a heart opening influence. He is a person who really makes you feel loved. He really can see the goodness in people. Mohamed is able to bring different cultures together. He acts like a bridge. He infuses the minds and hearts of the Americans with the love and wisdom of the Egyptians." (Friedemann)

Danielle Rama Hoffman and Friedemann Schaub are all about the work of unity, consciousness, and love. They initially met Mohamed in 2002

when they were on a tour in Egypt with Nicki Scully. When Nicki picked up their group at the Cairo airport, Mohamed and Emil were on the bus. "It was definitely good, big energy," Danielle said. So, their relationship with Mohamed began. "Emil brings Egypt to life," she added. It is people like Danielle and Friedemann who know the power of the Egyptian sites and are willing to allow their participants to have their own experiences— the type of experiences that Mohamed crafts and materializes.

Danielle and Friedemann now live in France, and each have their own business. Friedemann owns Cellular Wisdom, which offers a breakthrough program of mind-body healing. He has just published a very successful book called *The Fear & Anxiety Solution: A Breakthrough Process for Healing and Empowerment with Your Subconscious Mind.* Danielle, who owns Divine Transmissions, is a teacher and healer of metaphysics and the Egyptian Mysteries as well as the author of *The Temples of Light, An Initiatory Journey into the Heart Teachings of the Egyptian Mystery Schools.* She has just published a new book entitled *The Council of Light, Divine Transmissions for Manifesting the Deepest Desires of the Soul.* Danielle offers intuitive readings, seminars, classes, and products that are designed to elevate consciousness and open the heart. She is especially interested in helping healers to expand their business and align their business with unity consciousness and their true purpose. She wants these awesome teachers and healers to thrive by doing what they love and by sharing their gifts. Friedemann and Danielle travel as a team to Egypt to share their love of the Egyptian mysteries.

In 2005, Danielle and Friedemann brought their first group to Egypt. They flew to Cairo a few days before their group arrived to spend some time with Mohamed and prepare. Unexpectedly, Mohamed asked Danielle which temple she'd be willing to give up spending private time in. She answered, "That's like asking 'which of your children do you love the least?'" In true fashion, Mohamed managed to arrange that none of her children were ignored. Knowing Mohamed, he was likely impressed with her answer and appreciated that she understood the treasures Egypt has to offer.

For many years, Danielle saw Mohamed as a mentor. She would go to him with questions and felt that he had deep respect and understanding for her and Friedemann. He encouraged Danielle to write her book, and always assured her that she had his full support. He told her, "You are a little tree, and we are watering you every year." By watching Mohamed, Danielle grew as a tour leader and as a communicator. She learned how to do business in Egypt, even when it is not as efficient as what she is used to. Although things may not move as quickly as they do in America, she said, "The Egyptian way feeds such a deep aspect of my being, and I love having that family feeling. Mohamed really models aspects of open-heartedness that we talk about in our work."

Meanwhile, Friedemann described Mohamed's energy as "heart-opening." "He is a person who really makes you feel loved," he said. "He really can see the goodness in people." As Friedemann watched Mohamed on the boat, he saw how friendly he was to the staff, whether it was the mechanic, the captain, or the servers, as well as to his clients. He paid no attention to their rank or position; he simply treated them all with kindness and respect. "He just loves people, and so he focuses on giving attention to each one," Friedemann said. "Everybody loves him. People respond to him, not just as a business man, but as a human being." Friedemann described a very touching moment when Mohamed traveled on the boat again for the first time after his stroke. A band met him at the dock and played for him. "They wanted to celebrate him," he said.

Danielle and Friedemann would never leave Emil out of the picture. They spoke fondly of the jokes that Emil and Mohamed share, the way they tease each other with uproarious laughter, and the dynamic of their relationship. "In terms of their jokes, they love to make fun of each other." Danielle said. "This appears to be the Egyptian way. It is a sign of endearment. And they just keep one upping each other and bursting into leg slapping and bellows of laughter. They just love it."

"Mohamed and Emil have a competition going on," Danielle said. "Mohamed would give and give and give and Emil would give and give and give and that makes us want to give and give and give, as well." Friedemann spoke of Mohamed's generosity. He is well aware of and very impressed by the fact that Mohamed took care of his employees during the drastic economic slump that happened after 9/11. "This is a very different mindset than what we know in the West, where profit is the bottom line," Friedemann said. "Mohamed didn't turn people out. That is a remarkable thing to do, and it shows that he really cares. This is an extension of his heart."

Although Nicki usually handles the details of Danielle and Friedemann's trips, they always meet with Mohamed to formulate more specific plans once they get to Egypt. They sit with him and go back and forth, sometimes negotiating or hashing out their different ideas. As they described their process, I got a new aspect of the picture. Although Mohamed is a true magician when it comes to making things happen, he has his limits. "I have learned that Mohamed doesn't say yes to everything we ask for," Danielle said. "Mohamed is very generous, but he doesn't want to be taken for granted or pushed into anything." Above all, Mohamed wants to be treated with respect. Mohamed told Danielle and Friedemann about a woman who had thousands of dollars to spend, but didn't treat him with respect. She didn't value his opinion or care what he had to say, and he chose not to work with her.

Friedemann admires this different approach to business. "Quest Travel is motivated to make the trip amazing. If Mohamed chooses something special like entry into Una's Pyramid at Sakkara or a visit to the tomb to Seti the First in the Valley of the Kings, he will seemingly move worlds in order for it to happen. This is his love, but he needs to have a good feeling about it."

Danielle and Friedemann said that working in the Egyptian way takes patience. During a five-hour meeting, they might accomplish the equivalent of forty-five minutes of business. They described it as an art form: Mohamed's itineraries are like paintings. He takes his time with them so that he can follow his feelings and intuitions. On one trip, Danielle and Friedemann's group was originally not going to be able to visit Elephantine Island. But Danielle and Friedemann wanted to go and didn't want to give up the visit. They suggested making the trip in the early morning, which usually isn't done. It is difficult in Egypt to initiate a change to the status quo, there is a lot of work involved in changing a schedule. However, they worked together to create the best outcome and the early morning visit was arranged. Mohamed made it happen, which is no small thing.

On a larger scale, Danielle and Friedemann see Mohamed's work as a bridge that brings different cultures together. "He infuses the minds and hearts of the Americans with the love and wisdom of the Egyptians," Friedemann said. "Mohamed works with leaders that teach consciousness around the world and builds a network of mutual love and trust."

Friedemann and Danielle expressed their wish that the whole world could take advantage of this gift. "Mohamed has built a web of connection," Friedemann said, "with all of the people who work with him or travel with his tours. It is doubtful that anyone else can do this the way Mohamed does. No one else is the merchant priest that Mohamed is."

I asked the couple, "What do you want the world to know about Mohamed?" Danielle responded that Mohamed is an embodiment of the universal principle of love-in-action mixed with his own personality, and Friedemann nodded. "His gift for the world is that he brings your purest essence to the forefront. No matter how many shortcomings you have, you feel better about yourself, and you feel that amazing love catalyst, and the shortcomings don't matter. There is a joy, unconditional love, and grace. And he brings that out in you, so that you can actually feel the same. He basically ignites something that is already inside of you, and makes you experience it, and that is why you feel better when you are around him. He is a wonderful mirror. This is especially amazing because it comes from a man of a different culture, a different religion, and a different traditional upbringing. He is bringing acceptance and compassion into the world in a way that I haven't experienced."

Chapter 44: Dr. Jean Houston

"Nazmy is dedicated to people understanding the essence of ancient and modern Egypt."

Photograph courtesy of Jean Houston.

Jean Houston reminds me of Mohamed in the way she takes the time to really look at you, and into you. She encourages you and sees your potential. It is a rare gift when another human being looks at you with this kind of love, humility, acceptance, and understanding. She is a master at encouraging the seed she knows we all have within us to grow. With her dedication to human potential, she shares Mohamed's dream of creating change—within ourselves, our homes, our families, our work environments, our communities, our countries, and our world. She knows we can become world citizens and work to create peaceful solutions to our common concerns. When I talk with Jean, I feel as though I'm talking with Mohamed. Jean is a great guiding light, and she plans to be on the planet for a long time teaching and empowering us.

She is a scholar, philosopher, and one of the foremost visionary thinkers of our time and is one of the principal founders of the Human Potential Movement. She is a prolific writer and author of over twenty-six books. A powerful and dynamic speaker, Jean holds conferences and seminars with social leaders, educational institutions, and business organizations worldwide. With her intensive work in over forty cultures and one hundred countries, Jean has helped droves of individuals realize their place in and potential impact upon the global community. Those who come under her tutelage become involved in positive change and transformation.

Jean has shared her work through her International Institute of Social Artistry (IISA) which she founded with the United Nations Development Programme (UNDP). At the global level, she works diligently with individuals and groups to form competent leaders "that have wisdom, courage and compassion to tackle complexity and work effectively with other people" (*The Social Artist's Fieldbook, Developing Your Inner Capacities,* iv). She feels that without the development of leadership, important and necessary worldwide changes cannot take root. In this same text, she writes that it is her firm belief that:

> Developing national and local leadership capacities is necessary for both human development and decentralized governance. In order to be able to lead, individuals must understand their own motivations and expectations and be clear about their values. They must tap into their depths to develop a wide range of their human capacities. By strengthening and expanding themselves as individuals, they can better walk into a wide variety of situations with wisdom, courage, and compassion. Social artistry is a transformative approach to building leadership capacity that can effectively cultivate the kind of leaders necessary to facilitate change (v).

After I interviewed Jean for this book, I wanted to get to know her better, so I signed up for one of her three-day intensives in Seattle in 2011. She is warm, down to earth and approachable. She is keenly interested in helping each participant develop his or her potential, knowing that out of that potential people are motivated to create solutions to the problems that we face collectively.

Jean has great knowledge, and an amazing facility with language. Her work gave me tools for working through my fear and self-doubt, and for strengthening my confidence and courage. Social Artistry is a powerful teaching that can empower you to live out your dreams and share your gifts, and Jean is all about empowering and encouraging us to act upon our visions.

Having come to a basic understanding of her work, I also came to understand her great love and interest in Egypt.

When I interviewed Jean, she said Egypt is integral to her teachings. She has been fascinated with Egypt since she was a child. When she was ten years old, she saved her lunch money so she could buy a dictionary and teach herself how to read hieroglyphics. When she was young, she would always make a beeline for the Egyptian collections at the museums in Chicago or New York. "One of my favorite early memories," she said, "is of my father, who was a comedy writer, putting me on his shoulders as we went through the Field Museum in Chicago. As we went into the mummy room, he said, 'Hot dog Jeanie, mummies!'"

In the early '70s, Jean traveled to Egypt with her husband, Robert Masters. He was a profound spiritual Egyptologist, and Jean herself had a very large collection of ancient Egyptian antiquities. Jean, in fact, was trained by Freud's antiquities dealer, who was about 85 when she was twelve. He taught her how to date and care for antiquities, and she has been an antiquarian ever since. Her husband was devoted to Sekhmet and wrote a famous book called *The Goddess Sekhmet: Psycho-Spiritual Exercises of the Fifth Way.* Jean explained that she and her husband were the first to visit the living statue and understand its gifts for the world.

She met Mohamed officially in 2000, after he read her book, *The Passion for Isis and Osiris,* which explores the mysteries of ancient Egypt. He visited her in New York, and she quickly decided she would lead her tours through him. Even though Jean had a deep understanding of Egypt's magic before she met Mohamed and had traveled to Egypt for a long time prior to their meeting, she now works solely with Mohamed. One of the reasons she likes to travel with Mohamed is because he offers the opportunity for each group to have alone time at the sites. He listens to the needs of his tour leaders and helps them realize their teaching goals. He makes every tour unique by planning something special for each group. This is the reason why, for instance, I was able to go underneath the Step Pyramid at Sakkara in 2007, a site that is typically closed to the public. And we also had a two hour block of time just for our group in Seti the First's tomb in the Valley of the Kings, which is also usually closed. It is because of experiences like this that leaders such as Jean Houston return to Egypt time after time.

Jean takes large groups of students with her to Egypt. Jean's groups are composed of anywhere from seventy to more than one hundred people, so Mohamed is an integral part of her tours. Jean considers her trips to be part of an education or schooling in the mysteries of Egypt, and her requirements are complex. She sometimes needs temples to be open all night and she requires utter privacy so that she can share a higher level of information about the sites. "He always provides for that, which is remarkable," she said. She explained that working with Mohamed has made things much easier than anyone she traveled with previously. He is dedicated to people understanding the essence of ancient and modern Egypt," she said. "It is not as if modern Egypt goes by the boards. It is quite the contrary. We really see Egypt. We meet the people we need to meet, we see what we need to see, and, above all, it is done with such empathy, warmth, and love for his country and his great, great need to give this sense of Egypt to as many people as he can."

When I asked Jean about the effects 9/11 had on Mohamed and his business. "We were to go on a big trip," she said. "I had sent one of my employees to plan a big trip in September, but after 9/11 no one was about to travel to Egypt. So it was another seven years before I could get people to go again. Last April/May of 2009 I took a trip. Mohamed continues to have these trips unfold and to maintain the level of excellence that speaks to his dedication and the passion he has for his work."

As Jean pictures Mohamed, she sees him sitting on the boat, surrounded by a friend or two, drinking coffee and having a pastry. "Basically receiving the whole world as it comes in," she said. "He is like a kind and very benign king, and love is his religion. Mohamed is so tender and without ego, and is just utterly available to everyone." She described how Mohamed brings out the best in everyone, helping them grow. Our interview ended with exchanged birthday wishes—both Jean and I have May birthdays. What we also share is the understanding that Mohamed is an example of how people can use their gifts and resources for the betterment of us all. I'm grateful to Jean for her life-long belief in our potential as human beings and her passion for helping us to develop this potential. She is indeed an awesome and inspiring woman, someone who, like Mohamed, is a wonderful example and reflection of how we can uplift our world and create peace and understanding.

Chapter 45: Kathianne Lewis

"He is a heavenly man… Mohamed has to be good for their economy. He is a gift for the Egyptian people because so many people benefit from the business he brings. He is a gift for everybody…"

Photograph courtesy of Kathianne Lewis.

Kathianne Lewis sees Mohamed very much as a "New Age Muslim." On one of her trips to Egypt in 1994, when Mohamed was first starting his business, her group went to Mohamed's house, where Hanan cooked for them—and Mohamed shared the meditation music he had been creating. She calls him a "heavenly man."

Kathianne is the minister of the Center for Spiritual Living, a large and thriving Religious Science church in Seattle. Her church organizes trips to Egypt for very large groups. Mohamed described Kathianne as "a beautiful soul," and a letter from her sits framed upon his wall. "She teaches about the power of intention," he said. As I live in Seattle, I have gone to many services at Kathianne's church, so it was easy to drive over and chat with her about Mohamed.

Kathianne first traveled to Egypt with Power Places Tours. For her second trip and ever since, she's gone straight through Mohamed as her land carrier. For all her trips, she gives Mohamed an idea of what she wants, and he puts it all together. Each year, she wants the tours to be different. She said, with a chuckle, that Mohamed likes her groups because they try not to be "ugly Americans." They also tip well and try not to be too demanding, she added.

Both through her travels with Mohamed and her time in Egypt, Kathianne came to learn about the generosity of the Egyptian people. "This is how Egypt survives," she said. "If you have it, you share it. Part of their doctrine is to give three percent of their money to the less fortunate." Mohamed, she said, has given away a lot more than three percent. Kathianne said that Mohamed is one of the most generous people she has known. "This is true not only for the way he is with the people in our groups, but also with the people he cares for, as well as everyone around him."

While talking with Kathianne, I found that she considers Mohamed a spiritual brother and holds him in high esteem. Mohamed always tell us to go home and tell the American people what the Egyptians are really like.

Kathianne said. "Egypt is my homeland. It feels like my spiritual home. I resonate with it for many reasons. People change in Egypt. They heal. I make time before we visit a site for my groups to have individual process, for prayer, for group process, and for inward reflection. These are spiritual journeys. As for the sites in Egypt, they are all amazing. They have Jewish, Christian, and Islamic sites that feel sacred, as well as the ancient Egyptian sites. There is much love from all the people who take care of these places. Mohamed and Egypt together do such a wonderful job of providing us the experiences that open our hearts and minds."

Emil usually serves as the guide on Kathianne's tours. She talked about the friendship between Mohamed and Emil. She has been touched by their brotherhood and sweetness. "Mohamed really takes care of others and Emil helps him. They are both a lesson in amazing kindness," she said. "They are very funny, and they tell great stories."

It's easy to appreciate Egypt when Emil and Mohamed are constantly serving up wonderful surprises. Kathianne described how when she told Mohamed she wanted to see whirling dervishes, he quickly arranged a special dinner with entertainment and yes—whirling dervishes. "Mohamed makes it seamless, and it is heaven," she said.

When she travels to Egypt, she is highly aware of the positive exchange that is taking place. She and her groups benefit from the beauty of Egypt, and in exchange the economy and the people of Egypt benefit from the Americans who come. She also said, "Mohamed has to be good for their economy. He is a gift for the Egyptian people because so many people benefit from the business he brings. He is a gift for everybody and I love him, too. I wish we could go every year."

Kathianne also likes that Mohamed is willing to provide her with new adventures for each trip. "When we plan a trip, we negotiate. I ask for something beyond the usual six-night-cruise on the Nile. Since most people only travel to Abu Simbel as a day trip, it is not usual to stay overnight. But I like us to stay over at the beautiful resort at Abu Simbel which is so laid back. Mohamed makes this happen for us. As an extension of our next trip, we're planning to go to Petra in Jordan, which is one of the Seven Wonders of the World." Her biggest goal is to have a large boat for just her group. And she is sure that Mohamed will arrange this for her.

"Mohamed is so loved and so open-hearted," she said. "I got that immediately, and I hope that our groups give something back to him and his country—that it is reciprocal. It is so good to see another human being who is working on the consciousness of friendship and understanding and good will."

"I am so grateful that he teaches compassion," she said, "so that people can love and understand Muslims more. I learned that Islam is about compassion, which was something I didn't realize." Compassion is interwoven into the lives of the people. This is the fabric. The people are perfectly willing to fast during Ramadan, which is a holy time that lasts for a whole month. There is no eating and no drinking from sunup to sunset except for children and the ill. They do this to experience compassion and understanding for those who are poor and must do without. As Kathianne explained, a trip to Egypt is educational and can expand a person's views of Islam. It is a powerful prescription and antidote for our fears and prejudices as we learn that Muslims are peaceful people and that Egypt is a safe place to travel.

Chapter 46: Maureen J. St. Germain

"Mohamed carries a vision of peace and understanding through tourism in everything he does."

Photograph courtesy of Maureen J. St. Germain.

When Maureen was first planning a trip to Egypt, she had an intuition to call John Anthony West. She found his website—without really knowing why she should contact him—and saw that he was going to be in Egypt at the same time she was. She sent him an email, thinking he wouldn't respond, and asked if he'd be willing to give a lecture to her group. Soon enough, she heard back.

"This great man called me," she said, "and he had lovely words for my Flower of Life teachings, and we began a friendship. He helped me with my tour and gave me a good idea of what to do. He let me know what was possible." He also told her Mohamed was the right man for the job.

It wasn't until well after 9/11 that Maureen sent Mohamed a deposit, using her own money to secure the tour that she would eventually lead. In the process of making arrangements, Mohamed called her. She had no idea he was in the same time zone. When she put her hand on the phone, she knew it was him. She picked up the phone and said "Hello Mohamed." Together, they burst out laughing. "I have had a big heart connection with him ever since," she told me. "We both laughed for about a minute."

Mohamed wanted Maureen to go to Egypt to inspect the sites, wanting her to have some time with his company before her first trip. As she traveled to Egypt with Mohamed, she realized something. "I recognized him from other lifetimes," she said. "If this man loves you, you can do no wrong." Maureen lived in New York when Mohamed was there as a young man, and they actually worked at the Roosevelt Hotel at the same time. They didn't realize this until they became friends and began discussing their past; Mohamed worked in the restaurant and Maureen was the sales director.

Maureen is an international transformational teacher, author and intuitive. She works with individuals and groups to facilitate their awakening and transformation into the new reality that is emerging. It is her passion to help people grow and evolve, and her mission to help others manifest their heart's desire. Maureen's workshops are in demand all over the world, she has written several books, and she has led more than twelve tours to Egypt. She is insightful, compassionate, and funny. Known as the Practical Mystic, Maureen loves to share the knowledge she has gained from over 25 years of study as a seeker in ancient truths.

Like many tour leaders, Maureen was impressed by Mohamed's vision and generosity, especially in dealing with tour groups after 9/11. "Mohamed carries a vision of peace and understanding through tourism in everything he does," she said. Maureen explained that while hotels and tour companies laid off employees to make up for post-9/11 financial losses, Mohamed promised his staff they would be cared for. He had saved for a rainy day. He assembled his staff and told them, no pay cuts, no layoffs. "I will pay you until I cannot," he told them. "So don't fear, go back and tell your families not to worry. You are safe and your families are safe and we will recover and be even stronger."

Maureen emphasized how influential Mohamed has been in the Egyptian tour industry. "He built tourism in Egypt," she said. As she explained, Mohamed navigated the political terrain of Egypt's ever-changing rules and regulations, and created a system for all tour operators that insured predictable and precise scheduling for times in the temples. By building loyalty with his employees, clients, and the office of antiquities, he created a framework for travel. He was responsible for getting permits and putting a system in place that allowed groups to visit places like the King's Chamber, all the while ensuring there was no resentment from guards or other vested interests. After Mohamed pioneered the permits that allowed private times, he continued to turn around and give the guards their baksheesh, tips of cash! He always handles these details keeping in mind the good will of everyone involved.

But Mohamed has been just as influential to Maureen on a personal level. "He opened his heart to me," she said. "He taught me that loyalty is everything." Over and over, Maureen has been taken care of by Quest Travel, regardless of the size of the group or the circumstances. "Devotion to excellence and leaving no stone unturned is what Quest Travel does." Like other tour leaders, Maureen recognizes that Mohamed and his employees truly listen to guests on a trip. "If there is something special you want to see or do, they have been known to go to a location that was not on the itinerary because a group member had a life-long vision to be at a specific temple or site." Thanks to the connections with vendors, clients, and government officials, Quest Travel makes things happen, and the workers are willing to stick their necks out to support the lifelong dreams of the travelers. "They can open doors that no one else does," she added.

Maureen and Mohamed understand the healing power available at the sites in Egypt. On one of her tours, one of Mohamed's employees, Hatem, intuited that if he were the first one to hug Maureen when she exited the King's Chamber that his back would be cured, and it was!

There have been other healings in the Great Pyramid. Maureen shared that John Reid, a sound researcher, reported that his bad back was cured after lying in the sarcophagus in the King's Chamber. Those of us who have traveled to Egypt on spiritual tours have heard and experienced similar healing stories. But you don't have to be on a spiritual tour to have something like this happen. The mysteries of Egypt are open to everyone. This is one of the reasons Mohamed enjoys sharing these places with us. And this is one of the reasons that Maureen loves to share Egypt with her clients, and she is glad that she has a friend like Mohamed to support her in her work.

"Quest Travel also has a healthy respect for other people's belief systems, and they will work to help to support their tour leaders." On the other hand, when Maureen was in Peru, her guide wouldn't communicate with her or give her the information she needed. "Quest would never do such a thing," she said. "Because of that dynamic of respect, Mohamed promotes harmony within and exudes and promotes it outwardly."

I asked Maureen what she has learned from Mohamed. As usual, it all came back to the theme of activation. "Mohamed has a gift for pinpointing certain things for people," she said, "and he has said exactly the right thing to people to move them forward. He inspires people; he *sees* people. He inspires people to act."

When I asked Maureen what she wanted the world to know about Mohamed, she said, "He is a high priest of the highest order, and he is a phenomenal representative of Egypt." On a final note, Maureen has Mohamed to thank for her expanded linguistic abilities. One day, when Mohamed was talking to a co-worker about some arrangements in Arabic, she asked him if he would speak English instead. He looked at her and said, "Maybe you should learn Arabic." So she placed her attention on learning more Arabic and continues to do so.

Chapter 47: Robert Temple and Olivia Temple

"Mohamed is and has been a Force for Good." (Olivia)

"Mohamed is also a 'giver' rather than a 'taker'. He always wants to help people, to give things to people." (Robert)

Photograph courtesy of the Temples.

Robert and Olivia Temple have known Mohamed for more than ten years, ever since their first trip to Egypt when they attended a conference. Olivia's first memory of Mohamed is meeting him at the Mena House, and what she remembers most is his warm smile and his soft, lovely nature. "He is one of life's angels, because he is so understanding of people and can respond so kindly to different personalities," she said. "He is full of life. He spreads love wherever he goes, and he feels his way through things."

Robert Temple is the author of a dozen challenging and provocative books. He is especially known for his international best-seller, *The Sirius Mystery*. His books have been translated into forty-four languages. Professor Temple combines solid academic scholarship with an ability to communicate with the mass public, and his studies offer an alternative view of the history of Egypt. Olivia Temple is an artist and author, co-writing *The Sphinx Mystery: Forgotten Origins: Sanctuary of Anubis* with Robert. Robert and Olivia have also co-authored the first complete English version of Aesop's Fables. Both of them were kind enough to send some thoughts about Mohamed, and I pass them on to you.

Thoughts on Mohamed from Olivia

Olivia sent me the following piece of writing about Mohamed:

Mohamed was at the airport to meet us and took us in a Quest Travel mini-bus to the Mena House Hotel at Giza in Cairo. Robert was a guest speaker along with several other writers, including Robert Bauval, Graham Hancock, and Colin Wilson.

I liked the white streak in his [Mohamed's] very thick and oiled hair, and I liked his warm and sweet smile. He welcomed us all with a very gentle voice and a warm hand shake. He was beautifully dressed and smelled of jasmine, rose oil and sweet things—like a delicious cake. He had an office, whose address was Pyramids, Giza—how smart is that? His colleagues and the guides he provided for us were all dear people, kind, concerned, polite, and knowledgeable. There was Ihab, Medhet, and Emil, a charismatic and blue-eyed enchanter whose enthusiasm for the ancient Egyptian sacred places was almost alarming. He was to be our unforgettable guide.

Mohamed's concern was to make our trip the best experience for us. He is a real professional in that he makes this seem easy. He never gets in a state or shows anger or frustration. He will stage-manage every day, and, if necessary, get up in the middle of the night, to ease the path and make sure all will be well.

It seems that in this harsh and unjust world there have been sent angels, dotted amongst us like stardust, who make it all better. I think Mohamed is one of these. He is filled up with love, like a golden goblet overflowing with honey, and he wants this love to be shared. He gives it to everyone and he spreads it. That is his desire. He wants the people of the world to feel love, the love that knows no bounds. If love could dominate, if love could speak, if being Mohamed could make a difference, then there is hope. Mohamed is not only a Muslim; he is a man of all faiths. He is tolerant and uncritical and he is kind.

He should be known about and held up as an example. Without a doubt he is an influence, and a big one, on all the many people who have been to Egypt on his tours. I am trying to think of something to say about him that is not fulsome praise. He must do something wrong surely?

The day after 9/11, I received a fax from Mohamed. It was a heart-felt prayer that he had written to his fellow humans. That prayer made me weep and sealed my affection and admiration for Mohamed forever. Its content was so forgiving, so true and healing that I have included it here:

Dearest Friends,

With deep sadness and hurt Hearts we received the unexpected news of the horrific events that took place in various places in the USA and took the lives of many victims. All the Egyptian people, and our friends and families, did not sleep last night because of this lively nightmare they were following up with.

For those who love, please join me to Pray for those who have lost their lives today. Pray for those that are left behind. Pray for those who are laying in hospitals, burnt, broken, and bleeding. Pray for those who are laying in rubble, not knowing if they will be rescued before they die.

Pray for the perpetrators of these tragic and despicable acts of desperation. Pray for our leaders to practice restraint. Pray for forgiveness. Pray for the airline passengers who spent their last moments in terror. Pray for the heroes that died rescuing others. Pray for America. Pray for Peace. Pray for wisdom to find its way in the hearts of OUR USA President, our

generals, and the leadership of the world. Pray until you can't find another
prayer in your heart. Then give thanks...
—*For All Our Relations, Please Pray, Mohamed Nazmy*

Mohamed has opened the doors of the soul of Egypt. By encouraging and arranging for meditative time for groups of people in the secret sacred spaces, whether in the heart of the Great pyramid at Giza or in a tiny crypt at Dendera, he has assisted the release and flow of the energy (*and I dislike the over-use of that word, but it is the only apt word in this context*) and spirit of the ancient deities and people, and the mystery of the stones and places. A connection has been made and the best is brought out of people when they have experienced these places. Mohamed is largely responsible for this.

As a result, there are thousands of people whose lives have been affected profoundly and whose hearts and souls have grown with a positive exhalation of change. Mohamed is and has been a Force for Good. Long may he live!
—*from Olivia Temple*

Thoughts on Mohamed from Robert

Robert wrote about Mohamed with an amazingly accurate and powerful description:

The most striking thing about Mohamed is his amiability. It is the first thing I noticed about him when we initially met. It is not that he smiles a lot or grins a lot, but that he beams good will and friendliness from his face, which is better than a smile. In that sense I would describe him as radiant, since he radiates his good will rather than expresses it. However, a silent friendliness is also in my opinion an Egyptian characteristic. The Egyptian people are largely a silently sweet-natured people, as far as I have been able to judge. Perhaps Europeans were like that once, hundreds of years ago, who knows.

When people become too affluent they become spoiled like rotten fruit. In English we have an expression to describe ordinary people who have superior character; we say they are 'the salt of the earth'. That means that they are good people who are unspoiled and modest. Sometimes a more sophisticated person manages to combine this quality of being 'salt of the earth' with also being wise, professional and knowledgeable. I would say that Mohamed has the quality of being 'salt of the earth' in a highly sophisticated way. That means that he has preserved his innocence as a human being, innocence which is usually destroyed when a person ceases to be a simple person and becomes a complex person. The only way to preserve such qualities is to be free of ego. And that is certainly one of the secrets of Mohamed: he has little if any ego.

So no matter how intelligent and sophisticated he is, he remains very simple at heart. He has retained the magical innocence of childhood at the same time as he is able to cope with a complex modern world and run an extensive business. This is a very rare combination of character traits. I do not believe anyone who knows Mohamed could fail to trust him. Can you imagine Mohamed ever cheating anyone or lying to anyone? I cannot. That is why I call him a simple soul who is a complex man. Mohamed is also a 'giver' rather than a 'taker'. He always wants to help people, to give things to people. He is not grabbing for himself. But if you lack an ego, then there is no one to grab for, and all the radiation is going outwards, with none being sucked inwards, so that the result is a net outflow and a zero inflow. Imagine that Mohamed is Hapi, the Nile. Two streams flow from him, one to drain water away and one to drain water into the Nile. In Mohamed's case, only one stream flows: the stream that flows from him, not to him.

It is true that Mohamed runs a successful business; that he provides for himself and his family, and that he does it well. He knows how to earn money and achieve a profit. But he does this without exploiting people, as a natural productive activity, like the growing of grain. Apart from that, when did Mohamed ever grasp anything for himself? The highest ambition that I have ever encountered in Mohamed wanting something for himself is that he likes to have soft skin and he will always welcome a pot of the sort of moisturizer he likes as a gift from England. I think that is the only 'selfishness' of which he is capable.

I believe that Mohamed is descended from thousands of years of people who enjoyed helping crops to grow from the fertile soil of the annual Nile Inundation (which alas exists no more). I see him surrounded by flocks of wild egrets, looking with joy at the green shoots of plants, smiling at his patient water buffalo as it ploughs the black soil, breathing the fresh morning air and admiring the blue of the sky, the smell that arises from the ploughed earth, the aromas which drift from the Nile, and dreaming of a sacred temple, dreaming of the gods, dreaming of the sacred in every sense. Perhaps Mohamed has been a priest in a temple and learned silence and silent joy, has interiorized his piety, and has learned how to celebrate the beauties of a sacred cosmos. Is that where he learned how to beam good will and love and joy from his face? For how many ages has Mohamed gazed at sunsets and thought of eternity? For how many ages has he looked east at the rising sun, arisen in the night to wash and pray, bowed humbly, offered himself up to a higher power? In his every gesture, Mohamed shows his true nature. In his smiling eyes, we see his character. What higher praise can there be for a person than to say this of him, that he embodies the higher virtues in his own person. And that is Mohamed Nazmy.

—From his friend Robert Temple

Chapter 48: John Anthony West

"Mohamed is a greater force for peace that the UN! In fact he could run the UN."

Photograph courtesy of John Anthony West's Website.

Several people I spoke with told me that John Anthony West was one of the first people to persuade Mohamed to leave Sphinx Travel. I asked John if he'd encouraged Mohamed. "Encouraged him?" he said, "No. I bludgeoned him into starting his own business." Mohamed knew that it was a good idea, John explained, but he was legitimately fearful. Because of the up and down nature of the travel business, and because of the threat of terrorism in Egypt, it was hard for Mohamed to consider how he would support his family and his life in Egypt without his job at Sphinx Travel. John said, "Although Mohamed was working for this parasite, an awful man who owned Sphinx Travel, he was given a paycheck every month." Many of his clients begged him to leave. It wasn't until Mohamed himself woke up one day and knew that he was done working at the company that change came.

John is a well-known author, lecturer, and guide, known for his alternative ideas and investigations into the age of the Sphinx. As an independent Egyptologist, John has studied and written about ancient Egypt for over two decades. He is author of many books, including *Serpent in the Sky: The High Wisdom of Ancient Egypt* and his popular guide book *The Traveler's Key to Ancient Egypt, A Guide to the Sacred Places of Ancient Egypt.*

He first traveled to Egypt in 1978 in order to get photographs for his book *Serpent in the Sky,* and to examine evidence supporting or contradicting the agreed upon age of the Sphinx among conventional Egyptologists. He was very interested in learning more about the water-weathering hypotheses that places the age of the Sphinx at a much earlier date.

After that, he traveled back to Egypt many times as a guest speaker for other groups. In 1985, after John published his guidebook, he decided he wanted to lead his own tour. He didn't know anything about the process, and he didn't want to go with any of the typical New Age groups. The tourist board in New York recommended Sphinx Travel, and it seemed promising to John. When John arrived in Egypt, Mohamed was waiting at the airport, looking very dapper. He was greeting tourists, impeccably dressed with a white flash in his hair, sunglasses, his day-glow white suit, and a big smile. John said they have been best friends ever since.

Beyond his suave characteristics, there is a lot that John appreciates about Mohamed. "Mohamed has a real visceral, emotional sense of esoteric Egypt," John said. "He understands what ancient Egypt has to offer." John's group was one of the first that Mohamed worked with, and John said he would have been lost without him. "I wouldn't have known what to do," he said. "I would tell him what I wanted, and there was no fighting over the fact that I needed to stay more hours." John lectures in detail from both emotional and scholarly points of view. "Mohamed was fine with all of that, and he gave me special consideration."

For twenty-five years, John has seen Mohamed promote good will through his travel business. "Most people who bring tours are interested in making money," John said. "Having to take people around is secondary to that desire." John explained that in those scenarios, tourists are not getting an authentic Egyptian experience. Mohamed, however, ensures that travelers can soak up and get acquainted with the ancient sites, temples and tombs, while also getting to know the people of Egypt. "Money is not the most important thing. Mohamed wants to broaden your experience. He wants you to have an exchange with the people, and this makes a big difference," John said.

When I asked John what he has learned from Mohamed, he said he has gained vast knowledge about modern Egypt, but also something more. "He teaches peace through tourism," he said. "He creates bonds that weren't there before you started. He also does charity work for kids, and a percentage of his business profit goes to his foundation. Mohamed is a greater force for peace that the UN! In fact he could run the UN."

Part Eleven: The Present

Fig. Part Eleven.1. A rooftop view of the Mena House and the pyramids from Mohamed's apartment building.

In This Moment That You Have, Practice Peace

Chapter 49: Mohamed's Stroke in April of 2008

Mohamed believes everything is a gift from God, so when he had a stroke he accepted it with grace. He recuperated in France and worked hard at his rehabilitation so that he could get back to his life. He no longer has the use of the right side of his body due to paralysis caused by the stroke, but he has managed to walk again and to use his left hand. He has learned to type rather efficiently with his left hand and index finger, and I am always impressed by the way he sends rapid-fire texts with his left thumb. He can still do everything he needs to do although he has been forced to slow down. He is slow to walk from place to place, and steps are obstacles that take a bit of work. He still sits at his desk and does what he has always done, continuing with his life, following the beliefs he holds so dear.

He told me that he looks at people differently now, with a deeper understanding of their humanity, with a deeper love for all that they are. He has more time to reflect. "I still walk on the same road with the same vision," he told me as we sat in his office. "I am accepting and trusting always." Mohamed manages to stay in the moment and enjoy his life, continuing to be of service and promote peace. His vision remains the same.

"Even after his stroke," Jane Bell said, "Mohamed is a workaholic who wants to run his business, and keep to his mission and continue to provide transformative experiences for people. His goal remains the same—to use his business as a vehicle for creating peace and helping others."

I never get tired of hearing Mohamed's stories. His timing is perfect, and his stories always illustrate a point. When he told me he had a story for me that would summarize how he felt about his stroke, I leaned back in my chair and settled in.

Mohamed told me he used to listen to a man on the radio who had the most beautiful voice. When he mentioned the man to his brother, his brother grew excited and told him he knew the man and could arrange for them to meet. When Mohamed met the man from the radio, he was surprised to see he had no arms. When Mohamed asked, "How do you write?" the man answered, "I am very grateful for my mouth and my feet!"

Mohamed looked at me, his gaze both fierce and gentle. "This experience filled me with the spirit of appreciation for whatever situation I might face in my life," he said. "It taught me to be grateful for what I *do* have. This man used what he *did have* and never placed his attention on what he did not have."

Still, I had more questions. I was intrigued by his acceptance and positivity. Surely there was something he wasn't telling me. "Don't you just get frustrated and angry at times?" I asked him.

Although he said no, he admitted that he doesn't like having to receive the help of his friends and family for simple things, like tying his shoes, zipping his pants, or walking. He confided that receiving this help from those he loves is hard on his pride. It is clear, however, that those who help him do so because they love him.

When Mohamed was rehabilitating in Paris, many people traveled to France to visit him just to see his face break into that familiar, beautiful smile. His friends were able to give him the same gift that he so loves giving to others—the gift of joy.

Mohamed doesn't travel as much as he used to. He spends more time in Cairo, putting in additional hours at the office. After talking to those closest to him, it is clear they are the ones hit hardest by Mohamed's stroke, because they remember how things used to be. As for Mohamed, he just lives in the present. Being in the now seems to come naturally for him.

Since Mohamed's stroke, Emil has been there for him every step of the way. I look to Emil as my teacher when it comes to being a friend. He has fed Mohamed, dressed and bathed him, walked beside him as they slowly moved from the office to the car, helped him onto the plane or the boat, and always with nothing but kindness and patience and humor. I was awed by Emil's devotion and his immeasurable capacity to be there for whatever Mohamed needed, whenever he needed it, often without Mohamed having to speak a word. These men have been so close for so long, they communicate effortlessly.

After Mohamed returned from his rehabilitation in France, he kept to himself and stayed very close to the office. Several of my friends were on the first tour Mohamed joined after he had his stroke, and they all spoke of the love that people demonstrated for Mohamed on this tour. People came out in droves to see him and wish him well. Musical bands met him at the train station in Aswan and at the boat dock where he would often ferry across the Nile to the Afandina. One did not have to understand the language to feel the love that welcomed him everywhere he went.

There are many incidents to recount, but there is one that is especially touching and poignant. My friend Susan Webster, who lives in Seattle and has traveled to Egypt with Mohamed many times, told me a story that took place at the train station in Aswan. As the band played and people danced, an elderly man walked up to Susan, took both her hands in his, and said, "The gift of Mohamed Nazmy is a better gift than if you brought the gift of a million dollars."

Over and over again, I have heard heartwarming stories just like this one. Mohamed is important to so many people, and it soon becomes clear that he affects everyone he comes in contact with. Susan described Mohamed as a great light and said, "You know I join the many that leave space for him in my heart."

Out of that love comes concern. Jean Houston told me she wishes Mohamed would take his rehabilitation more seriously. Everyone I spoke to felt the same way—they all wished Mohamed would commit to healing and rehabilitation, delegate more work to others, eat better, take things easy, and stay away from stress. Those who love him try to help him, but not with great success. "That is not where his interest is," Jean said. "It is not with his body. He is with his mind and what he does in the world."

Jean for her part, has worked with Mohamed through psycho-physical regeneration, which was developed by Jean's husband, Dr. Robert Masters. Psycho-physical regeneration is a method for re-patterning the brain's mind system with certain kinds of movements and thoughts. Jean has worked long and hard with Mohamed, trying to train him on many of their trips. She has put him in contact with others who do psychophysical training as well, but is unsure how many of her suggestions he follows. Mohamed can be a stubborn man.

Eventually, Jean said what I did not want to say aloud. "Sharlyn," she said, "if he passes away, who is going to carry on?" Mohamed does what he does with such skill and love, that many fear there will not be someone who can take his place if he leaves this world. Jean tries constantly to convince Mohamed to come to the States and work more intensively on his health. As Jean explained, it is difficult for Mohamed to focus on physical recovery when his main way of working in this world is through the mind. He feels that he has rehabilitated himself to the point that he can still carry on with his vision. Jane Bell described Mohamed as a man of "great pride," which is often his Achilles' heel.

George Faddoul told me that when he first heard that Mohamed had a stroke, he didn't believe it. "In a business environment he [Mohamed] is the one to give out the anxiety, not receive it," George said. George wanted to do his part to help Mohamed, and he wanted to wish Mohamed a speedy recovery, so he was one of the many who visited Mohamed in France. George explained that Mohamed was positive about the stroke from day one. "There was never anything about 'poor me' or 'why me,'" he said. "This is Mohamed's nature."

All those who hold Mohamed dear to them kept Mohamed in their thoughts as he recovered. Maureen St. Germain told me another story: she asked a friend, Sherif, who was visiting Egypt if he would check in with Mohamed and see how he was doing. When Sherif returned, he showed Maureen a photo of him standing next to Mohamed, and Maureen burst into tears. Sherif had traveled many hours to find Mohamed. "I started to cry," she said. "I feel like I have not done enough for him in the recovery he had to go through, and I give him so much credit for coming through it all."

Maureen also explained that Mohamed's business was able to carry on its excellence because he has such a loyal staff. Emil and Ihab held tremendous weight as Mohamed recovered, because Mohamed normally has all decisions come through him. While Mohamed was in Paris recuperating, they stepped in and held the ropes.

"Emil missed Mohamed terribly," Jane Bell told me. "Emil really had to separate from his boss and friend and go ahead with his life."

Danielle and Friedemann also spoke about Emil's part in Mohamed's recovery. They explained that Emil would help Mohamed dress and eat, and truly suffered seeing his friend in such a weakened state. Danielle remembered Emil taking Mohamed on the first trip after his stroke and getting him to walk again. "It really felt like Emil brought Mohamed back to life," Danielle said. Let's not forget, however, the nature of Emil and Mohamed's relationship. Everything is done with a sense of humor. Emil made Mohamed walk the planks from boat to shore, braying like a donkey behind Mohamed to spur him on. With humor, persistence and love, Emil helped Mohamed regain confidence. In an email, Emil wrote that he had "mastered" Mohamed, meaning that he was now in charge of the rehabilitation, and he was going to be the enforcer so that Mohamed would have no choice, but to get back to his life.

Now, Mohamed is back to doing what he does, in spite of the lasting effects that have slowed him down. He is traveling again and often joins tours on their cruise on the Afandina. He went to many of the sites with us on my last visits. We went shopping in Cairo and he always met us for breakfast at the hotels. We traveled to Alexandria together and he did very well. He has even traveled to the States. He seems to walk faster and faster, having learned to negotiate the limitations of his body. He is back to life as usual. If anything, his stroke has deepened him, and made him even more grateful for all of his blessings, and for what he *can* do.

Chapter 50: The Revolution of 2011

The revolution in Egypt came as a big surprise to the world. For weeks, we sat on edge, watching the Egyptian people topple a dictator. An estimated two million people protested in Cairo. As I read news reports and blogs, it was clear these protests involved people from all walks of life, and that the utilization of social media was a new, powerful tool. In an interview, a woman from Cairo said she used to think bloggers were "spoiled brats of the Internet," but that she was now ever grateful to them. These tech-savvy young men are the ones who brought Mubarak down.

Fig. 50.1. Revolution graffiti. Photographer unknown.

One blog noted that it is common to hear Egyptians can endure anything. There is a common joke, "If a revolution fails, there's always next century." It was clear, however, that a big change had occurred. People—peasants from the country, young educated men, shopkeepers, members of the Brotherhood, the privileged, women—had come together to meet their challenges. Young men went out for supplies in their neighboring areas to keep the effort going. If food ran out, they went to another neighborhood and those people shared what they had. If the doors of the shops were closed to avoid looting, the shopkeepers would open if someone knocked on the door and acted respectfully. The military joined the protesters and cooked meals for those who stood their ground in the square. They set up makeshift hospitals to treat the wounded. Everyone stuck together, and they did not give up. They united around the belief that Mubarak and his government was no longer a viable option. A very diverse population had come together for one goal, and it is quite a remarkable accomplishment in spite of their differing political views.

On Friday, February 11, 2011, Hosni Mubarak resigned as president of Egypt, leaving Cairo for the Red Sea resort of Sharma el-Sheikh. After Mubarak's departure, Vice President Omar Suleiman, speaking on state television, said that Mubarak had decided to relinquish power to the military. The army ensured the Egyptian people that the thirty-year-old emergency laws would be lifted and that free and fair elections would be held. This assurance was given in an effort to end the worst crisis in Egypt's modern history. On the eighteenth day of the revolution, known as "Farewell Friday," hundreds of thousands of protesters gathered for a huge rally. When they heard the news that Mubarak had resigned, Tahrir Square and all of Egypt erupted in celebration.

Of course, those of us who have traveled to Egypt were in solidarity with the aspirations and struggles of the people, and we worried about Mohamed and all our friends at Quest Travel. I was able to speak to Mohamed and Emil by cell, and they assured me they were well. Mohamed was working with a group for John Anthony West, and the group decided collectively to remain in Egypt, move forward with their scheduled itinerary, and travel to Luxor. At the moment I called Emil, it was 8:30 P.M. in Egypt, and he was standing with John Anthony West's group at Luxor temple under its beautiful lights, safe and sound.

The day before Mubarak stepped down, I awoke in the middle of the night and felt compelled to get out of bed. I went to my desk, and wrote a mind treatment—a form of prayer taught through Religious Science and its founder Earnest Holmes. This is what I wrote:

> We see Egypt and the people relax and rejoice now as leaders come together to form a new constitution that guarantees the people their basic rights and freedom. We see Mubarak step down now so that new elections are held that represent the Egyptian people. We feel this and know the joy of this. And we send this now into the hands of Spirit for its manifestation and for the expression of love, unity, and freedom—all expressions of universal peace and liberation. It can be no other. And so it is!

That next morning, I awoke to the news that the Revolution had succeeded. Mine was one of the thousands and thousands of prayers that were fulfilled. During the entire eighteen days of this revolution, people around the world were glued to the television, Internet, and radio. I was relieved and so glad that the violence was over, and that the people of Egypt could get back to their lives and their livelihoods.

A Reassuring Letter from Mohamed

On February 13, 2011, Mohamed sent a message to his friends through Facebook:

My Dearest Friends around the World,

I am sure that you all were watching the drama unfold in our beloved Egypt over these past weeks. It has been spellbinding. And to see the actual fall of Mubarak today is such a thrilling and satisfying event. Truly, you share in watching history here and now. All free people around the world are cheering for us all as we reclaim our greatness and our independence after such a long siege of tyranny. What courage and spirit the great people of Egypt have shown the world. And to think that the world's young citizens, who live now in your cities, created a technology that has enabled us all to connect with each other and empower us to succeed in this revolution. It just proves how we are all connected to the core and for all time.

My prayers are that Egypt will find its way to a democratic and expansive future. The world is now cheering for us. I am proud to be called "Egyptian."

I am grateful and thankful for your emails and for this new dawn for Egypt and the Egyptian people. We are all happy for the change to what we want…. Hopefully tomorrow will be better than today…. We must do our very best from now on for the sake of Egypt and our future as well as the coming young generations who are the leaders for our future and our country….

—Bravo!!!! Love & many thanks and blessings, Mohamed

A Letter about the Revolution

One traveler who was on the trip with John Anthony West and Quest Travel during the revolution wrote this letter about her experiences and posted it on Nicki Scully's website:

Dear Friends & Family,

Our group returned to the US last night incredibly inspired by a magical 18-day trip to Egypt. We arrived in Cairo on January 28, just as the unrest was gathering steam. Soon after we got off the plane, we were notified that no one would be allowed to leave the airport. Spending 12 hours in (any) airport sounds nightmarish, but watching the crowds in Tahrir Square on Egyptian TV (in Arabic!) in the airport Burger King, we met lots of Egyptians who enthusiastically welcomed us, translated the news to us, and communicated their excitement and pride in the unfolding events.

Not knowing much about Egypt, my first worry was that deposing Mubarak might mean more restrictions for Egyptian women. Many women in Egypt wear bright colored head scarves, some wear burqas, and some don't cover their heads at all. One member of our group made friends with several young women in black burqas with only their eyes showing. They turned out to be biology majors in college and plan to become doctors! Other Egyptian women I spoke with convinced me that Egypt is very unlike other countries where radical clerics have taken over.

Egyptians love their army, and while there is worry in any kind of cataclysmic event, most everyone we talked to felt that no matter what, Mubarak had to go. They spoke of their dream of a free society with free and fair elections, freedom of speech and the press, and the opportunity to control their own destinies. My deep belief is that they are not going to surrender this newfound precious freedom to radical groups, or to anyone (or anything) else. And the women are strong.

Our tour company heroically managed to get us out of the airport late that night in a bus with the curtains closed. The next day, we convened at our hotel on the outskirts of Cairo, well out of the way of the demonstrations, and guarded (probably unnecessarily, but still welcome) by an army tank. After deep contemplation for 2 days about what might be safe to do, each person made a decision whether to stay or to go home.

Although events were unfolding unpredictably (such as the mass prisoner escape) I had a deep certainty that I HAD to stay. Thinking about leaving brought tears and I felt there must be some reason our group had succeeded in being there. I even hoped that we might somehow humbly be of service to the Egyptian people by holding our poise and a deep sense of hope for them for a peaceful resolution to the crisis. Ultimately, most of the group decided to stay.

After an initially tense ride through early morning Cairo past numerous neighborhood "checkpoints" (described in the news media as vigilantes, but actually courageous men protecting their homes with kitchen knives and sticks— with smiles and peace signs exchanged between us and them when they figured out who we were), we flew to Luxor and spent 5 days on a heart-melting cruise down the Nile. All the tomb and temple sites were completely empty—Luxor and Karnak, Philae, the Temple of Horus at Edfu, Hatshepsut, Valley of the Kings, etc., etc.—each one more incredibly moving than the last.

It did seem that there was no need to pray or meditate as we drifted up the Nile—we found it to be true that "the Nile meditated us." As the days went on, we couldn't imagine leaving. People would yell "Welcome to Egypt!" as we walked through Luxor and Aswan. As we moved past fear and into trust, it was clear to us that the Egyptian people's revolution was intelligent and targeted. (For those Enneagramarians, Egypt is a "9" culture and they finally got mad.)

I never felt in danger, but we were constantly aware that we needed to be sensible and stay out of the way! We were quite a novelty, though, since in most places we were the only tourists there. It's a sad time for the Egyptian economy, of which tourism is a huge chunk. Apparently, the norm is crowds of thousands, jammed tour buses, and all that that brings. We were able to walk around the empty sites, pray, climb into tombs, feed the temple dogs and cats, visit sites that have been closed to tourists for 20 years, sit between the paws of the Sphinx, and spend time with a pristine mummy still lying in his original tomb that has never been opened to the public. Many of us had incredible heart opening experiences. The Egyptian people are well aware that they are the guardians of these world treasures brimming with powerful energy. As our Egyptian tour guide said, "Egypt is beyond time and space."

We spent our next-to-last day in the completely empty Great Pyramid at dawn Friday morning meditating. Rus led us in prayer for the Egyptian people. Later that day, Mubarak resigned. When we got back to our hotel to eat breakfast, a HUGE double rainbow broke out over Cairo, and a few hours later Mubarak peacefully left the city. Our Egyptian tour guide told us she had NEVER SEEN A SKY RAINBOW BEFORE—(it almost never rains in Cairo—she had seen one once reflected in a waterfall). Happily, one of our party is a professional photographer. He has put together a beautiful slide show, which he has promised to post. Look for the rainbow!

So pack your bags and go to Egypt now before the tourists go back! I will never forget the sight of thousands of Egyptians, just standing there in the Square. I will never forget their generosity and kindness to 16 stray American, Canadian & New Zealand tourists whom they allowed to watch their poignant, elegant, restrained revolution.

Our return flight was cancelled, so we decided to go to Tahrir Square as a group on Saturday. We bought Egyptian flags as we drove through downtown Cairo. When they saw us waving them, people reached out their hands to clasp ours at red lights. When we got out, they crowded around asking us to be in pictures with them!! It was overwhelming. We will never, ever forget it. Though masses were still celebrating from the night before, many in the crowd had donned rubber gloves, medical masks and carried trash bags and brooms. They were cleaning up the square, just like they cleaned up their government. Long Live Egypt!

—*Many blessings, Peggy Mainor*

Chapter 51: The Revolution is Not Over

Not surprisingly, the travel industry suffered. About a month later, I was able to find a short video interview of Mohamed speaking about the travel industry on the Internet. It was reassuring to see him, but the message was sobering. Mohamed said the travel business in Egypt suffered a loss of between 3.5–4 million dollars. His interview was held at the magnificent Mena House. The only thing different than usual? It was empty. Tourists had stopped coming to Egypt.

In the next year, there was much political change. The organization of the Brotherhood was legalized and formed a new political party called the Freedom and Justice Party, becoming a strong voice in Egypt's political framework. On January 21, 2012 the first free parliamentary elections were held in Egypt in more than sixty years, ending in a victory for the Muslim Brotherhood's Freedom and Justice Party. The results came just days before the anniversary of Egypt's uprising that led to the end of Mubarak's regime and the temporary establishment of military rule.

Is It Safe to Travel?

After the revolution, many wondered if it was safe to travel to Egypt. As I was preparing to lead a tour in May of 2012, Mohamed wrote a letter which he titled *Egyptians Giving Birth to Egypt: Egypt Reborn*. Here is the letter that he wrote for the travelers in my group to reassure them:

My Dear Friends & Egypt's friends,

It gives me such a great pleasure to invite you to witness Egypt's birth, and to be part of this historical moment in Egypt and the lives of the Egyptian people. When you come to Egypt, we all write history together!!

Peaceful protest, demonstrations, governmental clashes, opinion conflicts, voting for constitutional law, and so many other changes are today giving birth to a New Egypt.

Egypt today is not only significant for its mysterious Pyramids, or its magnificent temples, or artistic breath-taking museums; today Egypt is more powerful through its people.

Egyptians have been always Egypt's main asset. During the Revolution what was accomplished was the Unity of Egyptians—the old, the rich and the poor, the civilian and the army—came together in the streets of Cairo and in Tahrir Square (Liberty Square) on Jan. 25th. This was the secret that paved the way for our today's freedom and newly born Egypt.

The Egyptian people created their peaceful unity in the January Revolution. Their tears for the martyrs quickly changed into sweet joyful tears when they witnessed their victory. Then they began cleaning the streets, painting the pavements, and planting trees. All of this provides the re-assuring factual evidence of just how peaceful & powerful these Egyptians are.

The warm smile, the welcoming hospitality, and the love of the Egyptians never changed over this time, and you can always feel it with your first step on to the streets of Cairo.

You can see the love between the Egyptians themselves expressed through the rich giving to the poor, and the sharing of food and clothes. You see more donations and more volunteers. There is an increase in the number of orphanages and non-profitable charity organizations. All of this proves that the Egyptians are all one loving connected people born in a free country with the right to be free.

Now, Egypt is yielding all the revolution's fruitful outcomes. The Egyptian parliament will be re-elected in a free election with international control and the presidential election is to take place along with fair and just penalties for all the ex-government members.

Today Egypt will become, and already is, a democratic society where the voices of the people determine what Egypt will be and will become again. Egypt today has a new face that shows expression rather than hides it; a face with eyes that sparkle with hope and gladness.

The strength of the ancient civilization has risen again like a phoenix from the ashes. Egypt will take its right position in the world now—no longer will we be held back.

The changing face of Egypt was like a woman giving birth—painful, messy, long and tiring and sadly with some blood. But the baby was born—the future Egypt has arrived. A new era has dawned.

So, we invite you today not only to a land of ancient civilization that has impressed the whole world since 7,000 years ago but also to a land of Egyptian youth, freedom and democracy where you can feel the heartbeat of the people which beats to a new sound—the sound of freedom.

Remember, the Giza pyramids are our meeting point to 'Welcome you Home' to Egypt.

—Blessings, Mohamed Nazmy

Political Elections, Morsi Elected as President, and his Removal from Office

I went ahead and led my first tour to Egypt in May of 2012, and we were well taken care of. Egypt was the same, only with far fewer tourists. It was obvious the economy was hurting. The streets were dirtier and the vendors were more aggressive. People complained of more crime. Still, my husband and I were both struck by the fervor and excitement we found in the people on the streets as they prepared for the presidential elections. With pride, they held up signs to let the world know who they would be voting for in June. It is hard to imagine that these people had never been able to vote for their own president before. The Presidential Election in June 2012 led to the election of Mohamed Morsi, a member of the Brotherhood.

People hoped for the best. They hoped Morsi would govern for all people. Some were happy to support a strong Muslim influence in the policies of their country, and some wanted to keep religion and state separate. Regardless, all were happy to vote and to have had an election. Over time however, many became angry with Morsi as he granted himself unlimited powers to legislate without oversight or review. He issued an Islamist-backed draft constitution that supported Sharia law. This, coupled with attacks on the free press and violence against peaceful protestors brought mass backlash. Morsi was deposed in July of 2013 due to unprecedented mass protests in the streets. It was clear that the revolution was not over.

The government then changed hands and was held in the possession of the army and a provisional government. The Brotherhood was denounced, and the population of Egypt was split. Many were happy with Morsi's movement toward implementing Sharia law into Egypt's governing principles, and felt the people had no right to end a democratically elected official. Others were outraged at the union of religion and politics, and wanted to return to a more secular system that protected the rights of women, Christians, and other minorities.

Violence erupted and many died on both sides, including innocent people who never took up arms. Many protestors died in the streets when the army moved in to clear the pro-Morsi demonstrators. Some were killed in mosques while praying. Police and military personnel died, as well as the Islamists who carried guns and shot at them. Street violence broke out between factions. Christian churches were burned. Some said the chaos would result in civil war. Some said the unrest would go on and on. The bombings began again as the Brotherhood headed underground, just like it did during Mubarak's rule.

Many are still resentful and angry at the West for initially supporting Morsi's election, and the Brotherhood is still angry at the United States for supporting the military overthrow of Morsi. The United States continued to give aid, saying that it was not a traditional coup but another twist in the people's fight for the kind of democratic government they hope to create. Morsi failed them with this when he began to take more and more presidential power while implementing a religious agenda.

Hard Times in Egypt

The last three years have been desperately hard for the Egyptians on all fronts. Fewer people are choosing to travel to Egypt. At first, Americans were told it was dangerous to travel to Egypt; a warning was posted and the embassy closed. Any nonessential personnel were asked to come home. Then, when Christian churches were attacked and burned, Europeans did not want to travel. The tourist industry has been ripped apart. This, of course, is a tragedy for a country that had already been devastated with the chaos of revolution and political upheaval. Much to my regret, I had to cancel my trip to Egypt that was slated for October 2013.

Mohamed's Views

I wondered how my friends at Quest Travel were surviving. What would happen? Would a true democracy for all people be able to grow from this turmoil? We hoped so. This is what Mohamed wrote on August 18, 2013 which he titled *Reincarnation through Revolution*— about the ouster of Morsi and the polarization of the Egyptian people:

My Dearest Friends and my Beloved Ones,

I am sure that your hearts are aching for your/our Beloved Egypt when you watch what's happening on TV. Accordingly I would love to share with you some of my thoughts and the truth of our feelings considering the current situation.

Revolutions all over the world, not in Egypt, have always been out of passion for your country, you revolt for peace and you revolt for justice. Egypt has always been a witness of revolutions, wars and victories.

No one on Earth would be happy or satisfied seeing blood, killing people or burning his country's entities; however, it still happens.

A year ago, the Muslim brotherhood had their chance and won the presidential elections hidden behind Morsi…. We believed that they would utilize this opportunity and do their best to achieve political success for the sake of Egypt.

However, and as time passed by, our dreams, wishes and hopes were all demolished and eradicated.

Yet, we kept on challenging ourselves, thirsty to reach our goals and top our revolution with success, development and a fully mature society living in peace.

I am not even in a place where I can judge that the Muslim Brotherhood are terrorists. However, I would be glad to clarify and ask; if they are Islam defenders, then their place isn't the presidential palace. But if they are political supporters and analyst, then they are for sure welcomed; however, they aren't welcomed under the title of any religion.

In a nutshell, country is for all and religion is for GOD. Mixing them just to hypnotize people is a complete disgusting action that reflects their weakness in both fields.

Violence of any kind is terrorism, threatening not only our present, but our future. Other countries' relationships with Egypt have become volatile due to what's happening; all of this for me is terrorism and violence.

One thing that we have to remember is that the gates are now open and the boundaries between people all over the world are erased; electronic platforms where all information is shared became as fast as the speed of light. Hence, we as people shall not be controlled or moved by the governments.

Political leaders' great achievements, recently, would be winning a war or controlling another country; completely forgetting about the internal peace of their people, dreams of their children, blood of their martyrs and deaths of their soldiers.

But it is my hope that while we are working to advance ourselves we should also spread these ideas of peace wherever we go. Our hand is open in friendship. We don't seek hostility. We don't want to be forced into it, but we are determined to protect our rights. My experience through more than 50 years has taught me that people of good will of all races can work together to bring about justice for all betterment of mankind.

Let's us all unite!

We have to remember, that Egypt is part of mother Earth and therefore is everyone's asset. We are born into this world with no boundaries, no country limits, no religion and no ID. We are all born as humans. We are all born to follow our hearts, create our own beliefs and build up our experiences.

Egypt is part of what we - humans - inherited; we need to preserve it & keep it safe. This will not only happen through Egyptians; but it will happen through each and everyone's support in this world. We need to help one another, support one another by joining together, by pushing forward and encouraging positive beliefs.

Egypt is safe & will forever remain safe. God promised us this from the day he created Earth.

Egypt now needs each and everyone's support; it needs our love, support and presence. Egypt is calling you, calling for your presence, inviting you with love to feel its warmth, to see the beauty of the Nile and to enjoy the Egyptian's smile. Looking forward to 'Welcome you Home' and to embrace you all with all the love and peace.

—*By Mohamed Nazmy*

And so life in Egypt went on. The last few years proved to be extremely challenging for Mohamed, Emil, and Quest Travel, but their persistence and hope remains constant. Although the tourism industry had suffered a death blow, they trust people will continue traveling to Egypt once the political scene calms. Mohamed is saddened by the violence and polarization, but he is excited about Egypt's movement toward stability with the election of their new president el-Sisi as of June 2014. Regardless of where one stands on the political side of things, the violence and suffering that has occurred brings sadness to the hearts of those who love Egypt and call it home.

The Presidential Election of June 2014

I traveled to Egypt again in June of 2014 and was able to spend a week in Alexandria with Mohamed and Emil. I was lucky to be there during the election of the new president. When the election was announced, I was caught in a huge bumper-to-bumper traffic jam in Alexandria on the way to dinner. Cars were at a stand-still as families waved their Egyptian flags from their car windows. Men, women, and children thronged the side of the street, holding up the peace symbol with their fingers as we did the same from our car windows. The people were jubilant, and the mood was ecstatic. Fireworks, drums, flags, and the smiling faces of hundreds are forever etched into my memory. I have never seen such celebration, and it was an immense joy to be a part of it. The announcement had just been made that Abdel-Fattah el-Sisi had been elected.

People had stood for days in long lines in order to vote, hoping for a chance to move toward a better life. To many, his election represents stability, law, and order. The people of Egypt had suffered with the sense of division that was created under Morsi, and they were relieved and hopeful that their new president would represent all people and get Egypt back on track, as he had sworn to do. I had witnessed a sea of Egyptians hopeful for a return to sanity, and to a secular government that protects the rights of all of its citizens and meets the needs of its people.

Many Egyptians feel that el Sisi will help Egypt regain stability and economic opportunity. I am hopeful as I see that the Egyptian people are in the process of forging their own style of government. We can join together with them as world citizens and support them as they make their way towards democracy and prosperity. What is true is that Egypt is unique and is following its own path, one that is driven by the Egyptian people themselves. They are defining their future. I am not saying that the current government in Egypt is not without its problems. As with any government, there is much to criticize, but it is not my intention within the scope of this book to elaborate. The story of Egypt continues to shape-shift.

May the wisdom of business people like Mohamed prevail; men and women who are passionate about their country and are doing everything they can to encourage the political process in a peaceful manner. Mohamed and Emil were glued to the television to see the election results and were extremely hopeful and enthused about Sisi's election. They see him as a leader who can reestablish law and order and get their country back on course. They are referring to this time as the birth of a new era.

We are Shape-shifting

On my three week visit in June, there was not a moment that I did not feel safe. I returned to Egypt again in September to lead a tour, and had the same experience. I am grateful to others who continue to lead tours to demonstrate that traveling to Egypt is still safe and of vital importance in the quest for peace and unity. The political scene has calmed, and there are as many life-changing adventures awaiting visitors as there ever were.

We are witnessing incredible changes on our planet, but always, the best of our spiritual teachings offer inclusion, forgiveness, care for our fellow humans and care for the planet that we live on. They also teach us about faith, trust, and love. This is true for the ancient teachings as well as the very best of Muslim, Christian, Jewish, Buddhist or pagan teachings.

Egypt is shape-shifting, but what remains clear to me is that we are world citizens—one people. There is room for difference, which makes life interesting and allows each human to find their own way and worship whatever makes the most sense to them. God does not choose sides. God does not have an agenda. God can be approached from many directions, and exists in all places at the same time. Cultures grow differently in different climates and express human nature in different forms. That is all.

Religions, national boundaries, race, gender, and even sexual preferences are losing their power to keep us separate. Like Egypt, we are changing— we are shape-shifting. This need to believe in separation is as outdated as war.

Through his life, his business, and his relationships, Mohamed Nazmy demonstrates how we can create peace. The metaphysical is alive and well in Egypt, but it is alive and well within our own hearts. If we open up to the mysteries, we, too, will be able to hear the words: "Your life is about service." It certainly can be.

This book is full of the principles of the Goddess Ma'at, which are balance, love, and light—principles that can be applied to our everyday lives in very practical ways. The ancient civilization of Egypt was founded upon these principles, and I am reminded of what Mohamed once said to me: Egypt and all it has to offer belongs to all of us.

I give my gratitude to the ancient teachings of Egypt, the sites and temples that still hold the energy, and our modern teachings of love and tolerance that come to us through our world religions. I am grateful for the development of Egyptian spiritual travel, and to all of the people who give their time and life blood for this work. I am ever grateful to Mohamed, Emil, and all the people who work for Quest Travel. I am grateful for all the connections with the people at the Mena House who are really Mohamed's extended family, as well as the staff at the many hotels, the crew of the Afandina, and every bus driver, escort, and guide. These people have become my friends. What a blessing and a gift.

I know many groups are planning to travel to Egypt again, and this warms my heart. Tens of thousands of people have traveled to Egypt and have been touched by Mohamed, Emil, and Quest Travel and we are all connected as Mohamed's Peace Ambassadors. We are a circle of like-minded souls and we are in this together. In writing, publishing, and promoting this book, I have been privileged to meet so many beautiful people—those who return to Egypt over and over, and those who have been just once, but were deeply affected. And there are those who want to go and will someday. We really do form a world community of love, laughter, and light. Now, you, the reader are invited to become part of this community that Mohamed Nazmy has spearheaded through his vision to create world peace. In this way, we are all one family.

I ask you to pray for Egypt and to pray for peace on our planet. We develop the solutions to our problems as we dissolve hatred, division, and intolerance one heart at a time. We can join together in our resolve to create peace, love and tolerance in our daily lives, wherever we are and in whatever endeavor we find ourselves. This is Mohamed Nazmy's vision. Consider yourself a Peace Ambassador—let's all become one and see what we can do together. I send love and light to each of you. Egypt is more than a geographical location. It is a state of mind, a clarity of intent, and a deep opening of heartfelt love, and it can be yours and mine at any moment just by tuning into the energy. Mohamed Nazmy encourages us to choose this truth, and to use our lives to create peace.

Chapter 52: Return to the Vision: Looking to the Future

In the anthology that Mohamed put together with George Faddoul, there is a chapter written by Shelli Wright Johnson, one of the group leaders who travels with Mohamed. Her description of faith:

> Sometimes you have to turn off your conscious mind and allow the subconscious to take over. Unlike the conscious mind which filters our thoughts, the subconscious takes any order given to it in the spirit of absolute faith and acts upon that order—especially those that have been charged with emotion and handed over with feeling. As the connective link between the bonds of the natural world and the boundless creative possibility of the supernatural, the subconscious, acts as the gateway to the activation of the Universal alchemical process (191).

Over and over, I saw Mohamed work with the absolute faith that Shelli describes. He trusts in God's plan of perfection, and the law of attraction comes into play. We can imagine ourselves as powerful beings who create our lives by purposefully choosing thoughts, feelings, and actions that uplift ourselves and others. In other words, we attract the vibration of whatever we are thinking or feeling. This is not really a complicated process. We become aware of what it is we desire, and we speak it, believe in the process, and then we receive. This is how Mohamed works his wonders.

One of Mohamed's favorite expressions is "If you can imagine it, you can achieve it. If you dream it, you can become it." His favorite song is John Lennon's *Imagine*, which he played for me when I interviewed him in 2010 and he played it again for me at my last farewell dinner in September of 2014. Another song he played for me on his computer was *You Raise Me Up,* sung by Josh Groben. Both songs are very inspiring. And another of Mohamed's favorite mantras is: "IF YOU MAKE A PROMISE YOU KEEP IT!"

Mohamed is a man like no other. He creates miracles every day. He works magic every day. And from now until his last moments on earth, he will be working for peace and touching hearts, minds and souls—every day. I do not mean to paint Mohamed as a saint. Like all of us, he has his faults and flaws. He is a taskmaster to his employees and he has a temper. He rails at inefficiency and expects perfection. His employees fear him for a reason, and they respect him for a reason. And it is not as if he has never had a nasty confrontation or a heated argument. Mohamed is also a very stubborn man. This stubbornness has helped him stay the course through difficult times, but it may also get in the way of his rehabilitation. People offer to help him, but he chooses to do things his own way. He is a very proud man and has accomplished much to be proud of, but Mohamed's pride sometimes gets the better of him. He has his own habits and patterns and is not open to a lot of change in that regard. Like so many successful businessmen, he has dedicated himself to his work, perhaps at the expense of his health and family.

Mohamed's friends fear that if he doesn't take care of his health he will have no choice but to end his work. Ultimately, they wish he would allow others in his business to carry more responsibility. Mohamed believes he cannot deliver the level of service necessary if everything does not go through him, and perhaps he is right. But the way the business was taken care of by those closest to him during and after Mohamed's stroke is a testament to the dedication that surrounds him. Ihab, the vice president of Quest; has said that between himself and Mohamed's children, they will carry on Mohamed's work.

One thing is true: Mohamed is irreplaceable. From the moment he had his vision in the Great Pyramid, he has dedicated himself to an invaluable mission. He has provided each tour-leader with the experiences they need for their groups to understand the utter sanctity of ancient Egypt. He has cultivated a rich web of friendships throughout the world among people who benefit from each other's work. People, who through their own study, scholarship, writing, teaching, and lecturing, spread the word and contribute to Mohamed's vision of building peace through understanding. Every time someone travels to Egypt with Mohamed, they become part of that growing community. They are changed, and they are more than willing to become one of Mohamed's Peace Ambassadors.

Thus, along with his stubbornness and his flaws, Mohamed's heart, spirit, passion, vision, quest, and kindness combine to make him the unique, charming, and dedicated man he is. He is loved and respected by so many. If you can call him a friend, you are blessed, and if he calls you a friend, he knows you are a blessing for him.

Given all he has done so far, I asked Mohamed what he hoped for the future. In 2012, he said that he wanted to resign from the business eventually and have his daughter run it. However, by 2014, Nancy has her own life and work, and Mohamed is less concerned with the idea of Nancy taking over for him. He wants to dedicate the rest of his life to being an ambassador of good will for the people. He wants to bring people together to promote peace. He wants to help the poor and the uneducated. He wants to be part of a larger effort. Most of all, he always hopes and trusts that the right situations, and the right people, will come into his life to help make this happen.

Mohamed told me that he likes to make plans five years at a time. But at the time of our interview, no one could know what would occur in Egypt in the upcoming years. We couldn't have anticipated a Revolution, the end of the Mubarak regime, the first democratic election in Egypt, and then the overthrow of the Morsi regime. There has been so much change in Egypt, and with it, turmoil and distress. The election of el-Sisi marks a new era in Mohamed's mind. Many of Egypt's people are envisioning a secular, democratic government. They are engaging in a huge experiment, and they hope for the best as they define their own future.

It is in that context that Mohamed's work goes on. He continues to aim toward making spiritual dreams tangible and promoting the spirituality of oneness. When I talked to Mohamed recently, I jokingly asked him when he was going to become President of Egypt. He assured me that he didn't need to be president to create change. Mohamed's title is Peace Ambassador, and he doesn't have to be the president to continue to dream big.

Mohamed's passion for making things better will never be stifled. He still wants to see the travel industry in Egypt improve as part of a mission to promote unity through travel. The travel industry is a core business for Egypt's economy, but Mohamed stressed that he would like to see better infrastructure and spending to support it, from facilities to transportation. Mohamed wants to encourage international companies to once again host their conventions in Egypt—the same conventions that used to bring thousands of people to his country. Mohamed is grateful for what tourism has done for him and his country, and wants to expand upon it in ways that would have a positive effect on the people of Egypt.

Mohamed is and will always be a very important asset to his country. With his deep concern for the youth of Egypt, he strives to ensure they have opportunities, education, and prosperity. Mohamed believes that no matter who is running the country, the travel business is an important factor in the development of Egypt's economy, Egypt's connection to the world, and the well-being of its people.

What Mohamed is doing in Egypt is inspiring, and it is one of my greatest hopes that many of you will travel there one day. Who knows? Perhaps you will travel with one of his many tour leaders, so that you can meet him, see the beauty and wonder of his country and have your own delightful experiences. On the other hand it isn't necessary for you to travel to Egypt to become a member of the family and make an impact upon your world.

Every time I think about turning my back on an opportunity to be kind or friendly or gracious or generous, I think of Mohamed, and I choose instead to extend my hand and smile. As I settle into the ups and downs of everyday life and the grind of my familiar responsibilities, I find I am not always feeling kind, friendly, gracious, or generous. I find myself being judgmental, critical, doubtful, and suspicious more than I would like to admit. My work begins with myself, but the profound and positive effect that Mohamed has had on me inspires me to do that work. Whatever the future holds, meeting Mohamed has been a highlight in my life.

Mohamed has taught me that fostering world peace starts with each individual through the practice of generosity. He has provided a model we can all follow. I think of his smile and hear his laughter, or picture him with Emil telling jokes. I can never seem to express enough the gratitude I have for Mohamed, for Emil, for Quest Travel, and for Mohamed's family, coworkers, and friends. They have all taught me the meaning of words like "openhearted," "trust," "faith," "love," and "generosity."

Travel is a marvelous way of updating one's thinking and instigating change, and for setting aside preconceived notions, judgments, and fears. It inspires people to continually investigate how they think, how others think, and to open up to new understanding and new truths. Then, they tell others, and those others tell others, and the understanding grows. As Mohamed would say, "We are all one." Mohamed also often exclaims: "My Egypt! Your Egypt! Our Egypt! " I keep these words close to my heart.

The Epilogue

This story has come full circle with my last tour to Egypt in September of 2014 which Irene Iris Ingalls co-led with me. There are two stories that really bring the story to a lovely conclusion. One story is so encouraging because it occurred on the heels of a really difficult time for Mohamed as the tourism business has been so deeply affected and tourists from the States have chosen not come. I was lucky that I had eleven souls who trusted me enough to travel to Egypt. They too, soon discovered how peaceful and safe it really is, and how their lives were enriched for making the journey with Mohamed and Quest Travel.

The first story demonstrates powerfully the magic of generosity. In the summer, Mohamed visited the new Children's Cancer Hospital in Cairo which his friend had told him about. They visited it together and when Mohamed saw the children and interacted with them, he knew in his true Mohamed fashion that he must make a donation in the name of his family. He didn't even blink an eye but wrote a check for a large amount. This donation would support a whole new wing in the hospital and the various rooms would be named after family members. This was very moving for Mohamed to be honored in this way. He had not expected this. Yet, he had no idea how he was going to pay for such a large donation. Times have been very hard in Egypt for the last three years. He had been keeping his business afloat, as well as supplementing his workers even when there was hardly any work. Last year they only did five tours if you can imagine.

Then out of the blue, a man from South Africa contacted Mohamed about running a tour for a large group, and could it be right away. At first Mohamed didn't feel like he could manage all of this at the last minute, but after many conversations with this Sufi teacher from South Africa, he agreed. The only stipulation was that Mohamed himself would have to stay with the group the whole time. Fifty five people came. Quest Travel hadn't had such a large group for quite some time.

And the most amazing fact is that the amount he received from the group was the exact amount he had donated to the hospital! This is another startling example of how manifestation and generosity work. It also started off the season with a bang of encouragement for all of his workers and for the travel business in general. Everyone prospered. It sounds almost unbelievable, but that is the magic of life with Mr. Nazmy. This goes right along with a favorite quote of mine by the spiritual teacher and writer Wayne Dyer, "If you ask with kindness in your voice and in your heart, "How may I serve you?" the universe's response will be, "How may I serve you as well."

The second story is personal. This book began with the words that Mohamed shared with my original group in 2007 when he asked us to become his Peace Ambassadors. It was his talk that he gave at our closing dinner that so impressed me and stirred up hope in my heart that we could create peace. It was hearing about his vision that was sparked by Anwar Sadat and Mohamed's father that so moved me and resulted in me wanting to write this book—not to mention the insistence from Thoth.

On the last evening of this last tour, our group met in a conference room at the Mena House to talk about our experiences in Egypt. I was deeply touched by the profound changes in every one. One woman said that it hadn't been so fun being a human being before this trip, as she was always in her head and never in her heart. We could tell by the lovely look on her face that she had experienced a profound change and that being in her heart was a good thing. Others too talked about the open-hearted experience of feeling safe, loved and cared for, as well as the spiritual understandings that they had come to about their own power and worth. Egypt had not let us down.

Then Mohamed shared about the new hope for his country with their new leader, and how they had suffered so much for the last three years. And yes, could we go home and tell our friends families and communities that is safe to travel to Egypt and that such a journey is well worth it. Could we become his new Peace Ambassadors?

Then he talked about his peace mission and how Anwar Sadat had met to further peace right here in this hotel. He said we would be seeing the room where the Mena House Conference was actually held—and then we would have our farewell dinner. As we walked through the halls of the magnificent hotel, and turned corners and walked through the maze of more long halls with their marbled archways, we finally turned the final corner to the great room that had held the Egypt-Israeli talks in December of 1979 which followed up the 1978 Camp David Peace Accord and the Egypt-Israeli peace agreement that was signed in March of 1979.

We stood at the entrance stairs that led down into the large room and peered through the giant Moroccan doorway into that famous room that was originally the Pasha's dining room. It had a two story ceiling with wood cut inlayed designs, and on either side of the room was a wood cut second story balcony that probably was used by the harem to view the king. I could imagine the ladies looking through the narrow wood cuts from their quarters on the second floor to see what the Pasha was up to. On every side of the room at floor level, were huge cut Moroccan door ways. And at the high ceiling above was a huge dangling Moroccan chandelier. It was breath taking.

And then the surprise hit us. There before us was set a long beautiful table beckoning us forward. The darkened room was lit gently by sconces on the side walls and the table was set upon a blazing golden rose table cloth with silver plates, flowers and candles. This was where our dinner was to be held. We were to have our own peace dinner in the very same room in which courageous leaders worked to create peace between Egypt and Israel!

And then came a really great moment in my life. As we all took our seats, and to our great surprise, Mohamed placed his iPhone on the table and played his favorite song by John Lennon, *Imagine*, and we all sang the words. Tears came to my eyes as we felt the power of this room and the souls of the men who gave their life blood to create peace. And I thought of this book and all that Mohamed Nazmy has created. As I said, the story had come full circle. As we sang the lines, *"You may say I'm a dreamer, but I'm not the only one. I hope someday you'll join us. And the world will be as one."*

Leave it to Mohamed to set up the perfect experience and to honor me for writing this book about his quest for peace following the footsteps of his hero Anwar Sadat, his father, and the dreams of others like Jimmy Carter and everyone who worked for peace and continues to do so.

Fig. The Epilogue.1. Our final dinner. Photograph courtesy of Ron Werner.

Fig. The Epilogue.2. Our peace dinner. Photograph courtesy of Ron Werner.

And to each of you who carries the hope in your heart that we can create a peaceful world. Please don't give up. We don't have to be a king or a president. I hope that you too are a dreamer, because you aren't alone. Imagine all the people living life in peace! We can make a difference with our generosity, open-heartedness, kindness, humor, and tolerance. And I thank Mr. Nazmy for another grand gesture, another perfect moment, and another tour that changed everyone in my group profoundly. I am grateful to share his story with you and to remind you we are truly one people and that we do make a difference.

List of Contributors and Their Websites

Visit the contributors' websites or emails to find further information on them: their tours, their work, their books, their services, and the products they offer such as guided meditations and related items.

Jane Bell
Presence of Heart
www.presenceofheart.com

Gregg Braden
www.greggbraden.com

Normandi Ellis
www.normandiellis.com

George Faddoul
QC Seminars
www.georgefaddoul.com

Jonny Hahn
Contact the author below

Sharlyn Hidalgo, MA
Alchemical Healing Arts
www.alchemicalhealingarts.com

Danielle Hoffman and Friedemann Schaub MD, PhD.
www.Egyptiscalling.com

Danielle Rama Hofmann:
Divine Transmissions
www.divinetransmissions.com

Dr. Jean Houston:
www.jeanhouston.com

Irene Iris Ingalls
www.lightlanguageart.com

Mark Lehner
www.Aera.org

Kathianne Lewis
www.sprituallivling.org

Tania Marie
www.taniamarie.com
www.spiritualskin.com

Greg Roach and Halle Eavelyn
Spirit Quest Tours
www.SpritiQuestTours.com

Maureen St. Germain
Transformational Enterprises, Inc.
www.maureenstgermain.com

Friedemann Schaub MD, PhD.
Cellular Wisdom
www.cellularwisdom.com

Nicki Scully
Shamanic Journeys, Ltd.
www.shamanicjourneys.com

Olivia Temple
www.oliviatemple.com

Robert Temple
www.robert-temple.com

John Anthony West
www.jawest.net

My initial editor:
Kelly Malone
http://www.wordsupcommunication.com

Quest Travel Contact Information:
Quest Travel: www.questtravelegypt.com
Mohamed Nazmy: president@questtravelegypt.com
Phone from the US to Egypt: 011-202-33768000 or 011-202-33768444
Fax: 011-202-33763810
Address:
Mohamed Nazmy
President Quest Travel
5 Emarat El Shams–Hadaik El Ahram,
Pyramids-Giza-Egypt

The Bibliography

Braden, Gregg. *Fractal Time: The Secret of 2012 and a New World Age*. USA: Hay House Inc., 2009.

---. *The Isaiah Effect: Decoding the Lost Science of Prayer and Prophecy*. New York: Three Rivers Press, 2000.

Bradley, John R. *Inside Egypt: The Land of the Pharaohs on the Brink of a Revolution*. New York, NY: Palgrave MacMillan, 2008.

Eavellyn, Halle. *Red Goddess Rising: A Spiritual Travel Memoir*. Spirit Quest World, 2012.

Ellis, Normandi. *Awakening Osiris: The Egyptian Book of the Dead*. Boston: Phanes Press, 2009.

---. *Dreams of Isis: A Woman's Spiritual Sojourn*. Wheaton, IL: The Theosophical Publishing House, 1995.

---. *Feasts of Light: Celebrations for the Seasons of Life based on the Egyptian Goddess Mysteries*. Wheaton, IL: Quest Books, 1999.

---. *Imagining the World into Existence: An Ancient Egyptian Manual of Consciousness*. Rochester, VA: Bear & Company, 2012.

Ellis, Normandi and Gloria Taylor Brown. *Invoking the Scribes of Ancient Egypt: The Initiatory Path of Spiritual Journaling*. Rochester, VA: Bear & Company, 2011.

Faddoul, George and Mohamed Nazmy. *The Modern Day Alchemist from the Land of the Pharaohs: Secrets of Manifestation Revealed to Awaken the Alchemist*. Sydney: QC Publishing, 2009.

Heirichs, Ann. *Egypt; Enchantment of the World*. New York: Children's Press, a Division of Scholastic, Inc., 2007.

Hidalgo, Sharlyn. *The Healing Power of Trees: Spiritual Journeys through the Celtic Tree Calendar*. Woodbury, MN: Llewellyn Publications, 2010.

Hoffman, Danielle Rama. *Temples of Light: An Initiatory Journey into the Heart Teachings of the Egyptian Mystery Schools.* Rochester, VA: Bear & Company, 2009.

Holmes, Earnest. *The Science of Mind: A Philosophy, A Faith, A Way of Life.* New York: Penguin Putnam Inc., 1998.

Little, Gregory L. et.al. *Edgar Cayce's Atlantis.* Virginia Beach: A.R.E. Press, 2006.

Mead, Michael. *Fate and Destiny: The Two Agreements of the Soul.* Seattle: Green Fire Press, 2010.

Naydler, Jeremy. *Temple of the Cosmos: The Ancient Egyptian Experience of the Sacred.* Rochester, VA: Inner Traditions International, 1996.
---. Shamanic *Wisdom in the Pyramid Texts: The Mystical Tradition of Ancient Egypt.* Rochester, VA: Inner Traditions, 2005.

Oakes, Lorna. *Temples and Sacred Sites of Ancient Egypt: A Comprehensive Guide to the Religious Sites of a Fascinating Civilization.* London: Southwater/Anness Publishing LTD, 2003.

Ravenwood, Kathryn W. *How to Create Sacred Water: A Guide to Rituals and Practices.* Rochester, VA: Bear & Company, 2012.

Romer, John. *The Valley of the Kings: Exploring the Tombs of the Pharaohs.* New York: Henry Holt and Company, 1981.

Schwaller De Lubicz, Isha. *The Opening of the Way: A Practical Guide to the Wisdom of Ancient Egypt.* New York: Inner Traditions International, 1979.

Scully, Nicki. *Alchemical Healing: A Guide to Spiritual, Physical, and Transformational Medicine.* Rochester, VA: Bear & Company, 2003.
---. *Power Animal Meditations: Shamanic Journeys with Your Spirit Allies.* Rochester, VA: Bear & Company, 2001.

Scully, Nicki and Linda Star Wolf. *Shamanic Mysteries of Egypt: Awakening the Healing Power of the Heart.* Rochester, VA: Bear & Company, 2007.

---. *The Anubis Oracle: A Journey into the Shamanic Mysteries of Egypt.* Rochester, VA: Bear & Company, 2008.

Scully, Nicki and Mark Hallert. *Planetary Healing: Spirit Medicine for Global Transformation.* Rochester, VA: Bear & Company, 2011.

Spear, Charlie. "Egypt: Land of Inspiration." *The State Journal,* Frankfort, Kentucky, 6 May 2011: A1-A7. Print.

St. Germain, Maureen J. *Beyond The Flower of Life.* New York: Phoenix Rising Publications, 2009.

Temple, Robert. *The Sirius Mystery.* New York: St. Martin's Press, 1976.

Temple, Robert and Olivia Temple. *The Sphinx Mystery: The Forgotten Origins of the Sanctuary of Anubis.* Rochester, VA: Inner Traditions, 2009.

Weeks Ph.D., Kent R. *The Lost Tomb: This is His Incredible Story of KV 5 and Its Excavation.* New York: William Morrow and Co., Inc., 1998.

Zuehike, Jeffry. *Egypt in Pictures.* Minneapolis, MN: Lerner Publications Company, 2003.